T + H + E

Gibson
SUPER
400

Art of
the Fine Guitar

T + H + E
Gibson
SUPER
400

Art of
the Fine Guitar

Thomas A. Van Hoose

GPI BOOKS

An Imprint of

 Miller Freeman Books

San Francisco

GPI BOOKS
Miller Freeman, Inc.
600 Harrison Street
San Francisco, CA 94107
Publishers of *Guitar Player, Bass Player,*
and *Keyboard* magazines

ISBN: 0-87930-230-5
Library of Congress Catalog Card Number: 91-61852

Designer: Brad Greene
Typesetting: Berna Alvarado-Rodriguez
Printed in the United States of America
First Paperback Edition, January 1995

95 96 97 98 99   5 4 3 2 1

DEDICATION

To all Gibson employees,
living and deceased

To the guitarists around the world,
living and deceased,
who have used the Super 400

To all those who truly appreciate
the art of the fine guitar

This book is respectfully dedicated.

Thomas A. Van Hoose, Ph.D.
September 27, 1990

Table of
CONTENTS

Foreword

Having known Tom Van Hoose for at least 15 years, I can think of no one better qualified to write the story of the Gibson Super 400 guitar. Tom has not only assembled what is probably the finest collection of Super 400s anywhere, but he has also devoted extensive hours of labor studying company records, catalogs, and other literature while researching virtually every aspect of the model from its construction to its place in the music scene.

The Super 400 is indeed a model worthy of such special consideration. It stands apart from virtually all other Gibson instruments as the most expensive guitar in the line from the time of its introduction in 1934 until recent times. At the time of its introduction, it was a radical departure from earlier guitars. Until then, Gibson, Epiphone, and others were making relatively small guitars, 16 inches wide and smaller. The Super 400, with its 18-inch width and super deluxe ornamentation, was a real trendsetter, not only at Gibson but throughout the industry. Soon afterward, Epiphone and D'Angelico introduced new large-body models. Like the Super 400, the Epiphone Emperor and the D'Angelico New Yorker had fancy binding and split-block inlays, and the New Yorker was X-braced as well. The Stromberg Master 400 also borrowed features from the Super 400 and from the Emperor.

Virtually everyone copied the Gibson model, and through the entire big band era, the Super 400 and its close relative, the Gibson L-5, were the epitome of orchestral jazz guitars. As the years went by, the Super 400 evolved, as will be explained in this book, from an orchestral rhythm guitar to a modern jazz instrument, eventually available in both acoustic and electric versions. Throughout this time, right on up until the late 1960s, the Super 400 maintained its position as the premier model in the Gibson line.

As a vintage instrument, the Super 400 is today highly sought, due not only to its historical appeal but to its excellent playing characteristics and its physical beauty. In my own experience as a dealer and collector, when I first started in the mid-1960s, arch-top guitars in general were in a relative state of eclipse compared to flat-tops, and what demand there was for arch-tops was primarily for cutaway models. In the later 1960s and early 1970s, the demand was for flat-tops and such rock-related electrics as semisolid-body Gibsons and solid-body Fenders. In recent years, however, the interest in arch-top guitars, both acoustic and electric models, has rebounded to the point where today many sophisticated collectors and musicians value fine quality arch-tops above all other guitars.

The demand remains for the flat-top and solid-body guitars, but in today's very diversified market there is a growing segment that really is seriously interested in arch-tops. Of the arch-tops, the Gibson Super 400 and L-5, the Epiphone Emperor and DeLuxe, and the D'Angelico and Stromberg guitars tend to command the most interest. In this group of instruments, however, the Super 400 stands out as the most enduring and historically significant of all, because it is with this model that the world was introduced to the first 18-inch-wide, deluxe-ornamented instrument.

Fine examples of the Super 400 to this day remain among the finest quality arch-tops, not only for their aesthetic and historic appeal but for their playing characteristics as well. Although the entirely handmade D'Angelicos and Strombergs may be in general more expensive and highly rated than the Super 400, when one sits down and plays them side by side, a good Super 400 holds its own and proves that it warrants the kind of attention that Tom is giving it. Tom's book certainly deserves a place in the library of every guitar collector and every lover of fine jazz guitars.

—George Gruhn

Preface

I first became acquainted with the Gibson Super 400 guitar while an undergraduate at the University of Texas at Austin in the 1960s. There I met blues guitarist Bill Campbell, who introduced me to the art of blues guitar playing through live performances and recordings of electric blues artists. Campbell also recommended the recordings of Kenny Burrell, whose blues-tinged jazz improvisation and accompaniment styles gave real direction to my early guitar-playing skills. I noticed that Burrell was pictured with a Gibson Super 400C on some of his album jackets and decided to find such a guitar after graduation in the hope of more closely emulating Burrell's unique musical qualities and mastery of the instrument.

I located a fine 1967 Gibson Super 400C through the American Federation of Musicians' monthly newspaper in 1975, and my pursuit of Burrell's sound began in earnest. The joy and difficulty of playing jazz guitar began to emerge simultaneously when I purchased and attached a gold DeArmond pickup to the instrument and began introductory jazz guitar lessons with John Perkins and the late Terrill Gardner. Eventually, professional commitments as a clinical psychologist prevented me from practicing and performing enough to attain real mastery of the jazz guitar, though I did achieve a level of musicianship that remains extremely satisfying and therapeutic in its own way.

During my musical development with the Super 400C, I became interested in the instrument's inherent craftsmanship and musical qualities. I also became aware of the subtle differences in different versions of the Super 400, especially after seeing Kenny Burrell perform with a Florentine cutaway Super 400CES. I purchased my second Super 400, a 1964 Super 400CES just like Burrell's, at Guitar Resurrection in Austin, Texas, in 1977. While playing and comparing both guitars, I became increasingly curious about the variations of the Super 400. Thus, my interest in collecting such guitars was born.

With the advent of vintage guitar shows in Dallas in 1978, I began to meet guitar dealers who helped me locate various acoustic and electric Super 400 guitars. The gradual expansion of general knowledge about vintage instruments during the late 1970s also affected my perception of the big Gibson arch-top. I began making notes about the instrument's similarities and differences, and an overview of the development of the Super 400 began to emerge. By 1980, I owned six different Super 400s, and the excitement of collecting and playing such fine instruments had firmly taken hold.

I decided to assemble a collection of Super 400 guitars, acoustic and electric, that would illustrate the evolution of this guitar from its auspicious debut in 1934 through its various changes up to the present time.

The idea for this book came as an outgrowth of my drive to complete my guitar collection and from the gradually increasing body of knowledge about the Super 400 that was generated by that pursuit. A trip to the original Gibson factory in Kalamazoo, Michigan, was undertaken in May 1984 to gather information for the book. There, the late Charley Wirz (who was working on a similar book on Gibson thinline electric guitars) and I encountered such a wealth of data and such a warm reception that both projects began to take shape quickly. Charley's untimely death in February 1985 plunged me into a period of grief that was extended by the deaths of my father and another close friend in the following year. By early 1987, I began working on the book again, and its form began to solidify after my second trip to Gibson's Nashville factory in 1988. With the support of the management of the new Gibson Guitar Corporation, work proceeded rapidly as book and collection became virtually inseparable.

In early 1989, Tom Dorsaneo of Miller Freeman Publications became interested in my forthcoming book, and now the book has become a reality for lovers of fine guitars everywhere. It is hoped that the reader will truly enjoy *The Gibson Super 400—Art of the Fine Guitar* on several levels—for its information, photography, and appreciation of the art of making such fine guitars. All the work contained herein, except where noted, is my own and has truly been a labor of love. I hope that this book will delight its readers as well.

— Thomas A. Van Hoose, Ph.D.

Acknowledgments

In the course of writing this book, I have had the pleasure of meeting and working with a variety of people involved in making and playing guitars. Each of these persons has given me inspiration and assistance as this book has steadily moved from an idea in 1984 to publication in 1991. In particular, I wish to thank the following persons for their contributions.

In the research phase, several persons provided invaluable information. Julius Bellson, historian emeritus for the Gibson Company, provided considerable time as well as excerpts from his personal records regarding the production process of the Super 400 and production data for the Super 400 and L-5 guitars. Ted McCarty, president of Gibson from 1950 to 1966, also provided valuable insights into the function of the company and the birth of the electric Super 400 guitar. He introduced me to Larry Allers and Gerald Bergeon, former long-time Gibson employees who freely volunteered their comments about the manufacturing process of these instruments. James Deurloo, who in 1984 was the manager of the Gibson Kalamazoo plant, arranged the above interviews and gave additional information about production of the Super 400. Now president of the Heritage Guitar Corporation, located in the old Gibson Kalamazoo factory, Deurloo also provided additional information about the birth of the Heritage Guitar Company and related topics.

I am especially indebted to Henry Juskiewicz, president of the Gibson Guitar Corporation for his support of this project. Tim Shaw and John Hawkins have provided additional information and behind-the-scenes assistance that have helped this project move along. A special word of thanks goes to James "Hutch" Hutchins of the Gibson Guitar Corporation, who has patiently assisted me over several years in completing various portions of this book, especially regarding information on Gibson's Nashville factory and the future of the Super 400 guitar.

Additional research information was provided by George Gruhn, who graciously wrote the Foreword of this book and who lent me several of his older Gibson catalogs for illustration purposes. Additional interview material was provided by Neal Penner, retired Gibson sales representative. Andre Duchossoir generously gave permission to reproduce selected data tables and other information from his book *Guitar Identification*. I also wish to thank Hank Thompson, Marty Grosz, and Rose Lee Maphis for their time and photographs. Maphis generously provided a photograph of her late husband, Joe Maphis, which is featured elsewhere in this book. Thompson and Grosz are both professional musicians who often play Super 400 guitars. Their comments and encouragement were especially helpful. Henry Van Wormer and Kevin Macy also provided artist photographs.

The idea of this book began to emerge as I was assembling my collection of Gibson Super 400 guitars. Soon the collection and the book became intertwined, and I would like to thank the following persons who have assisted me in assembling the collection of instruments featured in this book: Dave Hussong, John Sprung, Cesar Diaz, Mac Yasuda, Stan Jay, Shirley Robinson, Craig Swancy, Mack Hood, Jay Scott, Mike Larko, Jim Lehman, George Gruhn, Mark O'Hara, Bob DiPasqua, Joe Onorado, John Perkins, the Gibson Guitar Corporation, the late Charley Wirz, Hank Risan, and Danny McKnight. I would also like to thank the following persons for making instruments for me, which are featured in this book as well: Robert Benedetto, James D'Aquisto, and the Heritage Guitar Corporation.

Despite all the research I have undertaken, this book would not be a reality without the photographs it contains. I would like to extend a special note of appreciation to Bill Crump, who photographed the majority of the instruments presented in this book. Bill is an outstanding photographer with a love for the guitar; his unique perspective and experience with the instrument have been combined to render the beautiful photographs featured here. I also wish to thank Charmaine Lanham for her photographs in Chapter 4, "Restoration of a 1939 Super 400N." Charmaine photographed her husband Marty as he restored my 1939 Gibson Super 400N, and the sensitivity of her work is reflected herein. Finally, I would also like to thank Scott Grey, who was the first person to take photographs for this book.

Special thanks also go to Akira Tsumura, who graciously invited me to submit photographs of a portion of my Super 400 collection for inclusion in his book, *Guitars: The Tsumura Collection,* and whose excellent photography provided me with additional inspiration.

The following persons have graciously allowed me to have their instruments photographed for this book: James D'Aquisto, Robert Benedetto, Freddie Pigg, Willie Baker, Leon Chester, J. P. Ohnishi, Craig Swancy, Dr. Ken Ciuffreda, Joel Sanders, Bill Camp, and Gary Brunner. A special note of thanks is also extended to Gary Brunner, who has given me considerable advice and counsel as this book has proceeded along its path to completion.

I wish to extend a very special and personal note of thanks to my wife, June Van Hoose, for her ongoing support and understanding while this project was being completed. June's cooperation and assistance in the completion of this book have been sincerely appreciated, and her support has never wavered throughout the many years this book has been "in progress." The patience of our children, Elizabeth and Charles, is also appreciated. I also wish to thank the late Charley Wirz, because he provided much of the initial inspiration for the writing of the book. Charley's love of the guitar in all of its aspects—production, playing, and collecting—was truly contagious, and it is humbly hoped that some of his influence will emerge in this book as well.

Finally, I wish to acknowledge the generosity and patience of Margaret Price, who typed the manuscript many times as the book evolved and took shape. I am also grateful to Tom Dorsaneo, Matt Kelsey, Brad Greene, and Loren Hickman of Miller Freeman Publications for their commitment and assistance throughout the publication process, and to Dudley Jahnke of Algonquin Books for his encouragement and advice.

Introduction

A good deal of the romance that continues to surround the earliest history of jazz springs from the absolute mystery of it all. There were no interviews and no magazines to follow the comings and goings of the musicians who worked the smoky big-city clubs and dance halls, the colleges, Catskill resorts, river boats, and rent parties. Who could say with any assurance what the guitarists thought about what they were doing? Did they regard themselves as pioneers and have some sense of all that was to come? They left us only slim documentation—the recordings, of course, a few recollections and accounts of the era, a handful of pictures. Quite often, we don't even know who they were. Looking at an old photograph, we encounter anonymous rows of trumpeters and trombonists surrounding a smiling, nameless figure hunched over a small flat-top guitar, long-forgotten individuals who already were contributing to the endlessly rich traditions of jazz. Many of these bands never had the opportunity to record, and what do we really know about them? We can supply only our own endless speculation, imaginings, and dreams.

The cult of the guitar came to jazz relatively early, and this in itself seems remarkable, because the instrument was so new—still untried and open to invention. Guitars—parlor instruments, really—had been around for centuries, and a whole musical literature had developed around them, but the steel-string guitar was still a disreputable offspring and something peculiarly American, hardly more than a decade or two old. The guitar in jazz was like uncharted terrain that awaited serious exploration, as the electric guitar would be for music in the 1960s. Did its appeal lie in the inherent charisma of the instrument, or was it a reflection of the very youthfulness of jazz itself—still fresh, vigorous, accessible? If only someone had thought to ask. But things developed very quickly nevertheless.

The first fretted instrument to make its appearance in jazz was the banjo. But in the emerging mainstream of jazz orchestras and post-Dixieland swing groups, it disappeared quickly, being replaced briefly by flat-top and four-string guitars and, finally, by the more familiar arch-top instruments. In this atmosphere of accelerated growth, the guitars themselves also evolved swiftly, despite the absence of any precedent for this kind of development.

Gibson, a Midwestern firm that had been making harp guitars and mandolins since the late 19th century, was only carrying out the rather simple idea of linking a large mandolin-like body to a guitar neck when the company first introduced its early arch-tops. Still, with its big sound and vaguely orchestral appearance, the instrument had immediate authority.

The cleverness and obviousness of the solution seems dazzling, but this is the magic of history—people and events work together to create something unique to themselves and their times but that also has an effect on more durable traditions. And so we return to the musicians themselves, who managed to devise an entire stylistic vocabulary with extraordinary rapidity.

Think of this: Jazz guitar didn't exist before these musicians started playing it, and many of the ideas that were developed in the 1920s and 1930s remain integral to present jazz guitar traditions, having created a foundation for almost all jazz guitar styles that followed them. And think of this, too, because it surely is a factor in the development of the jazz guitar: No musician who took a guitar into a jazz group could be assured of public prominence, since at least until the 1940s the guitar was regarded primarily as a rhythm instrument that worked alongside the bass, drums, and often the piano. Celebrity was thus not an incentive. Although the opportunity to make records may have been available to a limited extent, no popular market for jazz guitar music had been developed, and so the musicians who pushed at the instrument's boundaries were laboring in relative obscurity. To the public, they probably were a relatively anonymous bunch, but musicians—and certainly other guitarists—must have been aware of the colossal achievements of Eddie Lang and Lonnie Johnson, of Carl Kress, Dick McDonough, John Cali, and others—instrumentalists who forged a style and a tradition almost singlehandedly, combining the excitement and discovery of the emerging jazz sound with, in some instances, a rigorous classical training. Could Eddie Lang have imagined a Pat Metheny, Sonny Sharrock, James Blood Ulmer, or John Scofield? Perhaps. Or perhaps not. But, in some way, they owe their musical existences to Lang. The Lang-Johnson duets, recorded some sixty years ago, still sparkle with originality and inventiveness. You can hear the foundation being put down; and in the decades that followed, jazz proved to be one of the most profoundly evolutionary of musical ideas, building on previous ideas that carry each other into the future.

But this is a book about jazz guitars—or, more precisely, about one guitar, the Gibson Super 400. In the half-century or more in which it has been available to musicians, the Super 400 has established itself as one of the great aristocrats of the instrument, a guitar whose elegance and purposefulness are obvious even to people who do not play the guitar.

Perhaps its very appearance at such an early point in jazz history—the first Super 400s were sold in 1934—answers some of our questions. Guitars took their place in jazz between World War I and the beginning of the recording era, and so the instrument took barely more than a decade of application to develop into something so wonderful as the Super 400—and during the very height of the Depression, at that.

At second glance, though, a great deal had happened in jazz before 1934. The players had been very busy during the preceding decade, even if much of the activity occurred beyond the surface of the music. The guitar already had begun to demonstrate the same kind of versatility that has marked its existence in all forms of music, from its basic rhythm role to the playful, improvisational virtuosity of the great duettists, from the lead voice that Lang was occasionally able to take with the Frankie Trumbauer band to the accompanying role that Lang also had played to singers Bing Crosby and Bessie Smith. Even though we have no way to know just how the players regarded their roles or their work, they must have been taken very seriously by the musicians around them. The era certainly had its stars among the band leaders and vocalists, but guitarists quickly and rather quietly had become almost ubiquitous.

And so the Super 400 assumes an important place in the history of jazz and, really, in the history of the guitar. In 1934, very few guitar manufacturers were in operation, and all were relatively small by modern standards. These companies didn't throw new models at musicians every year, seeking endorsements and calculating their marketing budgets. An entirely new instrument, and especially one as expensive as the Super 400, must have been quite an undertaking. The market apparently was ready. Until that time, jazz players generally relied on the Gibson L-5, the first workhorse arch-top, or they used the little steel-string flat-tops that were commonplace among hillbilly and rural blues players. The L-5 was larger and was favored for the ability to project its sound from the midst of an orchestra of horn and reed players.

As their opportunities increased, though, jazz guitarists must have longed for something more. Even the old Lang and Kress records, almost certainly made with L-5s, have an edginess of tone—a distinctive presence, but nevertheless a certain lack of sweetness and warmth, the very qualities that would have given their work the character of chamber music, which, in a way, it was. The appearance of an instrument like the Super 400 had a symbolic quality, even if it wasn't fully recognized at the time, because its mere invention argued for the importance of the guitar in jazz. One standard model was no longer adequate. There were enough players and they were serious enough to warrant something like this. The Super 400 must have emerged as a kind of signal—other companies and small shops entered the arch-top market soon afterwards, and the era of ever-changing models had begun. Since that time, probably no single instrument has dominated jazz guitar in quite the same way that the L-5 dominated the music during its first decades. Jazz guitar truly had come into its own, just as jazz itself—through band leaders such as Duke Ellington and soloists such as Art Tatum or Coleman Hawkins—was established as the virtuoso voice of American popular music by the end of the 1930s. We can assume an entirely pragmatic view of jazz history and suggest that Gibson, as a growing instrument manufacturer coping with the Depression-era economy, recognized an emergent market and followed good 20th-century business practice by introducing a flashier model with more running lights and taller tailfins, but the sense of occasion that accompanied the new Super 400 is difficult to ignore. It was a landmark. Something was afoot. The times were changing in American music.

Over the years, the Super 400 proved to be a versatile instrument and an adaptable one. Its combination of sweet tone and rich, resonant volume appealed to musicians outside jazz, and the Super 400 soon appeared in hillbilly groups and Western swing bands, becoming the trademark instrument of such respected stylists as Hank Thompson and Merle Travis, whose custom Super 400 is now displayed in the Country Music Association's Hall of Fame in Nashville. As the years slipped past, the Super 400 underwent other transformations as well, sprouting cutaways and pickups, trying out different finishes and ornamentation. Since World War II, it's been used by jazz soloists as different as Kenny Burrell and Larry Coryell, and despite stiff competition from other manufacturers and increased specialization in instrument design, the Super 400 has retained its unique position as a kind of Rolls Royce among arch-top guitars. Through everything, the Super 400 has maintained its dignity, emerging as a kind of representative of the long history of jazz guitar. Ours is a pluralistic age, in instruments as well as musical styles, and the Super 400 survives as royalty survives, with charisma and presence and a feeling for the richness and breadth and meaning of the past that can be earned only over time and with long, profound involvement in the traditions it represents. Perhaps only the D'Angelico New Yorker rivals it in this sense. We see a well-kept old Super 400 and it has connotations and associations—the uptown elegance of classic jazz, the authority of virtuosity, and a sense of maturity. This is the real thing.

Tom Van Hoose has been collecting Gibson Super 400s for a long time. He embodies the qualities of a traditional collector—he does not merely hoard or acquire, but, in an effort to compile examples of all the Super 400 model variations from the instrument's five-decade history, he has gradually honed a collection of first-rate guitars through a long, patient process of search, acquisition, resale, and trade. Along the way, he has become a scholar of the instrument's history, accumulating interviews, photographs, old catalogs, and all sorts of related information. Any important instrument amasses a whole history in the course of its life, just as people do; and, like people, it reflects in larger, more far-reaching ways the era in which it lives. A collection of this sort—like certain well-focused collections of art—speaks of individual taste, but it also reflects a period in history on a number of levels. The many different Super 400s that have gone out into the world can tell us something about our music, just as small, suggestive changes in certain kinds of violins or pianos reflect significant changes in the ways in which the classical repertoire is interpreted from generation to generation. If the profit motive governs the introduction of a new product, its success still speaks to the character and needs of its time. Much has been made of certain American stringed instruments—the Martin Dreadnought and Gibson mandolin come to mind for their having influenced the development of musical styles as much as they were influenced by them—but the Van Hoose collection may very well represent the first ongoing investigation of this sort in jazz and jazz-related music. It's an impressive accomplishment.

But something remains to be said about the Super 400, or at least about this particular collection. To discuss the instrument in purely historical terms seems rather cold and ignores some of the very qualities that made these guitars so immediately appealing. I first encountered the collection in 1983, when Tom had a selection of instruments on display in a booth at an early Greater Southwest Guitar Show in Dallas. It was in the old Wintergarden Ballroom, and there in the large room, filled with electric guitars and a dull cacophony of small amplifiers, where new manufacturers were still trying to sell the idea of brightly colored custom electrics and specialized hard rock and heavy metal tools, this little ring of Super 400s stood quietly, as immediate and as timeless as sculpture. In a place where fashionability and volume struggled to outdo each other, these instruments looked a little out of place, but they reminded the shiny, noisy hell-raisers around them of their history and lineage. They were there to let the fast, skinny little screamers know that the guitar didn't begin with Eddie Van Halen or even Eric Clapton. And people seemed to recognize that—the Van Hoose booth always had a crowd around it. Royalty claims its own, and is in competition with no one.

Like a true collector, Tom has always let the instruments speak for themselves. He is not a proselytizer and does not seek converts. As the years passed and guitar shows came and went, I got to know Tom, and I had the opportunity to sit in the booth on a number of occasions and play many of his guitars. It's a tribute to the Super 400 that once it's taken up and played it ceases to seem intimidating or imposing. The guitars play wonderfully, sound beautiful, and do not impose music on the player, readily accepting any kind of style. To sit among them, though, is to feel a presence, a power, the glow of their quality and the richness of their history. They insist on not being taken lightly, but they are gracious. They inspire.

Among jazz guitarists today, the era of the arch-top may be over. Its time of supremacy almost certainly has passed—loyalty to the instrument continues mainly among older players who emerged in the shadow of bop and who favor the smooth, even-handed consistency of the arch-top's sound as a vehicle for individual playing styles that have more to do with notes than varieties of tone or sonic textures. When younger players use arch-tops, it is usually in a specialized role, often intermingled with other guitar sounds. Arch-tops are hardly made anymore, and most of the manufacturers who do make them are mindful of the demands of the modern stage. An Ibanez George Benson guitar can, for instance, be played in an arena without feedback problems—something a Super 400 could never do without significant modifications.

For this reason alone, the Van Hoose collection—and this book—can be regarded as noteworthy events in the history of the jazz guitar. We are, at the moment, in the midst of a time when jazz musicians are reexamining the vast heritage of their music, either in the disciplined fashion of a Wynton Marsalis or with the probing revisionist sensibilities of players such as Henry Threadgill, David Murray, Chico Freeman, or Lester Bowie. The guitar needn't be exempt from this sort of thing. And, for any fan or musician who wants to look across the history of jazz guitar and learn from it, this is one major resource.

—*Bruce Nixon*

Chapter
I

The Prewar
Gibson Super 400
Acoustic Guitar

● **1935 Super 400**

First Model Super 400, 1934–1936

The collaboration of the Gibson engineering and marketing staffs played an essential part in the initial construction and appearance of the Super 400. Gibson planned the introduction of the Super 400 as part of a larger marketing strategy to boost overall sales and to broaden the company's market share. The Super 400 was the top of the line in a lineup of new and revised instruments that covered several price points in the guitar spectrum.

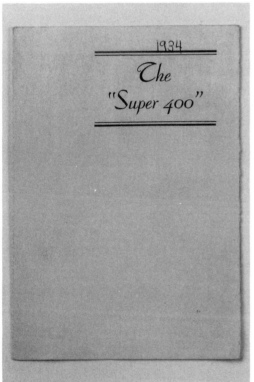

- 1934 Gibson Super 400 announcement folder, front
- 1934 Gibson Super 400 announcement folder, back

The additional instruments Gibson produced in late 1934 included the Advanced or enlarged L-5, the L-10, the L-12, and the L-7 guitars. These instruments all featured carved tops and backs, and the prospective instrument buyer suddenly found an array of instruments available that potentially appealed to almost every pocketbook, including those of musicians who could not yet afford an L-5 or Super 400 but who wanted a Gibson carved-top guitar at a more reasonable price.

The Super 400 was the largest and most expensive carved-top guitar available from any manufacturer at the time. The first model Super 400 was larger than its predecessor, the 16-inch L-5; it was also fancier in appearance. Such changes in guitar design in the 1930s were considered to be of major importance, and the interplay of marketing strategy and guitar craftsmanship became almost inseparable. Thus, the Super 400 was a guitar whose substantial differences in design and construction made it seem worth the price. The initial advertising flyer for the Super 400's introduction described the instrument in a very colorful and imaginative manner. Although the price of the guitar was $400, including a leather case and canvas case cover, the price was paradoxically used to demonstrate the quality of the instrument.

But why did Gibson introduce such an expensive guitar during

The "Super 400"

i

EVERY decade has its outstanding creations — a great and inspired leader, an amazing invention, an awe inspiring building, a record smashing horse. Their originality, character, finesse and inherent quality place them far above the ordinary — an inspiration to all but never duplicated in every measure.

ii

THE "Super 400" is an extraordinary guitar in every way — its price is a criterion of its quality.

The search for rare, old woods, and the infinite care in seasoning; the careful inspection and testing of every individual piece of material; the hand rubbed fine finish — the building of such a guitar cannot be hurried — time is not an element, for whether it takes two months or two years to build just one instrument, it must be perfect.

Tone — balanced, full and rich — ranging from a soft, sweet whisper to a vibrant, stirring, commanding power — but always, a pure, accurate guitar tone.

PRICE $400

Including: Solid brown leather, plush lined de luxe case with waterproof zipper cover.

GIBSON, INC., KALAMAZOO, MICHIGAN

SEE BACK COVER

● **1934 Gibson Super 400 announcement folder, inside**

such perilous economic times? Julius Bellson, Gibson's treasurer and historian until he retired in 1978, offered the following insights into the reason for the introduction of the Super 400. He stated that the Super 400 was introduced during Guy Hart's tenure as president of Gibson. Hart was instrumental in bringing out all of the Advanced instruments as well as the prewar electric guitars. Bellson stated that "there was an attempt to improve the volume of sales by coming out with something that was spectacular. You can't deny the fact that a Super 400 is a work of art and big showmanship" (Bellson, personal interview, 1984). The "showmanship" included the large body, the large headstock, and the distinctive inlays in the fretboard, the headstock, and even on the bridge. Also, the big guitar sported a hand-engraved tailpiece and was wrapped in a blue ribbon that said "Super 400" on it.

Professional guitarists eagerly embraced the new Super 400 guitar and utilized it in a variety of musical situations. In the hands of such players as John Cali of the Andre Kostelanetz Orchestra,

Robert Domenick with the Clyde McCoy Orchestra, Muzzy Marcellino with the Ted FioRito Orchestra, Clark Yokum with the Mal Hallett Orchestra, Eddie Deus with the Lloyd Snider Orchestra, and the great orchestra leader and entertainer Alvino Rey, the big guitar became part of the big beat of the prewar jazz and popular orchestras. The big sound of the big guitar also began to emanate over the nation's airwaves and through its movie theaters as the Super 400 quickly found acceptance with guitarists employed by radio stations and movie studios. Eddie Skrivanek of NBC radio and studios, Bobby Sherwood of the MGM staff, Berdell Mathis and Dick Roberts of radio and studio fame, Charles Marshall of the NBC studios in San Francisco, and Chic Gatwood of station WLW in Cincinnati are only a few of the guitarists who began using the Super 400 to project their distinctive musical sounds to audiences throughout the country. Even Rhubarb Red (also known as Lester Polfus or Les Paul), a radio artist of the 1930s, was at least pictured with a new prewar Super 400 in the 1937 Gibson catalog.

The Super 400 also began to find its way into the recording studios, as many of the above guitarists recorded music along with their bandmates during the 1930s and 1940s. Teddy Bunn and Al Casey made their presence felt in the studios, projecting a hard-driving rhythmic sense of jazz that would foreshadow the eventual emergence of the guitar as a solo instrument through the efforts of the great Charlie Christian and Oscar Moore.

Besides the better-known high-profile musicians mentioned above, many other guitarists who worked as performers and teachers of music also began using the Super 400. These included Francis Grinnell in Detroit, Jack Leonard in Portland, Bud Lee and Tom Anderson in San Diego, Lee Allen in Los Angeles, Cecil Ogle in Toledo, George Rose and Eddie Collins in Detroit, Herb Kratoska and Floyd Graham in Kansas City, "Gorde" Burch and Al Barnetts in Chicago, John Alaimo in Boston, Charles Amberger and Billy Vann in New York City, Evan White in Niagara Falls, and many others. Clearly the Super 400 was a force to be reckoned with in the acoustic guitar world of the 1930s and 1940s.

Materials, Construction, and Assembly

The Super 400 was made out of wood, plastic, mother-of-pearl, and metal. Manufacturers commonly used these materials in other stringed musical instruments of the period, but the wood in the Super 400 was of particularly high quality. Holly was used for the headstock overlay, and curly maple was used for the neck, the rims, and the back of the guitar. Mahogany was used to form the internal neck block, the end block, and the kerfing that helped join the rims to the top and back. Ebony was used for the fretboard and mahogany for the center neck strip. The finest close-grain spruce was used for the top of the guitar and for the internal top braces. Finally, rosewood was used to make the bridge. Plastic parts included an ivoroid plastic used to make the nut and the binding, a tortoise shell-colored plastic for the fingerrest, and a mottled plastic used as a special fingerrest overlay. Mother-of-pearl was used for all the inlays. Various metal parts included a steel truss rod, nickel-silver frets, and miscellaneous brass items such as the tailpiece, tuners, and screws. Early Gibson promotional material stated that the wood used in Gibson guitars came from around the world (Bellson, *The Gibson Story,* 1973).

However, a fine instrument is much more than the sum of its parts. Like any fine guitar, the Super 400 was a product of its materials, construction and assembly process, and a certain indefinable quality imparted to the instrument by its makers. The craftsmen appointed to assemble the Super 400 had been working in the same capacity on the Master Model series of Gibson instruments including the L-5 guitar, the F-5 mandolin, the K-5 mandocello, and the H-5 mandola. To assure the highest quality of construction and assembly, Gibson utilized a system in which each craftsman was responsible for a certain portion of the assembly process. Thus, some craftsmen only shaped and assembled necks, others carved tops and backs, and still others made various smaller parts that needed special fitting, such as pickguards and headstock overlays. In addition, certain craftsmen did the inlay work, while others did the assembly, binding, and finishing process. Such a division of labor allowed for considerable quality control that began with the Super 400 and extended downward through the carved-top guitar line to the least expensive guitars as well, since each craftsman performed essentially the same task on each type of guitar. It was this ongoing system of construction and assembly that allowed Gibson to introduce the Super 400 at a very high quality level and to keep its quality at a consistently high level for a long period of time.

The prewar Super 400 acoustic guitar range consists of three basic models. The first model is the noncutaway guitar in sunburst finish with the smaller upper bouts and 24¾-inch scale made from late 1934 through 1936. The first model is sometimes referred to as the "small" Super 400. The second model is the noncutaway guitar in either sunburst or natural finish, with the larger upper bouts and longer 25½-inch scale made from 1937 through 1941. The third model is the Premiere or cutaway guitar in sunburst or natural finish with the larger upper bouts, a single Venetian cutaway, and 25½-inch scale, made from 1939 to 1941. To facilitate an understanding of the evolution of each of these guitars, some general comments about the materials and construction of the Super 400 will be presented first. This discussion will be followed by a review of the specific prewar production models and their major components—headstock, neck, and body—to illustrate the evolution of the guitar during its brief production time. Finally, a summary of much of the prewar information will be presented, including production figures.

The overall assembly process of the Super 400 consisted of several operations performed either sequentially or simultaneously. First, proper woods were selected for the guitar and marked and set aside for Super 400s only. This was especially important for the tops and backs, since they had to be larger than any other guitar tops and backs being made by Gibson at that time. Once the woods were selected, several simultaneous operations began, including making rim assemblies; rough-sawing, carving, and shaping tops and backs; making neck assemblies; and beginning the headstock veneers. After craftsmen completed these operations, they assembled the tops and backs to the rims to form a complete body, attached the neck to the body, and attached the headstock veneer to the headstock. They carried out several different types of fitting operations during this phase of production work and also fitted other parts, such as bridges, tailpieces, and pickguards. Next, they applied the guitar's finish before attaching the miscellaneous small parts (tuners, pickguard, and tailpiece) to the guitar body and headstock. Finally, the miscellaneous parts were attached, the guitar was strung up and played, and then it was set aside either to be kept in stock or to be shipped to a dealer who had placed an order for that particular instrument. At any one time, several different Super 400s were in various stages of the assembly process.

Headstock: The instrument illustrated earlier was made in early 1935 and is representative of all of the features of the first model Super 400. Beginning with the headstock, the guitar's design is both elegant and ornate. Seven-ply binding outlines the contours on the front of the headstock, and the headstock overlay is made of blackened holly. The "Gibson" inlay at the top of the headstock is a very graceful script style commonly referred to as the "prewar"

● **1935 Super 400 headstock, front**
● **1935 Super 400 headstock, back**

script. This inlay is made of mother-of-pearl and was delicately cut from a solid pearl blank with a jeweler's saw and inlaid horizontally into the face of the headstock veneer in a very precise fashion. Directly beneath the Gibson inlay was a new inlay design unique to the Super 400. This design consisted of four triangles separated by a rectangle, all carefully inlaid into the headstock veneer so that the rectangle appears to separate or split the triangles. This headstock inlay pattern, referred to as the "split-diamond inlay," was later used on the Les Paul Custom, the ES-355, and the Johnny Smith guitars. The newly designed truss-rod cover partially repeated the split-inlay pattern. The truss-rod cover, of black plastic, is bound with white trim on the outer edges and contains an inlaid center parallelogram similar to the larger pearl inlay in the split-diamond design directly above it. Taken together, the Gibson script, split-diamond inlay, and truss-rod cover present a rather striking horizontal/vertical motif on the headstock. A simpler split-inlay pattern, with two proportional triangles divided by an elongated hexagonal figure, is inlaid directly into the center of the back of the headstock.

The brass tuning machines were made by the Grover Company and were a fancier version of a similar tuning machine offered previously on the L-5 guitar. They utilized a single worm gear, which was not enclosed or lubricated, and featured rather delicate engraving on the gear plate and on the brass tuning buttons. These tuners are often called "open-back Grovers." (It should be noted that these early Grover tuning machines did not seem to keep the guitar in tune very well, and many owners of first model Super 400s replaced them with the larger and more efficient Grover Imperial tuning keys or the later Kluson Sealfast enclosed tuning machines officially introduced on the Super 400 during 1938–1939.) All parts of the tuning machines were gold-plated, including the slotted screws. The rather small size of the tuners seemed to emphasize further the large size of the headstock, adding to its unusual character. The engraving and plating of the tuners also contributed to the overall appearance of the headstock as a very fancy piece of work. When viewed from the side, the headstock can be seen to taper gently from approximately a ¾-inch thickness at the neck juncture to a ⅝-inch thickness at the far end of the headstock. From this viewpoint, the highly figured curly maple of the headstock can also be seen.

● **1935 Super 400 tuners**

Neck: The neck of the first model Super 400 continued the theme of ornate, high-quality craftsmanship. The neck was constructed of two pieces of book-matched curly maple with a center strip of mahogany that is visible from the back of the neck. Gibson called this design the "two-piece" neck, although others often called it the "three-piece" neck because of the mahogany center strip. Gibson design engineers felt that making the neck out of two pieces of book-matched curly maple with a center strip of mahogany would strengthen the neck and prevent warpage, as well as provide a rather distinctive appearance. The two-piece neck continues a design pioneered on the original L-5 guitar. The Super 400's neck utilized Gibson's patented adjustable truss rod, which began slightly above the nut and was placed in a channel in the neck under the fretboard. The truss rod terminated in the heel of the neck and was adjustable at the headstock only. The back of the neck on this instrument has a subtle ridge, and the neck feels fairly thick by today's standards. In Gibson's original announcement about the instrument, they described the neck only as "highly figured curly maple" with an "ovaled ebony finger board." The neck joins the guitar body at the

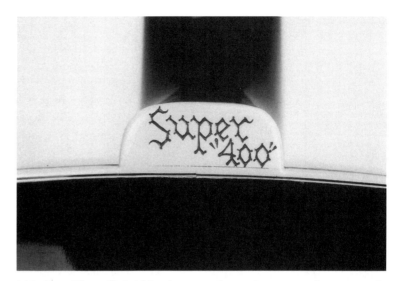

● 1935 Super 400 heel cap

14th fret. The celluloid heel cap on the neck was another unusual feature of these prewar Super 400s. The thick heel cap was engraved with the words "Super 400," a feature Gibson has not offered on any other carved-top instrument before or since.

The ebony fretboard features 20 nickel-silver frets and is bound with three-ply binding consisting of a thin white layer next to the fretboard followed by a thin black layer and then a thicker, more rounded white layer at the outside edge of the fretboard. On the left side of the fretboard binding are shell dots inlaid into the binding at the 1st, 3rd, 5th, 7th, 9th, 12th, 15th, and 17th frets. These position markers correspond to the fretboard inlays at the same position on the face of the fretboard. The three-layer binding terminates in a graceful point at the end of the fretboard just past the 20th fret, and this termination is executed in a very precise fashion. From the 14th fret, where the neck joins the body, to the 20th fret is a section of the fretboard called the fretboard extension, which is clear of the guitar body. Gibson installed a matching piece of curly maple under the fretboard at the 14th fret that joins it to both the neck and the body and tapers upward from the body to the base of the fretboard. When viewed from the side, the fretboard extension appears clear of the body from the 16th fret past the 20th fret. This maple piece was used to support the fretboard extension and to minimize any inhibition of top vibration.

Gibson continued the split-diamond theme of the headstock for the fretboard inlays by utilizing a complex pattern that resembles split blocks of mother-of-pearl. Where the L-5 had utilized simpler one-piece blocks of mother-of-pearl inlays at the standard fretboard positions, the Super 400 introduced a sequence of eight alternating three-piece and two-piece inlays that enhanced the appearance of the instrument and required substantially more cutting and fitting as well. The three-piece inlays appeared at the 1st, 5th, 9th, and 15th positions, while the two-piece inlays appeared at the 3rd, 7th, 12th, and 17th positions. The nickel-silver frets seem thin when compared to those on instruments from the late 1950s onwards. The fretboard does have a notable radius, which gives the tactile impression of an arched shape when playing the instrument. The nut was made of an ivoroid plastic material, and most of these nuts have yellowed considerably with age. The guitar has a 24¾-inch scale length, measured from the nut to the center of the bridge, which is unique to the first model Super 400 only. All subsequent models of the Super 400 used the 25½-inch scale.

Body: The body of the first model Super 400 continued the theme of ornateness and high quality described above. The most obvious feature of the guitar's body, when viewed from the front, is its width—a full 18 inches across the lower bout at its widest point. By comparison, the standard Gibson L-5 (1924–1934) was only 16 inches wide at the lower bout. The Super 400's wider 18-inch body presented a truly striking appearance even when compared to the Advanced L-5, introduced in late 1934 with a new lower bout width of 17 inches. The top of the guitar was initially carved by machine and finally shaped by hand and was made of the finest spruce available. One of the early sales pitches for the Super 400 reminded dealers and potential customers that the guitar got its name not only from its price ($400) but from the fact that a spruce tree approximately 400 years old was needed to make the Super 400's wide top. Gibson decided on a uniform grain width of 16 grain lines to the inch for the top, and because the finished instrument had to be 18 inches wide across the lower bout, the actual top width prior to assembly and finishing had to be between 18½ and 19 inches. To find spruce of this grain width and total width required a tree that was approximately 400 years old.

● **1935 Super 400 body**

When viewed from the side, the top appears to have two pronounced arches, the first rising up underneath the fretboard extension and the second rising up under the tailpiece. The middle area of the top appears to be somewhat flat by comparison to these two areas, and this unusual top contour is often misinterpreted as a "sagging top," as if the braces had come loose inside the body. However, this was the standard carving pattern for the first model Super 400 top. The top of the Super 400 was braced underneath with two spruce braces in an X-pattern. This was a change from the parallel bracing of the 16-inch L-5, and was thought to produce more volume and a different tone than the smaller guitars were able to muster.

One rather interesting minor variation on the first model Super 400 is related to the thickness of the top. Gibson began to experiment with the guitar right away, offering both a thin-top version and a thick-top version. The difference in thickness between the two tops was approximately 1/16 inch, and the thin-top version had a somewhat lower, thinner bridge base than the thick-top version. Gibson's thinking was that the thin-top model would achieve the sound of the small-bodied L-5s, while the thicker-top model would project a somewhat different or "richer" tone because the top was thicker and the bridge was higher. However, Bellson noted that there was really no noticeable difference in the tone of the instruments, so Gibson standardized the instruments with one uniform top thickness and one uniform bridge size. There is no accurate count of the number of thick- or thin-top models available. (The 1935 Super 400 illustrated elsewhere in this book is apparently a thick-top version of the guitar.)

The f-holes in the top were rather small, considering the overall size of the instrument. In fact, they were roughly the same size as those available on the 16-inch L-5, although the Super 400 f-holes were bound with triple-ply white-black-white binding, which makes them look even smaller. Seven-ply ivoroid binding was used to unite the top with the sides of the instrument's body, again in an alternating pattern with four layers of white binding and three layers of black binding. The two-piece bridge was made of rosewood, with a base that was carefully hand-fitted to its position on top of the guitar. The bottom of the base was carefully contoured to match the contours of the guitar

top exactly, and the base rose upward with a taper on each end, terminating in a central flat area that supported the compensated rosewood bridge saddle. Brass posts and small brass wheels were utilized to hold the bridge saddle in place and to elevate it on the treble and bass sides of the instrument. Each end of the bridge base had a triangular pearl inlay pointing towards the bridge posts, and the bridge saddle had a longer triangular pearl inlay on its front and back. In continuing the themes of triangles and ornateness, the Gibson design engineers seemed to have left almost no space untouched!

The tailpiece for the new instrument was made of brass and was attached to the guitar body at its end on the rim joint, hinging over the top but not actually touching it except at the binding. This tailpiece, in its ornateness alone, stood in stark contrast to the much simpler L-5 tailpiece of the same time period. When examined closely, the tailpiece reveals the following details. "Super 400" is engraved in a calligraphic fashion in the center of the crossbar. Etched diamond shapes adorn each end of the crossbar and continue downward on the long hinged top piece. These diamond shapes are surrounded by an intricate etching pattern. When a first model Super 400 tailpiece can be found in excellent condition, it is apparent that a great deal of hand finishing went into this particular piece of hardware. The entire tailpiece was gold-plated, with the various geometric figures being highly polished while the surrounding areas had a satin-brushed appearance. Such differences in texture imparted a contrasting effect, when viewed from the front, that focused one's attention on the intricate etching patterns. The end of the tailpiece

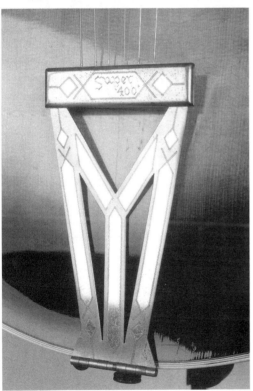

- 1935 Super 400 f-hole
- 1935 Super 400 bridge
- 1935 Super 400 tailpiece

featured a large triangle, pierced in the center by a hole for the large ebony end pin, which itself had white inlaid circles in the center. This end piece was attached to the longer top portion of the tailpiece by a pinned hinge. The tailpiece was secured to the body with three screws located at the apex and along the sides of the triangular figure. These tailpieces were manufactured outside the Gibson factory to Gibson specifications.

The sides of the guitar body were also made of highly figured curly maple and were formed on the bending iron. The sides of the guitar are joined at each end of the body, although the top joint is invisible because it is covered by the heel of the neck. The rims terminate at the bottom end of the body in a single seam that is barely visible past the end of the tailpiece. Despite the large lower bouts, the sides of the body flare out less dramatically at the upper bouts, much in the same manner as the body on the 16-inch L-5. This disparity between the upper and lower bout sizes and the location of the bend in the sides provide a very comfortable playing position when the player is seated.

When examined closely, the back of the guitar reveals a notable feat of luthiery in the almost perfect book-matching of its two curly maple pieces. Most of the first model backs that I have seen have been made of curly maple with a fine ribbon-curl grain pattern. The sunburst finish on the back begins with a dark brown at the outer edges and gradually changes color to a beautiful gold-amber tone in the center, perfectly highlighting the ribbon-curl grain of the back. Unlike the top of the guitar, the back has a single-arch pattern that begins at each end of the body and at the rims, arching up towards a higher plane in the center. The rims are bound to the back of the guitar in a three-ply binding pattern of alternating white and black layers that is similar to the top binding but less ornate.

The plastic pickguard on the Super 400 utilized a new type of celluloid overlay material that had a very dramatic appearance. Basically, the pickguard was made of a tortoise shell–like plastic with a veneer of nitrocellulose acetate on top that gave the appearance of floating pieces of reddish-brown and white plastic. This pickguard material is often referred to as "mottled" or "marbleized" by Gibson workers and guitar enthusiasts. The pickguard was rather long and was bound on all edges in five-ply white-black binding. The forward portion of the pickguard was secured on the guitar with a large, gold-plated screw that passed through the top left corner of the pickguard directly into the guitar top beside the fretboard extension. There was a large plastic support block glued to the underside of the pickguard at this point that also rested on the guitar top. The back portion of the pickguard was secured to the rim of the guitar with Gibson's threaded rod and bracket assembly, as used on the L-5. This assembly elevated and stabilized the pickguard over the guitar top. These brass metal parts were also gold-plated, and the brass bracket or "foot" that attached to the rim had a triangle and parallelogram etching pattern engraved on its face. One end of the threaded rod was secured to the bracket with a blind nut, and the other end was threaded into a plastic block attached to the underside of the pickguard.

● **1935 Super 400 pickguard**

Although the 1934 Gibson announcement flyer on the Super 400 gave the body size as 18½ inches wide, 21¾ inches long, and 4 inches deep, the true measurements of the initial instruments are somewhat different. The instrument is actually 18 inches wide at the lower bout, 22 inches long when measured from each end of the body, and 3⁷⁄₁₆ inches deep at the rim. (It is possible that Gibson actually measured the body depth at the center of the body or at one of the two arched points in the top mentioned earlier.)

Finish: On the first model Super 400, the top, rims, back, and neck were finished in a golden sunburst called "rich cremona brown." The instrument was very dark around the edges of the top and back, progressively lightening in color to a golden area in the center of the top surrounding the f-holes and the bridge. The finish lightened on the back in a similar fashion, highlighting the highly figured book-matched curly maple. Some of the early first models have what appears to be a hand-rubbed sunburst finish similar to the finish applied to the earlier L-5 guitars of 1924–1934. Most first models have a sprayed-on lacquer finish, the technique that was utilized on all subsequent Super 400s. The natural finish was not offered on the first model, and would not become available on the second model Super 400 until 1939, when several changes and options for the guitar were announced.

Case: The case for the first model Super 400 was manufactured for Gibson by the G & S Company in Chicago, and was called the Masterkraft Case. It was manufactured with the same care with which the guitar itself was made, being built in a very sturdy fashion of preformed arched plywood that was covered on the outside with genuine leather and lined on the inside with plush purple velvet. The exterior leather covering was very smooth and uniform in texture, with an embossed line approximately 1 inch from the edge of the case on the top and bottom that followed the contour of the case all around. The case had five nickel-plated brass latches to secure the lid to the case body, with one featuring a lock and key. The latches were made by the Excelsior Company of Stamford, Connecticut. A large leather-covered handle was attached to the left side of the case between the second and third latches. The case had two nickel-plated brass hinges on its right side to allow the top to be opened and closed, with four small brass buttons to lean the case on when standing it up on its edge. The case also had four large brass buttons on the bottom. When the lid was opened, it was held in a vertical position with a velvet strap attached inside the lid and case body. The two hinges were covered inside the case with matching purple ribbons, and the case contained an accessory pocket just forward of the neck support that was used to store picks, straps, strings, and so forth. To protect the fine leather on the Super 400's case, a canvas and vinyl zipper cover was included that was carefully fitted to the case. This cover had zippers that worked in opposite directions from the protruding handle of the case and also had a flap that helped secure the top and bottom part of the cover on the case beneath the handle. In my experience, it is extremely unusual to find one of these case covers with a first model Super 400 case, since the covers did not appear to

● **1935 Super 400 pickguard bracket assembly**

be very durable. Also, it should be noted that the leather case and canvas zipper cover were included in the $400 price for the instrument.

Second Model Super 400, 1937–1941

Following the initial sales success of the first model Super 400, Gibson design engineers continued their efforts to increase the instrument's popularity. Possibly through feedback from players, but more certainly through pressure from upper-level management at Chicago Musical Instruments (CMI), the design of the first model Super 400 was altered in such a fashion that in 1937 the instrument presented a distinctly different appearance. In the factory announcement folder of 1937, however, no differences are apparent. This is the first of many instances in which the initial advertising for a revised or new model Super 400 does not match the actual instrument as introduced. Usually, the error was in the use of older copy and photographs depicting earlier instruments. In fact, the instrument pictured in the 1937 product announcement is the same instrument

- **Joe Maphis with his prewar custom Super 400**
- **1937 Super 400 catalog description**

utilized in the 1934 announcement folder, and the condensed 1937 ad copy is also very similar to that used in 1934. Between 1937 and 1941, when production ceased because of wartime demands on materials, manpower, and production facilities, the second model Super 400 continued to evolve in such a manner that two distinct variations appeared. These variations were the 1937–1941 sunburst-finish and the 1939–1941 natural-finish guitars. Additional changes included increase in body size, scale length, and f-hole dimensions.

Sunburst-Finish Variation

Headstock: The headstock of the second model Super 400 is identical to that of the first model, utilizing the same seven-ply binding to outline the headstock contours. The same materials are used throughout—holly headstock veneer, mother-of-pearl inlays, and curly maple headstock pieces. The same inlay patterns were also used on both the front and back of the headstock. The only notable change in the headstock was the addition of the larger Kluson Sealfast tuning machines. These machines were actually introduced in 1938 or 1939, replacing the engraved Grover Sta-Tite tuners that were standard for both the first model Super 400 and the second model through approximately 1938. Of course, it was commonplace for guitarists to replace the smaller, open-back Grover tuning machines, since they did not keep the instrument in tune very well. Also, Gibson began to offer the Kluson Sealfast tuning machines and the large Grover Imperial tuning machines as options in their various prewar catalogs, often encouraging guitarists to "dress up" their Super 400s with the addition of these larger, flashier, and more dependable tuning gears.

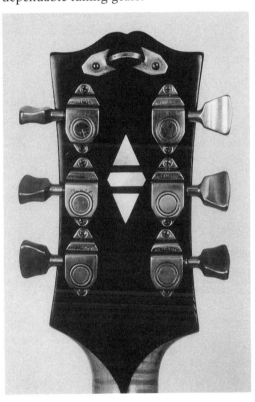

- **1939 Super 400N headstock, front**
- **1939 Super 400N headstock, back**

In 1939, the large Kluson Sealfast tuners, offered as an option two years earlier, were now issued as standard equipment on the Super 400. These tuners had the advantage of being sealed and internally lubricated and kept the instrument in tune to a far more consistent degree than the previous open-back Grover tuners. The tuners utilized amber-colored plastic buttons, and optional gold-plated brass buttons could be ordered.

Neck: The neck of the second model Super 400 retained the same appearance as that of the first model, except that it was slightly longer to accommodate the increased scale length of 25½ inches. This change required an increase in the length of the neck and the distance between the individual frets. Additional changes in the second model neck include a less-pronounced fretboard radius and a slimmer neck contour resulting in the standard neck width of 1¹¹⁄₁₆ inches at the nut. These subtle changes made the second model

● **1939 Super 400N tuner, Kluson Sealfast with optional metal button**

● **1939 Super 400PN tuner, Kluson Sealfast with amber plastic button**

Super 400 much easier to play than the first model, while the aesthetics of the original design—binding, inlays, and materials—were retained.

The same inlay patterns were utilized, and the same materials were also included throughout—ebony for the fretboard, a two-piece book-matched curly maple section for the neck itself, two "wings" of matching curly maple for the edges of the headstock, and a center mahogany strip separating the two halves of the neck. The heel cap was also engraved with "Super 400," and the neck joined the body at the 14th fret. This basic neck design was continued with minimal changes through approximately 1960. The same style three-ply binding was used on the fretboard, and the same shell dots were inlaid into the binding at the fret spaces that corresponded with the fretboard inlays.

Body: It is in the body of the second model Super 400 that the most dramatic changes were apparent. The upper bouts of the body were enlarged from 12¼ inches to 13⅝ inches across, theoretically to increase volume and improve the aesthetics of the instrument. The instrument's top initially retained its X-braced pattern. The f-holes were altered to be somewhat more open or wider than those on the

● **1939 Super 400N body**

first model, also to increase projected volume from the guitar. The instrument continued to utilize the same celluloid pickguard with the marbleized overlay and the same engraved "foot" that secured the pickguard to the rim. The instrument retained the same rosewood bridge base, with triangular inlays at each end, but the triangular inlays on the front and back of the bridge saddle were eliminated. The instrument also featured the same hinged tailpiece used on the first model Super 400, with the same engraving pattern. The back was constructed of two highly figured pieces of curly maple in a variety of grain patterns—flame, ribbon, and bubble. Use of a particular pattern depended on the availability of each pattern and/or a customer's particular request. The binding used on the front and back of the guitar body was the same as that used on the first model Super 400—seven-ply white-black binding on the front and three-ply white-black binding on the back of the instrument.

As production of the second model Super 400 began to increase, Gibson engineers continued to make further changes in the instrument to enhance its already notable appeal. In 1939, several additional changes were made in the instrument. Some were permanent, while others were offered as options for the first time. The permanent changes in the instrument included a change in the top bracing pattern from the X-bracing utilized from 1934 to a parallel bracing pattern. I have examined several instruments from 1939 and have found both X-braced and parallel-braced instruments in approximately the same numbers. According to Julius Bellson, the parallel bracing was introduced at the request of top management, heralding a return to a similar bracing pattern used on the 16-inch L-5s. Additional permanent changes included the standardized use of the larger Kluson Sealfast tuning machines and addition of the new Varitone tailpiece sometime during 1939.

The Varitone tailpiece got its name from its ability to vary the tone of the instrument. This was accomplished by inserting an Allen wrench into a hole in the top of the tailpiece and turning an Allen screw in a small, cylinder-shaped piece of brass attached to the underside of the tailpiece that contacts the top about one inch above the end of the body. As the Allen screw in this cylinder is raised, it forces the cylinder down onto the top of the guitar, which exerts an upward pressure on the tailpiece, raising it slightly away from the top of the instrument. Conversely, by screwing the Allen screw down into the brass cylinder, the tailpiece's height could be lowered closer to the top of the instrument, with some relief of the upward tailpiece pressure. Such changes actually do produce an audible difference in the tone of the instrument. When the tailpiece is elevated, the guitar has a slightly more treble quality. Conversely, when the tailpiece is lowered closer to the top, the instrument seems to produce more sound in the midrange and lower frequencies. Apparently the sound differences are due to varying pressure on the bridge as the strings are either elevated or brought down towards the top by the large crossbar on the end of tailpiece.

The 1941 Super 400 illustrated in color plate 3 neatly summarizes the final steps in the evolution of the prewar Super 400 guitar in sunburst finish. At first glance, its physical appearance is extremely similar to that of the 1937 model described earlier (see also the 1938 model shown in color plate 1). The only external differences that can be easily noted are the change in the f-holes of the 1941 Super 400, which have been lengthened slightly from those of the 1937 model. Also, the Varitone tailpiece is evident on this guitar instead of the hinged tailpiece utilized on the 1937–1939 models. However, there is a more significant change in this instrument that is not apparent on first inspection. This guitar uses a parallel bracing pattern instead of the X-bracing pattern utilized on the earlier first model and second model Super 400s. Also, this particular instrument has the now standard Kluson Sealfast tuning machines with the large amber buttons. Aside from these changes, this instrument is identical in every other detail to the 1937 second model Super 400. Construction of the instrument follows the same process, and the individual sections of the guitar—headstock, neck, and body—are all constructed and finished in the same manner. This particular instrument was one of the last sunburst Super 400s made during the prewar years and is representative of the instrument as it evolved to its final prewar stage.

Finish: The second model Super 400 was offered only in the sunburst finish in 1937 and 1938. However, in 1939 Gibson officially offered the natural finish as an extra-cost option. It will be described below.

Case: The second model Super 400 utilized the same style case as the first model, an arched plywood case covered in genuine leather, which was furnished with a canvas case cover. However, the case was somewhat larger in the upper bout area to accommodate the revised upper bout size of the second model Super 400. Cases for the second model were made by Geib Case Company. It features the standard five nickel-silver latches, as well as the plush-lined interior of purple crushed velvet with a single purple strap designed to hold the guitar case lid open at a 90-degree angle from the case body. The case has the standard pocket for accessories extending from the neck support towards the headstock enclosure. It has the standard brass bumpers on the bottom side of the case, as well as the small embossed line in the leather top that follows exactly the outside edge contour of the case lid.

Natural-Finish Variation

Finish: Among the options offered on the 1939 Super 400 was a very striking new finish. For the first time, Gibson officially announced the introduction of the natural finish as an option on the Super 400 for $10 extra. The Gibson craftsmen had to select the spruce and curly maple body components carefully to maximize the appearance of the instrument while minimizing any flaws in the wood such as mineral streaks and knots, which previously could be covered with the darker portions of the sunburst finish. In other words, wood in the natural-finish instruments had to appear virtually flawless and much more evenly matched than some of that found in the early sunburst instruments. The ad copy illustrated here is from the 1941 Gibson catalog. The catalog copy, as well as the highly retouched instrument photographs, describe the "regular" finish and the new "natural" finish in very

- 1941 Gibson catalog,
  Super 400 and
  Super 400N
- 1939 Super 400N front

colorful language. The particular instrument shown here is a 1939 Gibson Super 400N, one of only seven such instruments reportedly shipped during the prewar years. This particular instrument is also featured in some detail in Chapter 4, but will be described briefly here to illustrate the various changes in the second model Super 400 that were new in 1939.

Headstock: When viewed from the front, the headstock of the 1939 Super 400 appears exactly like that of the 1935 and 1937 Super 400s insofar as the inlay patterns and binding. The headstock was constructed in the same manner as the earlier designs. On the back of the headstock, the reader will notice the brass loop screwed to the upper portion of the headstock. This is part of the optional "neck cord assembly," which could be either purchased and installed by the owner or ordered installed at the factory. It allowed the owner to attach an optional Gibson-supplied silk neck cord or some other type of guitar strap at the end of the headstock and at the opposite end of the guitar on the tailpiece. Also, notice the larger Kluson

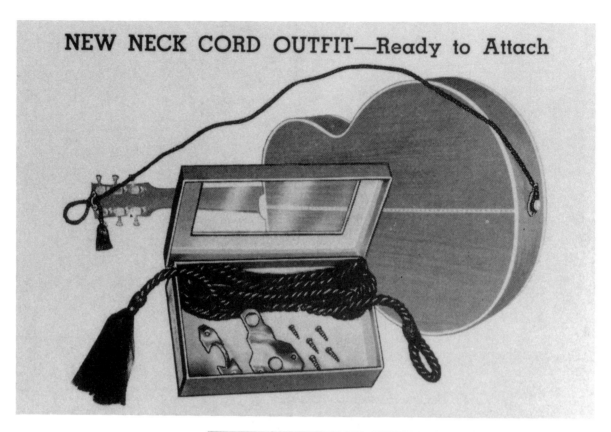

NEW NECK CORD OUTFIT—Ready to Attach

- 1941 Gibson catalog, neck cord
- 1941 Gibson catalog, Kluson Sealfast tuner

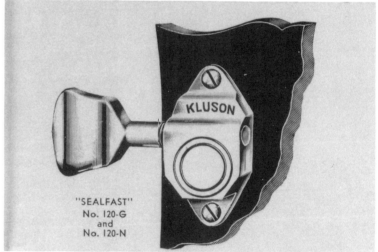

Sealfast tuning machines with their large metal buttons. These buttons were also an option ordered with this particular guitar, in place of the standard buttons made of amber-colored plastic.

Neck: The neck of the 1939 Super 400 is similar to that of the 1937–1938 guitars in all respects, including materials, inlay patterns, width, length, and thickness. However, on this particular instrument, the extension piece under the fretboard is somewhat thicker than in earlier observed instruments, yet still is free of the top of the guitar past the 16th fret.

One minor detail on this particular instrument that differs from the 1937 second model Super 400 is the introduction of the five-ply

binding around the fretboard. All previous versions of the Super 400 guitar utilized a simpler three-ply binding of two narrow bands of white and black with a wider, beveled outer band of thicker white material. This particular instrument features two narrow white bands and two narrow black bands of binding plus the wider, beveled white binding at the outside edge of the fretboard.

Body: The body of the 1939 Super 400 also retained all of the features of the 1937–1938 guitars except for the addition of the Varitone tailpiece as described above. The f-holes initially remained the same but were elongated somewhat in 1940; their width remained the same. One change was introduced regarding the method in which the pickguard was attached to the upper bout of the guitar. In 1939 Gibson changed the attachment from a simple screw into the top of the guitar to an attaching screw that passed through a plastic block underneath the upper part of the pickguard, entering the extension piece under the fretboard. On the illustrated 1939 model, someone had apparently thought about screwing this fingerrest into the top, because a hole was made for the top screw and a small screwhead was glued into the screw hole. However, this pickguard is actually screwed into the side of the fingerboard extension and not into the top, as it appears to be.

When one examines the back of this instrument, it is apparent that highly figured curly maple was utilized in conjunction with the natural finish. The same highly figured curly maple was used on the rims of the instrument, and the neck also features book-matched tiger-striped maple. The arching of the top of the 1939 Super 400 closely followed the arching pattern first introduced on the first model Super 400, with a large pronounced hump at the middle of the upper bouts falling off to a rather flat area down between the f-holes and then terminating in a smaller arched surface rising underneath the elevated tailpiece. Again, the reader is reminded that this pattern does not necessarily mean that the top is sagging, though the braces should always be checked to verify this. This instrument, like all the prewar Super 400s, was furnished with the standard leather-covered plywood case and a canvas case cover.

The 1941 Super 400N illustrated in color plate 3 represents the final stage of the evolution of the prewar natural-finish Super 400 noncutaway guitar. However, since only seven Super 400Ns were reportedly shipped between 1939 and 1941, the evolution of features took place rather quickly. This 1941 Super 400N differs from the earlier 1939 Super 400N in only three major respects. First, the f-holes are somewhat longer than those on the 1939 model. Second, the Varitone tailpiece is now standard equipment. (I have seen a 1939 Super 400N with a hinged tailpiece exactly like that utilized on the 1934–1939 Super 400s as standard equipment.) Third, this particular instrument features parallel bracing as opposed to X-bracing. But perhaps the most striking aspect of this particular instrument is its almost brand-new condition. This instrument surely represents the height of Gibson's efforts in the noncutaway Super 400 guitar, containing the latest features of the time and an exquisite tone that sets it apart from many instruments that I have examined and played. It is supplied with a mint-condition, leather-covered Geib hard-shell

● **1939 Super 400N,**
f-hole
● **Marty Grosz**

case and a later black canvas cover, a replacement for the original tan canvas cover, which was lost many years ago.

This instrument was constructed of the same materials as its predecessors and featured the same detailing in fit and finish on the headstock, neck, and body of the guitar. As on the 1939 model, highly figured curly maple was utilized for the two-piece carved back, the rims, and the two-piece neck. The materials in this instrument are breathtaking and with the natural finish form a rather stunning statement regarding the art of the fine guitar. The retail price of this instrument in 1941 was $426 with case and case cover.

Case: These "later" second model Super 400s were also supplied with the Geib leather-covered plywood case and canvas case cover. The case was priced separately from the guitar for the first time (see Table B-11 in Appendix B), while the case cover continued to be included at no extra charge.

● 1940 Gibson catalog, Super 400 Premiere and L-5 Premiere

Third Model Super 400 (Premiere), 1939–1941

The year 1939 was a banner one for Gibson, for it also marked the introduction of the cutaway body design on several of its carved-top guitars. This cutaway design was the rounded or Venetian type and was achieved with some difficulty by bending the right rim sharply inward, then straightening it out again to join the side of the interior neck block. The cutaway presented a striking change in the visual appearance of carved-top instruments and offered the guitarist access to most of the frets. To an intrepid few, it offered access to the entire fretboard! This new Super 400 cutaway model was called the "Premiere." The Premiere or third model Super 400 was offered in two variations, the first with the standard cremona-brown sunburst finish and the second utilizing the new natural finish.

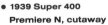
- **1939 Super 400 Premiere N, body**
- **1939 Super 400 Premiere N, cutaway**

Body: The body of the third model Super 400 Premiere presented a radical departure from the body of the second model. The upper bout width of the second model was retained, but a single Venetian cutaway was introduced in the right upper bout. The cutaway was designed to give the guitarist greater access to the upper register of the instrument, while also broadening the product line. To my knowledge, all third model Premieres have parallel-braced tops with the longer f-holes seen first in 1939. Internally, the neck block was somewhat smaller to accommodate the cutaway. The very first Premieres from 1939 have the fretboard extension resting flush on the guitar top. By 1941 the neck angle had been altered, and the fretboard extension was again clear of the top as on the first and second model Super 400s.

The third model cutaway was formed by bending the right rim somewhat sharply, with extra parallel-grain bracing on the inside of the cutaway. The first Premieres featured an unusual top carving pattern around the cutaway that looks somewhat "bulged" in appearance. By 1941, the top contour had been changed so that the top area around the cutaway had a flatter and more gradual slope.

The cutaway was bound into the neck joint with the usual seven-ply alternating pattern of white-black plastic binding. The cutaway also required a shorter pickguard, which was usually made of the same tortoise shell–like plastic with the mottled overlay. In a very few instances, the pickguard was made of a white patterned plastic and bound in the usual manner. The engraved foot and rod assembly was carried over from the second model.

The tailpiece for the Premiere was the new rigid model incorporating the Varitone adjustment feature. All Super 400 Premieres also utilize the Varitone tailpiece instead of the hinged variety, and these early Varitone tailpieces have the words "PAT. APPLIED FOR" stamped into the upper portion of the tailpiece extension that screws into the

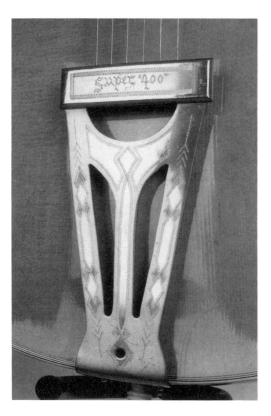
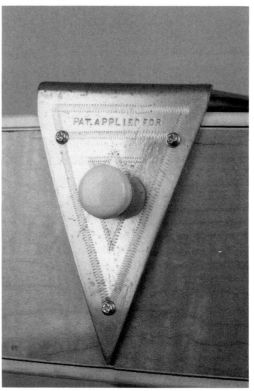

- 1939 Super 400 Premiere N, Varitone tailpiece
- 1939 Super 400 Premiere N, tailpiece

rim of the guitar (a PAF tailpiece, no less!). Many years later Gibson eliminated the Varitone from the rigid tailpiece because its usefulness in altering the tone of the guitar was questionable, and overzealous owners would sometimes tighten the Varitone screw so much that the top would crack under the tailpiece.

Natural-Finish Variation

Just like its noncutaway relative, the Super 400 Premiere in natural finish had to be constructed of the most flawless woods available, since the rather clear finish could not hide any knots or mineral streaks in the wood. Hence, the natural-finish Super 400 Premieres tend to have spectacular wood on the back, rims, and neck, which show off the many variations of curly maple to its best advantage. The Super 400 Premiere shown in color plate 2 is a 1939 model, the first year of the natural finish and of the cutaway design. Interestingly, all Super 400 Premieres were introduced with parallel bracing instead of the X-bracing found on some 1939 Super 400 noncutaway instruments. Also, the 1939 Premiere features the now standardized f-hole of 7⅝ inches in length and 1³⁄₁₆ inches in width, instead of the shorter and wider f-holes noted on the 1939 Super 400 noncutaway guitar mentioned above.

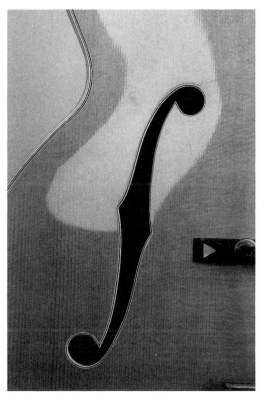

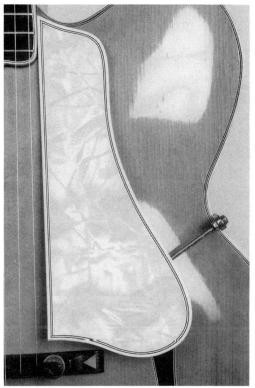

- **1939 Super 400 Premiere N, f-hole**
- **1939 Super 400 Premiere N, pickguard**

The detailing on this instrument is magnificent in every respect. Since the lighter areas of a natural finish cannot hide any flaws or reworking, all of the outside glue joints are visible and are not only intact but very finely done. Aside from the cutaway feature and the lower neck angle, the 1939 Premiere appears very similar in construction to the standard second model Super 400 noncutaway guitar. The headstock, neck, and body all appear to be constructed in exactly the same manner, with the exception of the pitch of the neck on the 1939 Premiere. These very early Premieres had a somewhat lower neck angle than the later ones, and the fretboard extension appears to rest exactly on the top of the guitar with only a small curly maple spacer between the underside of the fretboard and the top of the guitar. This spacer makes contact with the top of the guitar at all points. This particular instrument also features an unusual pickguard, although it is original to the instrument. Instead of the usual mottled celluloid, this pickguard is made of a pearloid-like plastic and bound in the standard five-ply manner. This type of pickguard material is occasionally found on other prewar Super 400s and on other Gibson carved-top instruments, but it is extremely rare and was probably used on an experimental basis only.

On the 1939 Premieres, the top is carved in such a manner that it rises dramatically under the fretboard extension, tapering down to a flatter area between the f-holes and finally rising slightly in a less pronounced arch under the tailpiece before tapering rapidly down to the rim. This profile, when examined from the side, is very similar to the top-carving pattern on the first model Super 400. The back of this instrument features highly flamed book-matched curly maple with

● **1939 Super 400 Premiere N, bridge detail**

extremely strong striping as well as some medullary patterning, which is visible when viewed from a certain angle. A noticeable arch is felt in the carving pattern of the two-piece back, in which the arching pattern begins about an inch from the rims and rises rapidly into a noticeable swell in the center of the back. This back is carved very symmetrically all around the instrument. Also, because of the rather shallow neck angle, the heel cap on this particular instrument is smaller than those found on subsequent instruments. In all other respects, the instrument features the standard appointments of the Super 400 second model guitars, including the bridge and Kluson Sealfast tuners. The tailpiece is particularly striking, with alternating dull and bright patterns and an intricate etching pattern of various panels over the top of the tailpiece as well as a set of simpler designs on the end of the tailpiece that attaches to the rim of the guitar. A six-pointed star is featured in the very center of this tailpiece extension, which itself is pierced by a large hole containing the ivoroid end pin.

The retail price of this instrument in 1939 was $425, including the leather-covered hard case and canvas case cover. This particular instrument is accompanied by a black leather-covered case with an unusual appearance. Instead of the standard light brown leather, this case is covered in a black alligator-grained leather with an orange band painted around the entire rim of the case top, just above the case latches. Although the case has four regular nickel-plated brass latches and one locking latch, these latches are of a different design than those utilized on the standard Super 400 cases described earlier. These nickel-plated latches are exactly like the smaller ones utilized on the 16-inch L-5 cases in the late 1920s and were manufactured by the Eagle Lock Company of Terryville, Connecticut. The interior of this case is lined in a reddish-orange plush velvet, with an internal case pocket just forward of the neck support. This is an original Gibson case for this instrument, although this style of case is encountered very infrequently. Occasionally this type of case was also used with the prewar L-5, L-12, and other fine carved-top guitars. This case also features a much sturdier metal handle instead of the usual leather-covered handle that was more prevalent on the brown leather cases.

Sunburst-Finish Variation

The 1941 Super 400 Premiere illustrated here, like the 1941 second model noncutaway Super 400 mentioned earlier, represents the final evolution of the prewar cutaway Super 400 guitar and all its features. Compared to the 1939 Super 400N Premiere, this instrument appears similar in almost every respect except for the finish and the pitch of the neck. On this instrument, the neck angle appears somewhat more elevated, and the curly maple spacer underneath the fretboard extension contacts the top of the guitar at the neck joint but rises slightly above the top at approximately the 17th fret, thus clearing the body for the last three frets. This instrument possesses the standard pickguard made of the mottled celluloid material. When viewed from the side, the carving pattern of the top of this instrument is very similar to that of the 1939 Premiere, as is the carving pattern of the back of the instrument. However, this instrument features a book-matched curly maple back featuring an attractive bubble maple pattern rather than a striped or flamed maple design. Because of the higher neck angle on this instrument, the heel of the guitar and the corresponding heel block are somewhat larger than those on the 1939 model. All other features of this instrument are identical with those of the 1939 model, including the various metal and wooden appointments on the guitar.

This instrument also comes with the standard light brown Geib hard-shell case covered with leather, with the purple plush-velvet interior and the standard case pocket located just forward of the neck support. On this case, as in some others, the Geib Company label is embossed on a circular medallion of thin brass that is glued to the top of the case pocket cover. This case also has the standard nickel-plated latches noted on most earlier cases, made by the Excelsior Company of Stamford, Connecticut. The case also features the four standard brass bumpers on the bottom and the standard leather-covered handle with the metal insert attached to the handle anchors on the case. This particular case is in very good condition but shows considerable wear, and it illustrates clearly what happens to these leather-covered cases when they are not protected by a case cover. The case has various scuff marks, water stains, and other marks of an indeterminate origin. However, it is structurally quite sound and has kept the instrument in its current excellent original condition.

● 1941 Super 400
Premiere, cutaway

Summary

In late 1934 the Gibson Corporation stunned the fretted instrument world with their unveiling of the Super 400 guitar, at that time the largest carved-top guitar in production by either a major company or individual luthiers. The first model Super 400 was unique in two main respects—it was 18 inches across its lower bouts, and its level of ornamentation was much fancier than that of any other guitar available at that time. All first model Super 400 guitars, from late 1934 through the end of 1936, are essentially similar in all respects. They have a unique body style consisting of a small 12¼-inch upper bout and a much larger 18-inch lower bout. The hand-carved spruce top was braced underneath in an X-pattern. The small f-holes were bound in triple-ply binding, and the guitar top had a unique carving pattern that appears depressed in the center when viewed from the side of the instrument. The two-piece, book-matched, carved curly maple back was highly figured, and the entire guitar was finished in

● **1941 Gibson catalog, various artists**

● **1941 Gibson catalog,
various artists**

a rich cremona–brown sunburst. The guitar scale length was 24¾ inches, and the instrument was equipped with a hinged, engraved gold-plated brass tailpiece and small engraved gold-plated brass Grover tuning machines. The instrument was offered only in the sunburst finish, and the price for the instrument was $400 including a plywood case covered in leather and lined with a purple plush material. This case was enclosed in a canvas zipper case cover made to order for the guitar and case. Approximately 92 of these guitars were made from late 1934 through the end of 1936.

In 1937 the Super 400 was altered substantially to produce the second model Super 400, made with some changes from 1937–1941. The width of the upper bout was increased from 12¼ inches to 13¾ inches while the lower bout retained its 18-inch width. The guitar's scale length was also increased from 24¾ inches to 25½ inches. The only other major change was a subtle widening of the f-holes, though their length initially remained the same. From 1937 to 1939, the second model Super 400 retained the X-braced top and hinged

29

brass tailpiece of the first model, and was offered only in a sunburst finish.

However, in 1939 the natural finish was offered on the noncutaway Super 400 as an option for the first time. Several other changes also occurred in 1939. Approximately halfway through the year, Gibson changed the top braces to a parallel bracing pattern, and has retained essentially that same bracing pattern to the present day. The hinged brass tailpiece was replaced by the new Varitone tailpiece, which was rigid in its design but allowed the musician to subtly adjust the timbre of the instrument by loosening or tightening the tailpiece at the end of the guitar. Sometime during 1939 the f-holes of the Super 400 were lengthened from 7 inches to 7¾ inches. The larger and more reliable Kluson Sealfast tuning machines were introduced in 1939. Thus, the second model Super 400 includes both a sunburst and a natural-finish variation, a transition from X-bracing to parallel bracing in instruments of both finish types, and the various other changes detailed above.

The third model Premiere, or cutaway Super 400, was offered for the first time in 1939. This instrument presented still another major change for the working musician to contemplate, the cutaway upper bout on the right side of the instrument. This cutaway allowed access further up the fretboard than earlier guitars did, and became instantly popular among musicians of the day. The Premiere was manufactured from 1939 through 1941 and was available in both the sunburst and the natural-finish variations. To my knowledge, all Premieres were parallel braced and featured the longer f-holes of the period and the rigid Varitone tailpiece. The scale length on these guitars was also 25½ inches. Approximately 29 sunburst Premieres and 18 natural Premieres were produced during 1939–1941. During these three short years, the guitar evolved fairly quickly in two key respects—the neck angle and shaping of the cutaway. On the 1939 Premieres, the neck angle is very "shallow"—that is, the fretboard seems more parallel to the top of the instrument and the fretboard extension actually rests directly on top of the guitar. The cutaway areas for the top and back were carved in such a manner that they seemed to swell right where the top and back met the bent rim to form the cutaway. By 1941, the neck angle had been elevated slightly so that the fretboard was not parallel to the top of the guitar. The fretboard extension did not rest on top of the guitar now, so vibration of the top was less inhibited. Also, the carving of the top and back around the cutaway area was smoother and without the characteristic swell of the 1939 models. Both cutaway and noncutaway guitars were furnished with the standard plywood case, covered in leather and lined with a plush pink or purple interior. Occasionally a black leather case with an orange plush lining is also encountered with the Premiere model. By 1941, the sunburst Premiere cost $441.25 and the natural-finish Premiere cost $452.25.

For all intents and purposes, production of the Super 400 guitar stopped in 1941 when the United States formally entered World War II. Production of the Super 400 and the L-5 guitars, as well as various other types of instruments that required a considerable amount of handwork,

• 1945, "Bobby Dick and his Super 400 guitar"

was halted so that essential materials could be conserved and "war work" could be performed. Like many manufacturers around the country, Gibson was asked by the U. S. government to fabricate certain parts for various items used in the war effort. One contribution of the Gibson staff to the U. S. war effort was the application of their expertise in bending guitar rims to making wooden glider skids. When they were assigned this task, the Gibson staff learned by experimentation that only pressing the five plies of wood required for the glider skids would not keep them permanently bent, and that often the tips of the glider skids would "spring back." Julius Bellson stated that the Gibson staff then began to prebend the tips of the glider skids on their guitar rim-bending forms. After the skid tips were prebent, the plies were then glued together, and the ends did not lose their shape or spring back. Apparently other manufacturers who worked with wood were having a difficult time retaining the shapes of these glider skids, so Gibson was asked to consult with various other manufacturers to teach them how to bend the skids properly.

The Gibson Corporation also made at least two other parts for war weapons. The first was a plunger for the Crosley Company, a proximity fuse trigger with a phosphor spring that when heated would expand and explode. Gibson also manufactured some guide rods for the Guide Lamp Company in Anderson, Indiana, a division of Ford Motor Company. The guide rods were used in the M-3 submachine guns in conjunction with twin recoil springs to keep the breech block on track as it recoiled from the backward pressure of each round that was fired. Once again Gibson offered some innovative consulting ideas by convincing the Guide Lamp staff to use a duplicate set of measuring tools like Gibson's so the quality control on these particular rods would be very high. Unfortunately, at the war's end, Guide Lamp did not respond to Gibson's query regarding possible cancellation of a pending order of tons of the rod material, so Gibson was stuck with a lot of metal rods that were eventually sold for scrap.

It should also be noted that the main reason many guitars were not produced was twofold—first, all the efforts of the factory staff were needed to produce parts for the U. S. war effort; and second, use of some of the materials in the Super 400, such as ebony and brass, were restricted because of the war. The amount of metal that could be used on an instrument was limited to no more than 10 percent of the total weight of the instrument. Gold or nickel plating was not allowed. Bellson stated that "we [could] no longer make what we considered to be a Gibson instrument, so we gave it up and went on to war work." Production of the Super 400 did not resume until 1947.

Briefly, the following summarizes the number and types of Super 400s shipped during the prewar years of 1934–1941.

First Model, 1934–1936	92
Second Model, Sunburst, 1937–1941	309
Second Model, Natural, 1939–1941	7
Third Model Premiere, Sunburst, 1939–1941	29
Third Model Premiere, Natural, 1939–1941	18
Total, 1935–1941	455

Thus a total of approximately 455 prewar Super 400s were shipped, including all models.

Chapter
II

The Postwar Gibson Super 400 Acoustic Guitar

● **1949 Gibson
Super 400CN**

As World War II headed towards
its inevitable conclusion, monumental changes began to occur at
Gibson that would forever alter the company's course as a leading
musical instrument manufacturer. In 1944 the Chicago Musical
Instrument Company (CMI) acquired a controlling interest in
Gibson, Inc. CMI was a distributor of high-quality musical
merchandise and foresaw the tremendous profitablity that could be
achieved by Gibson with an infusion of additional capital. M. H.
Berlin, founder and president of CMI, became secretary-treasurer of
Gibson as well in 1944. Following Berlin's association with Gibson
in a key leadership role, many new policies were instituted that
correctly anticipated the incredible postwar demand for Gibson
products. Besides several top-management changes, plans were
formulated to implement sizable production increases and the
simultaneous introduction of new types of guitars once World War II
ended. According to Julius Bellson, Berlin "authorized the addition
of approximately 15,000 square feet of milling and production area,
purchased new equipment and machinery, and the construction of
an enlarged, improved lumber storage." (Bellson, *The Gibson Story,*
Chapter 23). Additional changes included a rather dramatic shift
to the use of authorized Gibson franchise dealers located in different
geographic regions of the country in place of the earlier distribution
policy of selling Gibson instruments through territorial agents
who often functioned as music teachers. This policy also correctly
anticipated the great increase in demand for Gibson products
following World War II. To meet the anticipated increase in
production, the Gibson work force was increased considerably
and war work was finally discontinued in 1945.

Several events occurred immediately after World War II that
dramatically affected the production and expansion of the Super 400
guitar line. The first event was the introduction of a complete line
of electric arch-top guitars, including the very fine ES-5. The ES-5
was the predecessor of the Super 400CES and the L-5CES, whose
evolution and development will be discussed in Chapters 3 and 6.
Secondly, Theodore McCarty joined the Gibson management staff
in 1948. McCarty's contributions to the development of various
Gibson products are legendary, and his specific contributions to
the development of the electric Super 400 guitar will be discussed
in Chapter 3.

Besides internal changes in Gibson's product line and the addition
of Ted McCarty, the changing musical scene also had considerable
influence over the eventual direction of the Super 400. A rapid
decline in popular and jazz orchestras and the burgeoning interest in
small combo jazz groups led many guitarists to utilize the acoustic
Super 400 in this new context. Emerging guitarists with great talent

- 1960 Gibson catalog artists including Norman Brown
- 1960 Gibson catalog artists including George Gobel and Bill Haley

and promise included Kenny Burrell, who would go on to play the Super 400C and the Super 400CES as his main instruments for long periods of time; sideman Bill DeArango; and outstanding rhythm player and accompanist Marty Grosz. Besides the obvious acceptance of the instrument as a jazz guitar, the Super 400 began to find its way into other avenues of musical expression. The acoustic Super 400 began to be a featured rhythm instrument for the emerging field of Country and Western music. Several performers such as Sonny James, Hank Snow, Don Gibson, Leon Payne, Billy Grammer, and George McCormick began using the acoustic Super 400 as a rhythm and accompaniment instrument with some success. Also, the late Joe Maphis used his acoustic Super 400 as an amplified guitar with telling effect as he expanded the boundaries of country music by incorporating elements of jazz, Western swing, blues, and other influences in his highly original and stunning playing style. Entertainers in a "popular music" vein at different times in our recent musical history have also utilized the Super 400. George Gobel utilized a prewar Super 400N as an accompanying piece that seemed almost as big as he was! Norman Brown, the outstanding accompanist with the Mills Brothers, played a Super 400CN with the vocal group for many years. Currently Country and Western artist Lyle Lovett plays a Super 400CN as one of his main instruments, and Charlton Johnson, rhythm guitarist in the Count Basie Orchestra, swings with a postwar noncutaway Super 400 as well.

Gibson commissioned a series of engineer's drawings, produced between August and November of 1945, depicting various subassemblies of the Super 400 noncutaway acoustic guitar as part of its efforts to resume production of the Super 400 after the war. Careful examination of these engineer's drawings makes it apparent that the overall concept of the Super 400 remained relatively unchanged, although its ornamentation was simplified somewhat. This simplification of ornamentation resulted in some cost savings on the instrument, which allowed a slight increase in the profit margin on each guitar without necessitating a premature rise in the price for postwar guitar customers. Initially, the Super 400 lineup of postwar acoustic guitars included the fourth model noncutaway guitar and the fifth model cutaway guitar, both offered in sunburst and natural finish.

Fourth Model Super 400,
1947–1955

The fourth model Super 400 acoustic guitar is a noncutaway guitar whose general appearance is similar to the corresponding prewar second model in most respects.

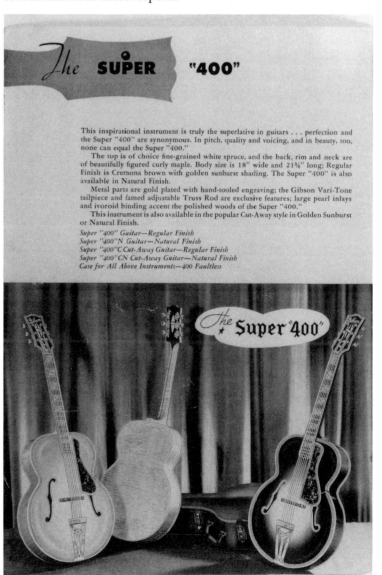

● 1950 Gibson catalog,
Super 400 and
Super 400N

37

Headstock: The very first fourth model Super 400 instruments were assembled in 1947 and shipped in 1947–1948, and reflected a curious combination of prewar and postwar features that were unique to that period of manufacture only. By 1949, Gibson had completed the transition from prewar to postwar design standardization of the Super 400, and the ornamentation remained largely unchanged from that point forward for the acoustic models. On the very first postwar production models of 1947–1948, the headstock featured the older Gibson script logo inlaid horizontally into its face just as on the prewar guitars. The headstock also featured the same mother-of-pearl split-diamond inlay on the face and the simpler split

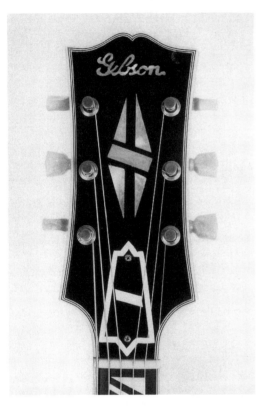

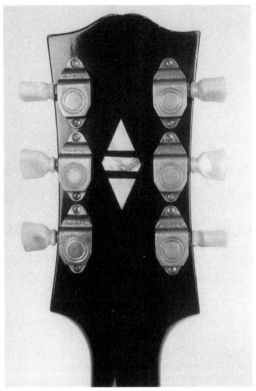

- 1947 Super 400 headstock, front
- 1947 Super 400 headstock, back

logo on the back, and the same truss-rod covers were used. The Kluson Sealfast tuners were continued, but the plastic tuning buttons were smaller and less ornate than the prewar tuning buttons. The seven-ply binding was continued, and the same wood materials were carried over—holly for the headstock overlay and curly maple headstock pieces. The headstock shape also remained unchanged from its second model predecessor. By 1948, the prewar headstock logo had been dropped and the more modern Gibson slanted inlay, which was continued through the end of production of the fourth model Super 400, had been adopted.

Neck: On these first postwar guitars of 1947, the neck inlays remained the same and the simple three-ply fretboard binding was also retained. By 1949 this fretboard binding had been expanded to five-plys, though the fretboard inlays remained unchanged. The scale length remained at 25½ inches, and the guitar continued with the three-piece curly maple neck construction described in the discussion of the second model noncutaway guitars. The neck width remained

● **1947 Super 400 heel cap**
● **1947 Super 400 pickguard**

1¹¹⁄₁₆ inches at the nut, but the new fourth model neck was somewhat thicker in cross section than the second model neck. This slight increase in cross-sectional thickness is reminiscent of the first model neck, though not quite as thick overall. By the time the fourth model was discontinued in 1955, the cross-section thickness had been reduced somewhat. However, the heel caps on the postwar Super 400s were not engraved with "Super 400" as on the prewar guitars. The fretboards of these first transitional guitars were usually ebony, although Brazilian rosewood was used in 1948–1950 because of postwar ebony shortages.

Body: The body of the fourth model Super 400 retained almost all of the features of its corresponding prewar relative, with the same dimensions in all key areas. Parallel bracing of the top was retained, and the f-hole size had been standardized by this time. The particular guitar illustrated in color plate 4 has an unusual plastic pickguard that was standard Gibson material but is very seldom encountered. This material is pictured on the very first Super 400 advertising flyer of 1934 and is occasionally seen on these instruments during the prewar and early postwar years. It is a streaked brownish plastic rather than the mottled type. The pickguard featured the same threaded rod and vertical bracket for attachment to the guitar rim as the prewar models, except that the engraving on the vertical bracket or "foot" was omitted. The guitar continued to feature the solid-base rosewood bridge, but all inlays on the bridge base and saddle were eliminated. Another simplification involved elimination of the intricate engraving patterns on the Super 400 tailpiece. The engraving of the postwar guitars was limited to the words "Super 400" on the crossbar, which was boxed in by a small wavy line pattern. Also, some very small intertwined engraving lines were impressed into the large tapering portion of the tailpiece over the top of the guitar. The Varitone tailpiece tension device was retained, but the roller cam was enlarged in diameter, which later proved to be a mistake because owners of these instruments would tighten down the Varitone device so much that tops of the instruments would occasionally split along the center seam underneath the tailpiece. The Varitone thus lost its effect on the tone of the guitar.

The curly maple backs and sides of the instrument body remained the same, with the same high-quality woods, workmanship, and finish that characterized the prewar guitars. This instrument was supplied with a hard-shell case that is consistent with the transitional nature of the instrument. The case was a Geib model built along the same pattern as the leather-covered prewar cases, but was instead covered with a brown canvas-like material. The guitar came complete with a canvas-lined, vinyl zipper case cover, which was sturdier than the strictly canvas prewar covers. Approximately 64 sunburst and 27 natural-finish fourth model Super 400s were shipped in 1948, some of which had the transitional prewar–postwar features described above.

By 1948–1949, the fourth model Super 400 had evidenced some additional changes, some of which remained with the instrument until the end of production in 1955 while others were altered along the way. The prewar Gibson script logo was replaced by the more modern slanted Gibson logo, which is still used in a similar form today. The guitars from 1948 through 1950 usually had rosewood instead of ebony fretboards, because ebony was a very scarce wartime commodity and ebony stocks could not be easily replenished until approximately 1950 or 1951. The pickguard material was standardized, continuing with the mottled plastic material used on the prewar guitars. The nonengraved threaded rod and bracket assembly was used, and the pickguard was pinned to the fretboard extension as on later prewar guitars. In other respects, the fourth model guitar in both its sunburst and natural-finish variations remained relatively unchanged until the end of production of these guitars in 1955.

Finish: Production of the fourth model noncutaway Super 400 reached 240 units by 1955, with 154 sunburst-finish and 86 natural-finish guitars being shipped. The sunburst-finish and natural-finish variations of the fourth model Super 400 are essentially alike in all respects except for their finishes. Features were quickly standardized after 1947, with only the brief substitution of rosewood for ebony as fretboard material during 1948–1950. The natural-finish fourth models generally have more highly figured wood for backs, rims, and necks, as was the custom for the prewar natural-finish guitars.

Case: The fourth model Super 400 initially utilized a plywood Geib case identical in construction, contour, and fittings to the second model case, except that the postwar case was covered with brown fabric instead of leather. In fact, no postwar Super 400 cases were leather covered. In 1949, Gibson began using Lifton hard-shell cases, also made of plywood, with four case latches and covered with the more familiar brown fabric material used on other Gibson cases from that period. The vinyl and canvas case cover was still offered as an extra-cost option, a practice begun during the end of prewar production. (See Table B-12 in Appendix B for details.)

Fifth Model Super 400C, 1950–Present

The fifth model Super 400 was the postwar cutaway acoustic guitar officially called the Super 400C (cutaway). This instrument

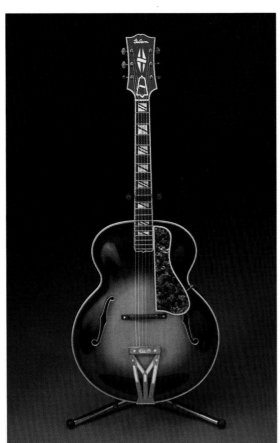
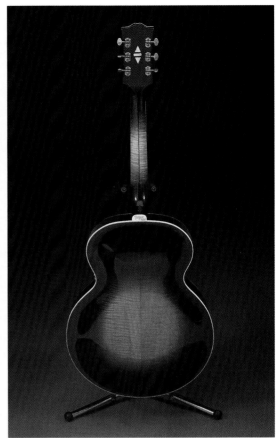

Plate 1
- 1935 Super 400, front
- 1935 Super 400, back
- 1938 Super 400 and leather case

Plate 2
- 1939 Super 400 Premiere N, front
- 1939 Super 400 Premiere N, back
- 1941 Super 400 Premiere, front
- 1941 Super 400 Premiere, back

Plate 3
- 1941 Super 400, front
- 1941 Super 400, back
- 1941 Super 400N, front
- 1941 Super 400N, back

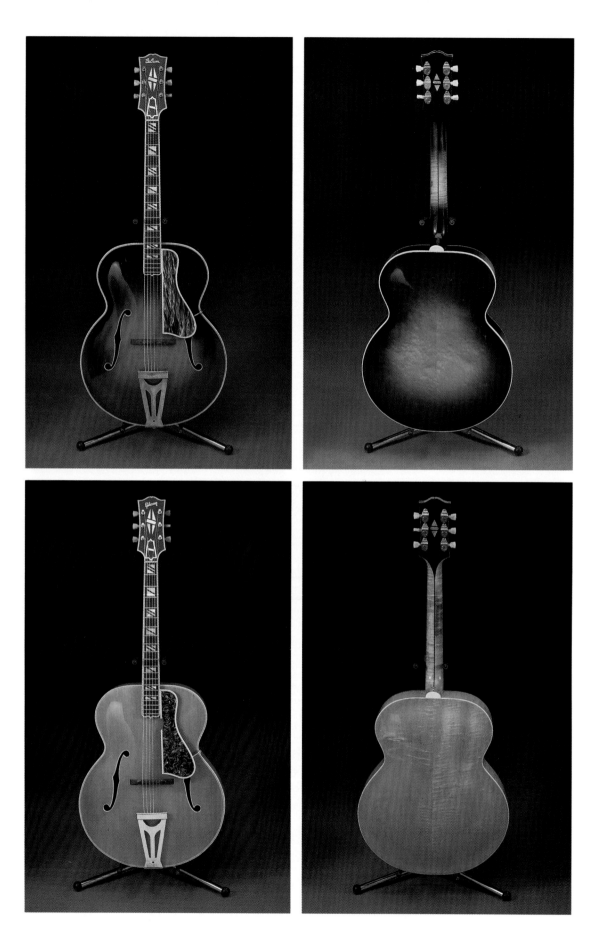

Plate 4
- 1947 Super 400, front
- 1947 Super 400, back
- 1949 Super 400N, front
- 1949 Super 400N, back

Plate 5
- 1949 Super 400CN, front
- 1949 Super 400CN, back
- 1964 Super 400C, front
- 1964 Super 400C, back

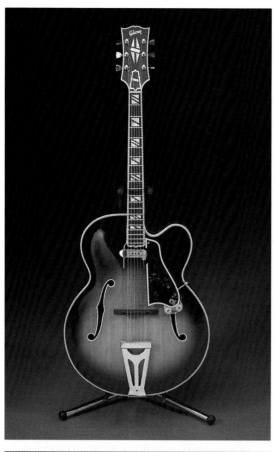
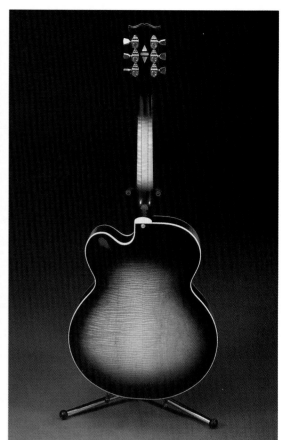
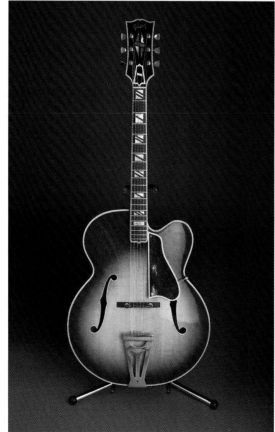
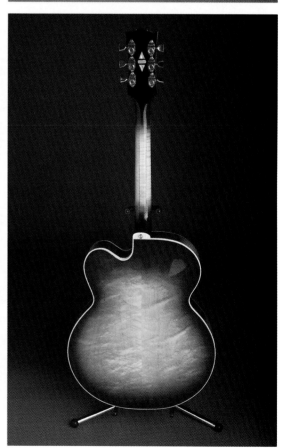

Plate 6
- **1967 Super 400C, front**
- **1967 Super 400C, back**
- **1969 Super 400C, front**
- **1969 Super 400C, back**

Plate 7
- **1977 Super 400C WR, front**
- **1977 Super 400C WR, back**
- **1953 Super 300, front**
- **1957 Super 300C, front**

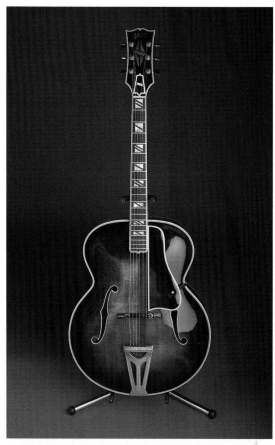

Plate 8
- 1978 Super 400, front
- 1978 Super 400, back
- 1978 Super 400N, front
- 1978 Super 400N, back

was initially similar to the prewar third model Super 400 Premiere in most respects, but Gibson has made enough changes in the instrument over the years that the current Super 400C appears very different from the 1939–1941 Premiere. Changes in the Super 400C

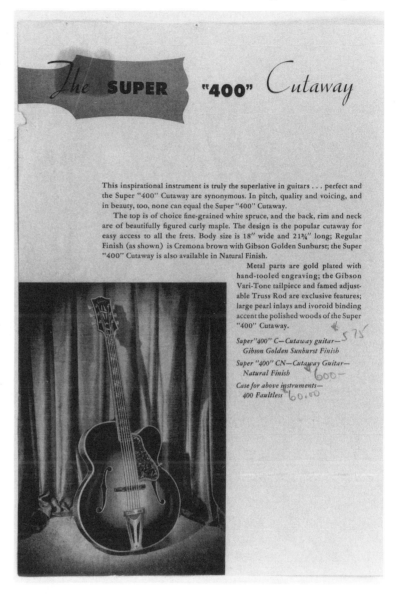

This inspirational instrument is truly the superlative in guitars . . . perfect and the Super "400" Cutaway are synonymous. In pitch, quality and voicing, and in beauty, too, none can equal the Super "400" Cutaway.

The top is of choice fine-grained white spruce, and the back, rim and neck are of beautifully figured curly maple. The design is the popular cutaway for easy access to all the frets. Body size is 18″ wide and 21¾″ long; Regular Finish (as shown) is Cremona brown with Gibson Golden Sunburst; the Super "400" Cutaway is also available in Natural Finish.

Metal parts are gold plated with hand-tooled engraving; the Gibson Vari-Tone tailpiece and famed adjustable Truss Rod are exclusive features; large pearl inlays and ivoroid binding accent the polished woods of the Super "400" Cutaway.

Super "400" C—Cutaway guitar—Gibson Golden Sunburst Finish

Super "400" CN—Cutaway Guitar—Natural Finish

Case for above instruments—400 Faultless

● **1957 Gibson catalog, Super 400C**

from 1949–1990 include simplification of ornamentation, changes in headstock logo and contours, changes in neck design, a change in the cutaway shape, and miscellaneous changes in fittings, finishes, and cases. Some of these changes were designed to cut production costs slightly, allowing for more gradual price increases. Other changes were typical of changes throughout the Gibson product line. Whatever the reason, changes in the postwar Super 400C continued to occur throughout its production right up to the present. These changes will be discussed in detail in the appropriate sections of the remainder of this chapter.

Headstock: The headstock of the Super 400C was at first almost exactly like that of the Super 400 Premiere, except that the postwar

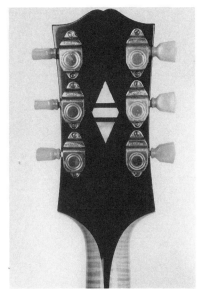
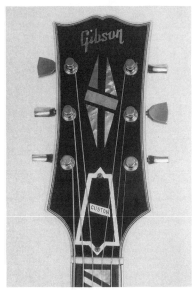
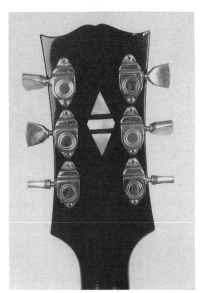

**Headstock changes,
postwar acoustic
Super 400 guitars**

- 1949 Super 400CN
  headstock, front
- 1949 Super 400CN
  headstock, back
- 1964 Super 400C
  headstock, front
- 1964 Super 400C
  headstock, back
- 1977 Super 400C
  headstock, front
- 1977 Super 400C
  headstock, back

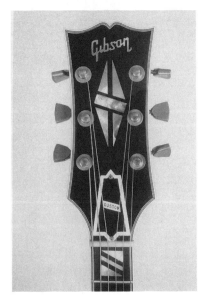

Gibson slanted logo was used instead of the thick prewar horizontal logo. The headstock featured the same prewar contour from 1949 until about 1960, when the ends of the headstock became more pronounced or "pointed." The same blackened holly veneer was used until about 1970, when a more course-grained overlay of fiber

● **1949 Super 400CN tuner**
● **1964 Super 400C tuner**

veneer was substituted. Binding remained five-ply, and the pearl split-diamond inlays on the front and back of the headstock were continued. The truss-rod cover retained its classic art deco shape, but the word "Custom" was etched on the white diagonal parallelogram beginning in the early 1960s. Tuning machines were again the gold-plated Kluson Sealfast model, initially using a plastic button that was simply pressed onto the tuner post. This button was used on several other postwar Gibson guitars, including the L-5, L-7, and early Les Paul Standard and Custom, and is often called the "single-ring Kluson" button for its one "ring" just where the button was inserted onto the tuning post. These plastic buttons were replaced by gold-plated brass buttons of the same shape in 1958. The Kluson Sealfast tuning machines were continued on the Super 400C until the late 1970s, when a similar Schaller tuning machine was substituted and continued to the present day.

Neck: The neck of the first postwar Super 400C guitars was almost exactly like the neck of their prewar relative, the Super 400 Premiere. The neck was made of two book-matched pieces of highly flamed curly maple, with a center mahogany strip. Neck width and contours for the very first Super 400Cs were exactly like those of the 1939–1941 Super 400 Premieres. However, the neck of the Super 400C was thickened in its circumference around 1950, and continued to be rather thick in most respects until around 1958. The width of the neck did not change to any significant degree, however. The fretboard on the first postwar Super 400Cs, from 1949–1950, was usually made of Brazilian rosewood, again because of the immediate postwar shortage of ebony. Around 1950, the Super 400 fretboard reverted to ebony, which has remained the fretboard material to this day. The same split-block fretboard inlay pattern was used as on the prewar Super 400s, and all inlays are made of mother-of-pearl. One interesting difference in trim involves the heel cap on the postwar Super 400C. This heel cap was not engraved with the words "Super 400" as on the prewar guitars. Also, the heel of the neck was more rounded rather than rectangular in cross section, so the heel actually appeared somewhat smaller. However, Gibson returned to the more rectangular heel shape in the mid-1970s, and this shape continues to the present.

Three major changes occurred in the neck of the Super 400C guitar during the postwar period of 1949–1990. The first major change occurred in approximately 1960. In the latter part of that year, Gibson switched from the three-piece neck to the current five-piece version, with three pieces of book-matched curly maple separated by two slender mahogany strips. The second major change occurred in approximately 1967, when the neck was narrowed at the nut from $1^{11}/_{16}$ inches to $1^{9}/_{16}$ inches. This loss of $^{1}/_{8}$ inch in neck width produced an instrument that felt somewhat awkward to many guitarists, because the large body size contrasted sharply with the very narrow neck. This change, supposedly made to make the instrument easier to play, was not appreciated by guitarists, so Gibson returned to the standard neck width of $1^{11}/_{16}$ inches in late 1969. The last change in the Super 400 neck occurred in relation to the guitar headstock; that is, a volute was added to strengthen the neck–headstock joint in approximately 1974–1975. If a player was not used to this "hump" on the back of the neck–headstock joint, its presence became immediately apparent when playing the guitar in the lower register. Many guitarists objected rather vociferously to this addition to the neck, and guitarists and collectors continue to treat this Gibson "innovation" with scorn. The volute was phased out in 1980–1981. Scale length of the Super 400C neck remained fixed at 25½ inches, as had been the case for all prewar guitars except the first model Super 400.

Body: The body of the postwar Super 400C has remained relatively unchanged from its introduction in 1949 to the present day. The top continued to be made of carved spruce, and the back continued to be made of a book-matched set of curly maple carved plates. The rims were also made of curly maple. The types of curly maple utilized in the back of the Super 400C included bird's-eye maple, quilted maple, straight-grained curly maple, and the very thin ribbon-curl maple that presents the appearance of a fir tree. Likewise, the rims of the guitar utilized curly maple and its various

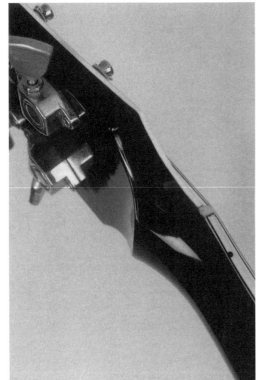

- 1977 Super 400C WR Volute
- 1964 Super 400C cutaway detail
- 1977 Super 400C WR cutaway detail

configurations. In general, the woods on the Super 400C from 1949 through 1969 continued to be rather highly figured in nature, especially on the natural-finish guitars. Rather plain curly maple began to appear in most of the Super 400 guitars produced from the mid-1970s through the early 1980s. As this material was finally used up, more highly figured wood was once again featured on the Super 400C from the early 1980s up to the present time.

Structurally, the body of the Super 400C remained almost exactly the same, except for a slight alteration in the shape of the Venetian cutaway that is usually not noticeable unless a Super 400C body from 1949–1970 is compared with a Super 400C body from 1973–1989. The subtle difference seems to be in a more "closed" cutaway configuration on the latter guitars. The tops continue to be parallel braced, and all interior fittings—mahogany end blocks and kerfing, spruce braces—remained exactly like those of the prewar Super 400s. The first pickguard on the postwar Super 400C was made of the same mottled plastic overlay / tortoise plastic base as on the Premiere. This pickguard was continued until all the mottled material was used up by approximately 1964. After that, the tortoise plastic pickguard

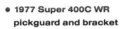

● **1977 Super 400C WR pickguard and bracket**

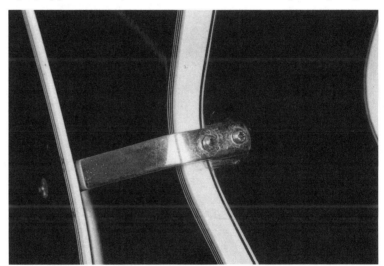

material was used without the overlay and continues to the present day. The forward edge of the pickguard was fastened to the fretboard extension with either pin or screw until about 1964. After that, the forward edge was screwed directly to the guitar's top with a single gold-plated Phillips screw, with a small plastic ring between the bottom edge of the pickguard and the guitar's top. The pickguard was attached to the guitar's rim with the standard threaded rod and bracket assembly until about 1973–1974, when this bracket was replaced with a simpler one-piece bent brass bracket. The bent bracket was attached to the rim with two screws, and it was joined to the pickguard with a gold-plated screw that passed through the top of the pickguard, meeting a gold-plated nut below the bracket. This new bracket and mounting arrangement continues today and has real merit for its simplicity and greater rigidity. The origins of this bracket design are from D'Angelico, Stromberg, and Epiphone.

The bridge on the Super 400C was initially the same rosewood

SUPER 400 C

A superlative instrument, flawless in appearance and performance. Designed with carved top and back in modern cutaway style, its rare beauty, response, and magical tone are the fruits of Gibson's expert craftsmanship.

Features: Carved top of finest close-grained spruce, and carved back of highly figured curly maple with matching rims and white-black-white ivoroid binding. Slim, fast, low-action, three-piece curly maple neck with adjustable truss rod. Ebony fingerboard and peghead with large pearl inlays. Rosewood adjustable bridge. Exclusive Super 400 adjustable tailpiece. Gold-plated metal parts and Sealfast individual machine heads with metal buttons.

18" wide, 21¾" long, 3⅜" deep . . .
25½" scale, 20 frets

Super 400CN Natural finish $675.00
Super 400C Sunburst finish $650.00
400 Faultless plush-lined case $60.00
ZC-4 Deluxe zipper case cover $35.00

Super 400-C

- 1960 Gibson catalog, Super 400C
- 1962 Gibson catalog, Super 400C
- 1966 Gibson catalog, Super 400C
- 1970 Gibson catalog, Super 400C

adjustable model used on the Premiere, but without the triangular base inlays. The base was solid, and the saddle was compensated. This bridge was used from 1949–1975, when an ebony adjustable bridge was substituted. The "new" ebony adjustable bridge was the

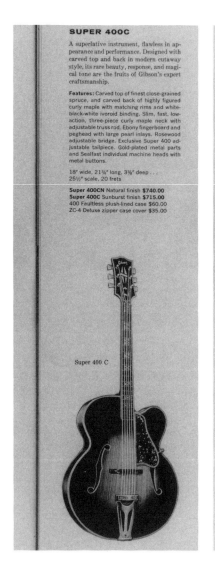

SUPER 400C

A superlative instrument, flawless in appearance and performance. Designed with carved top and back in modern cutaway style, its rare beauty, response, and magical tone are the fruits of Gibson's expert craftsmanship.

Features: Carved top of finest close-grained spruce, and carved back of highly figured curly maple with matching rims and white-black-white ivoroid binding. Slim, fast, low-action, three-piece curly maple neck with adjustable truss rod. Ebony fingerboard and peghead with large pearl inlays. Rosewood adjustable bridge. Exclusive Super 400 adjustable tailpiece. Gold-plated metal parts and Sealfast individual machine heads with metal buttons.

18" wide, 21¾" long, 3⅜" deep . . .
25½" scale, 20 frets

Super 400CN Natural finish $740.00
Super 400C Sunburst finish $715.00
400 Faultless plush-lined case $60.00
ZC-4 Deluxe zipper case cover $35.00

Super 400 C

SUPER 400C

A superlative instrument, the ultimate in appearance and performance. Designed with carved top and back in modern cutaway style, its rare beauty, response, and magical tone are the fruits of Gibson's expert craftsmanship.

FEATURES: Carved top of finest close-grained Spruce, and carved back of highly figured Curly Maple with matching rims and white-black-white ivoroid binding. Slim, fast, low-action, five-piece Curly Maple neck with adjustable Truss Rod. Ebony fingerboard and peghead with large pearl inlays. Rosewood adjustable bridge. Exclusive Super 400 adjustable tailpiece. Gold-plated metal parts and machine heads with gold buttons. 18" wide, 21¾" long, 3⅜" deep; 25½" scale, 20 frets.

Super 400C   Sunburst finish

Super 400CN   Natural finish

400   Faultless plush-lined case
ZC-4   Deluxe zipper case cover

SUPER 400C

The Super 400C is the ultimate in appearance and performance. Exceptional tone quality and fast-action response have made the 400C the professional's choice. Designed with carved top and back in modern cutaway styling.

FEATURES: Carved top of finest close-grained spruce, and carved back of highly figured Curly maple with matching rims and white-black-white ivoroid binding. Slim, fast, low-action, five-piece curly maple neck with adjustable truss rod. Ebony fingerboard and peghead with large pearl inlays. Rosewood adjustable bridge. Exclusive adjustable tailpiece. Gold-plated metal parts and machine heads with gold buttons. 18 inches wide, 21¾ inches long, 3⅜ inches deep; 25½ inch scale, 20 frets.

Super 400C—Sunburst finish
Super 400CN—Natural finish

400—Faultless plush-lined case
ZC-4—Deluxe zipper case cover

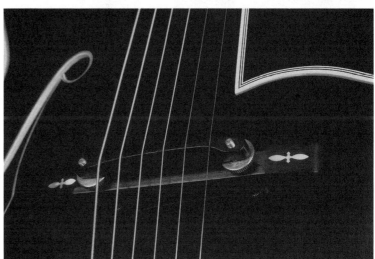

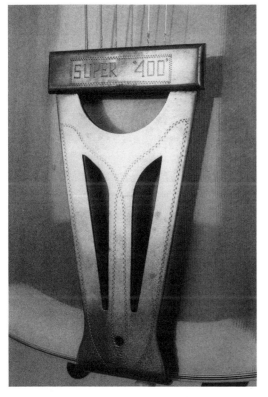

- 1949 Super 400CN bridge
- 1977 Super 400C WR bridge
- 1949 Super 400CN tailpiece

same as had been used on the Johnny Smith guitar, with a solid ebony base containing two bow tie–shaped pearl inlays on the ends. The ebony saddle was compensated, but in a more gradual manner than on the earlier rosewood saddle. In general, the bases of these ebony bridges were much thicker than their rosewood predecessors, and they seem to inhibit sound transmission somewhat. Finally, the Varitone device was eliminated from the large brass Super 400 tailpiece in about 1973–1974. This was another simplification that was a genuine improvement, since the postwar Varitone had dubious tone impact, and its misuse often resulted in tops cracking beneath it. The simpler tailpiece featured the simpler postwar engraving pattern, which remains in use today.

Finish: The Super 400C was initially offered in the golden sunburst and natural finishes from 1949 through 1975. To use up some of the plainer curly maple Gibson had on hand, in 1976 optional new finishes of ebony and wine red were offered. These finishes were used to cover very plain woods and actually made the plainer guitars look somewhat attractive in a flashy kind of way. The ebony and wine red finishes were discontinued in 1980.

Case: The postwar Super 400Cs were initially supplied with

● **1964 Super 400C tailpiece**
● **1977 Super 400C WR tailpiece**

Super "300"

Many of the famous Gibson Super "400" features have been incorporated in the Super "300"—it is the same extra large size: 18" wide and 21¾" long.

Choicest woods—spruce, figured maple and rosewood—are used in the Super "300". Other Gibson features are: beautiful pearl inlays; ivoroid binding; elevated celluloid finger-rest; individual enclosed machine heads; super size specially designed tailpiece; adjustable rosewood bridge and Gibson Adjustable Truss Rod.

Gibson rich Cremona brown finish is highlighted with Golden Sunburst shading on top, rim, back and neck.

Super "300"—Guitar—Regular Finish
300 Case for Super "300"

● **1950 Gibson Catalog Super 300**

Lifton plywood hard-shell cases covered in a brown cloth-like material. These were lined with pink plush lining, and the case covers were offered as an extra-cost option. The brown Lifton hard-shell case gave way to a Lifton hard-shell case covered in black vinyl-like material with an orange lining in approximately 1962–1963. This case was continued with few changes until the early 1970s, when a plywood case that seemed somewhat cheaper in design and finish was introduced with a black vinyl covering and a red coarse-velvet lining. This case was continued until the early 1980s, when Gibson began purchasing its cases from Canada. The Canadian cases resembled the original brown Lifton cases in that they were covered in brown vinyl and had a pink plush lining. Also, the interior featured a guitar-shaped piece of pink velvet stitched to cloth hinges that was laid over the guitar's face once the guitar was placed down in the case. This extra flap in the case, often called a "bib" or "diaper," is sometimes detached by owners who are not too impressed with them. These later Canadian cases are very sturdy, and are a definite improvement over the black cases of the mid-1970s.

The Super 300 and Super 300C

Before summarizing the postwar Super 400C production, it is important to discuss briefly the Super 300 guitar. Gibson introduced the Super 300 in 1948 as a less-expensive version of the Super 400. The instrument was produced in both noncutaway (Super 300) and cutaway (Super 300C) versions. Gibson shipped a total of 214 Super 300s, all of which were listed as noncutaway guitars. The Super 300C was made only during 1957–1958, and is considered extremely rare. All Super 300s and Super 300Cs were offered only in the golden sunburst finish. All critical dimensions of both guitars are the same as their more expensive Super 400 counterparts. The only real differences between the Super 300 and the postwar Super 400 are in ornamentation and figure in the curly maple neck, back, and rims. These differences are noted below.

Headstock: The headstock face inlay of the Super 300 instruments was much simpler, with the small pearl "crown" replacing the pearl split-diamond inlay of the Super 400. Nothing was inlaid on the back of the headstock. The standard postwar slanted Gibson logo was utilized, and the headstock was bound with a single layer of white binding. Tuning machines were the Kluson Deluxe models, nickel-plated, with small oval plastic buttons that were later replaced with the Kluson "single-ring" or "butterfly" buttons. The first Super 300 truss-rod covers were bell-shaped and made of a single layer of black plastic. On later Super 300s the truss-rod cover was a two-layer black-white laminate, also bell-shaped.

Neck: The neck of the Super 300 was of the same three-piece construction as the Super 400 neck. However, the Super 300 used much plainer curly maple in its construction, usually with very little figure. The fretboard was made of Brazilian rosewood, with parallelogram pearl inlays like those on the L-7. The fretboard was bound in single-ply white plastic. The smaller nickel-silver frets were used, and the scale length was 25½ inches. The neck heel had no plastic cap.

Body: The noncutaway Super 300 had the same body dimensions and construction as the postwar noncutaway fourth model Super 400. The top was carved spruce, the back was a two-piece carved curly maple affair with rather plain wood, and the rims were plain curly maple. Three-ply binding was used on the top and back of the guitar's body. The f-holes were unbound, and the tailpiece was nickel-plated brass with no engraving and no Varitone. The body of the Super 300C was exactly like its noncutaway relative except for the Venetian cutaway, which had the same shape as the cutaway of the 1957–1958 Super 400C. The rosewood bridge was exactly like that of the postwar Super 400, with a solid base and compensated saddle. The pickguards were made of the standard three-ply black-white-black plastic offered on other postwar Gibson guitars, bevelled on all edges and attached to the fretboard extension with a screw or pin and to the body with the brass nickel-plated rod and bracket assembly.

Finish: The Super 300 and Super 300C were offered only in the golden sunburst finish.

Case: The standard Lifton hard-shell plywood case was offered with the Super 300, lined with pink plush velvet and covered with brown cloth or vinyl.

Summary

By the end of World War II, Gibson was already making plans to reintroduce the various guitar models that the company manufactured before the war. Also in the works was an ambitious plan to launch an entire line of new models specifically aimed at the small but growing electric guitar market. Gibson management correctly anticipated a tremendous postwar demand for their products, and of course the Super 400 was no exception in this regard. When the postwar acoustic Super 400 guitar was introduced in 1948, two distinct versions of the guitar were available. The noncutaway Super 400 guitar (herein called the fourth model) was offered in the golden sunburst finish with a natural-finish option. Likewise, the cutaway fifth model Super 400 guitar, formerly known as the Premiere but now labeled the Super 400C, was also reintroduced in the golden sunburst finish with the optional natural finish as well. Thus four versions of the acoustic Super 400 were available immediately after the war for guitarists to choose from. The fourth model Super 400 was produced from 1947 through 1955, when it was discontinued. A total of 154 noncutaway guitars in sunburst finish and 86 guitars in natural finish were shipped during this time period.

The noncutaway Super 400 guitar was dropped in 1955 because of its declining popularity, due in part to the company's emphasis on the cutaway acoustic and in part to the enormous success of the electric Super 400, introduced in 1951. The noncutaway Super 400 was also closely associated with the large orchestra, whose numbers declined rapidly after the war as the public's musical interests changed, drifting somewhat until the sharp rise in popularity of Country and Western music and the birth of rock and roll. However, Gibson did make two noncutaway Super 400s in 1978—one sunburst, one natural—for a trade show. These guitars were sold and eventually came to rest in the Freddy Pigg collection.

The fourth model Super 400 was essentially identical to the prewar second model noncutaway Super 400 in most key respects. The fourth model Super 400 differed from its prewar predecessor in that it utilized the more modern postwar headstock logo, and in general evidenced some subtle simplifications in ornamentation to facilitate a slight reduction in cost of manufacture, which was coupled with a gradual increase in price.

The fifth model Super 400, or Super 400C, was introduced in late 1949 and has continued in production with several evolutionary changes since that time. Approximately 355 Super 400Cs were produced in sunburst finish and 194 were produced in natural finish from 1950 through 1979, the last year for which official hand-tallied records of production were kept. Beginning in 1980 Gibson changed over to a computerized record-keeping system, but when the Norlin Company sold Gibson to its current owners in 1986, there was some confusion regarding access to the data via the company's computers. It is not known whether this data was lost, or whether only Norlin employees knew how to access the data so that access to the data was denied by default. I have made several visits to both the Kalamazoo and Nashville Gibson factories, and despite these visits and much correspondence, my findings on the known production totals for the years 1980 through 1989 remain rather incomplete.

The Super 400C evolved in a parallel fashion with the noncutaway Super 400 through 1955 and continued its evolution after that time. Major changes in the Super 400C included the switch from a three-piece to a five-piece neck in mid-1960, the radical narrowing of the neck to 1 9/16 inches at the nut in 1967, and the addition (and later deletion) of the volute at the headstock–neck joint in approximately 1973–1974. Otherwise, construction of the Super 400C remained essentially unchanged except for a slight alteration in the shape of the cutaway. Incidentally, to my knowledge no Super 400Cs were offered by the factory with a Florentine or sharp cutaway. All Super 400Cs produced are apparently of the Venetian or rounded cutaway variety. Woods used in the Super 400C back and rims became rather plain from the mid-1970s to the early 1980s, but when production of the Super 400C was ended at the Kalamazoo plant in 1984, the last instruments from that period had rather outstanding wood in all respects. However, most instruments produced in 1984 were of the Super 400CES variety. Miscellaneous changes occurred in appointments such as the pickguard material, minor simplifications of the tailpiece, a change from a rosewood to an ebony bridge, and so forth. The Super 400C was offered in the golden sunburst finish with a natural finish as an option, and in 1976 the wine red and ebony finishes were offered so that Gibson could use up its remaining stocks of plain wood available for the large Super 400 body.

Finally, the Super 300 and Super 300C were part of Gibson's new product line introduced in 1948. Initially only the Super 300 was offered, and the Super 300C was added in approximately 1957 for only two years. These were essentially plainer versions of the Super 400 and Super 400C guitars, with identical dimensions but plainer woods and ornamentation. They look rather like Gibson L-7 guitars, with the same fretboard logo and headstock inlays as the postwar L-7 and L-7C. Briefly, the following is a summary of the number and types of Super 400s shipped during the postwar years of 1948–1989.

Fourth Model, Sunburst, 1948–1955	154
Fourth Model, Natural, 1948–1955	86
Fifth Model, Sunburst 1948–1989	358+
Fifth Model, Natural, 1948–1989	195+
Total, 1948–1989	793+

Thus, a total of a least 789 Super 400Cs were produced between 1948–1979, with a very small number being made between 1980–1989.

Chapter
III

The Postwar
Gibson Super 400
Electric Guitar

~

● 1952 Gibson
Super 400CESN and
Gibson GA50
amplifier

Although Gibson first introduced a small line of electric steel guitars and electric-acoustic guitars prior to World War II, the Super 400 and L-5 guitars were not officially offered in an electric version until 1951. However, the initial acceptance of the prewar electric guitar led the Gibson company to prepare a revised and expanded line of electric guitars to be

GIBSON FINGERREST PICK-UP UNITS

100-SN *Single Nickel (L-7, S-300).*
101-SG *Single Gold (L-5, L-12, S-400).*
102-SCN *Single Cutaway Nickel (L-7C).*
103-SCG *Single Cutaway Gold (L-5C, L-12C, S-400C).*
104-DN *Double Nickel (L-7, S-300).*
105-DG *Double Gold (L-5, L-12, S-400).*
106-DCN *Double Cutaway Nickel (L-7C).*
107-DCG *Double Cutaway Gold (L-5C, L-12C, S-400C).*

● **1959 Gibson catalog, McCarty pickup**

introduced when war work was ended. This initial line of postwar electric guitars was expanded greatly over the years, moving into such diverse areas as the solid-body guitars, the semisolid or thinline guitars, and the electric arch-top and carved-top guitars.

Before World War II, Gibson first introduced a small line of Hawaiian or steel guitars with companion amplifiers. Shortly thereafter, the first official Gibson arch-top electric guitars—the ES-100, ES-150, ES-250, and ES-300—were unveiled. These guitars were all noncutaway arch-top guitars with a single pickup whose design varied from model to model. (Gibson also offered two attachable pickups that allowed the owner of an acoustic arch-top to amplify the instrument by attaching the pickup over the guitar's top via a rod that clamped onto the strings between the bridge and tailpiece.) These prewar electric arch-top guitars apparently sold very well, so Gibson planned to upgrade and reintroduce the electric arch-top as soon as World War II had officially ended.

In 1947, Gibson introduced their first line of postwar electric guitars, consisting of the ES-125, the ES-150, the ES-300, and the ES-350. The instruments varied in price and manner of decoration, and the ES-350 was different because it was a cutaway guitar while the other three models were not. All four instruments had bodies made of laminated maple with mahogany necks and rosewood fretboards. Each guitar had a single P90-style pickup, the earliest of which had nonadjustable pole pieces.

In 1948, Ted McCarty joined the Gibson company, and one of his first priorities was to expand the potential number of Gibson's electric guitar models in a quick and inexpensive way. He invented an ingenious pickup/pickguard assembly known now as the McCarty pickup, consisting of a very thin single-coil pickup with nonadjustable, flat pole pieces mounted in a laminated pickguard along with volume and tone controls and an input jack. The McCarty pickup assembly was offered in single- and double-pickup versions, for cutaway and noncutaway guitars, and for guitars with nickel-plated parts and gold-plated parts. The pickup was officially introduced on the L-7 guitar as an option, and these early electric L-7s were labeled the L-7E or the L-7PE, with the letter *E* designating their electric status, while *P* indicated Premiere, or cutaway, body style. In reality, these were stock L-7 guitars that had the McCarty pickup assembly supplied with them at the factory instead of a conventional acoustic pickguard. An additional advantage of the McCarty pickup assembly is that it could be ordered through any Gibson dealer and retrofitted to older Gibson carved-top guitars and carved-top instruments of other makers, such as Epiphone, D'Angelico, Stromberg and Gretsch guitars. It is not unusual to find McCarty pickup assemblies installed on these various makes of guitars, even in the present vintage guitar market.

In 1949, Gibson expanded their electric arch-top guitar line further by adding two very significant instruments, the ES-175 and the ES-5. The ES-175 was initially introduced with a single P90 pickup, while a double-pickup version was made available approximately two years later. The ES-5 was offered in its original form as a three-pickup instrument with a single master tone control and three individual volume controls. This instrument was the final precursor to the electric Super 400 and L-5 guitars, which were introduced in late 1951.

When interviewed in Kalamazoo, Michigan, in May of 1984, Ted McCarty stated that under the management of CMI there was constant pressure to be "creative," to come up with new instruments and new ideas regarding instruments every year. These ideas usually had to be translated into at least working prototypes by the time the major music merchandising conventions were held in March and November of each calendar year. Gibson, Inc., and its parent company, CMI, were both heavily influenced by customer input from their beginnings through the late 1960s. Some customer input that Gibson had been receiving about the electric arch-top guitars was that customers would prefer a true electric version of the Super 400 as a separate instrument. Before the electric Super 400 was introduced, guitarists who liked this instrument had to content themselves with retrofitting a pickup to the guitar, such as the DeArmond, the earlier Gibson EP-17 or EP-21 attachable arch-top pickups, or the McCarty pickup/pickguard assembly. However, these pickups did not seem to provide the exact tone that many professional instrumentalists were looking for. Finally, McCarty and some of the Gibson design staff began working on a purely electric version of the Super 400 cutaway guitar. This instrument, christened the Super 400CES (Cutaway Electric Spanish) guitar, was introduced at a trade show in New York along with the

● 1960 Gibson catalog, various artists including Muzzy Marcellino with Art Linkletter

companion L-5CES guitar in late 1951. These instruments were different from all prior prewar and postwar electric arch-top guitars. Although the tops of these instruments were made of carved spruce and the backs were made of book-matched carved curly maple in the same manner as the tops and backs of the Super 400C and L-5C acoustic guitars, the tops were carved somewhat thicker than their acoustic counterparts to inhibit top vibration and make feedback more manageable. In the same vein, the top of the Super 400CES was braced with two long parallel braces or tone bars and several small braces that ran between the long braces to make the top even more rigid. Small "strut" braces were also added at the tips of the long tone bars where they tapered into the underside of the top close to the end of the guitar. The resulting tone quality of these instruments was considerably different from that of any amplified acoustic Super 400 yet made and seemed to provide exactly the right response to professional guitarists' demands (McCarty, personal interview, 1984).

The introduction of the electric Super 400 guitar seemed to be the answer to many guitarists' prayers and dreams. Here was an instrument with truly great electric-acoustic tone qualities that could be used in a variety of musical contexts. Many jazz guitarists began "electrifying" their Super 400 acoustic guitars with the addition of either the Gibson-made McCarty pickup or the independently manufactured DeArmond single-coil pickup. The electric Super 400 guitar attained wide acceptance fairly quickly, and many guitarists, including Kenny Burrell, began to switch to this kind of instrument since it provided more tone and volume and less feedback than acoustic guitars equipped with various types of pickup assemblies. Besides jazz greats such as Burrell, other guitarists who have

● Hank Thompson
● Joe Maphis and
   Merle Travis

embraced the Super 400CES at various periods during their careers include George Benson, Eric Gale, Larry Coryell, Louis Stewart of Ireland, and Frank Evans of England. Country and Western players also welcomed the Super 400CES just as they had taken to the acoustic Super 400 at an earlier time. Merle Travis, one of the first Country and Western musicians to adopt it, used the Super 400CES as he developed his unique "Travis" picking style, involving moving bass lines, melody, and chords all working together in an intricate and very pleasant musical context. Travis had a special Super 400CES made for him, appropriately called the Gibson Special, that featured extensive personalized ornamentation on the headstock and fretboard and a long-armed Bigsby tailpiece for special vibrato effects. His good friend, guitarist and singer Hank Thompson, also ordered a similar Super 400CES, which he continues to play with great effect. Jerry Reed utilized the Super 400 to record some early album material and made the guitar really sparkle in his unique musical style.

Besides jazz and Country and Western music, the Super 400 occasionally found its way into a blues context. The late Pee Wee Crayton used a custom-made Super 400CESN with a single Charlie Christian pickup mounted in the neck position. Robben Ford, a stunning new blues talent, utilized a Florentine cutaway Super 400CES and he was able to coax great feeling from the guitar on many occasions. Finally, the "new music" of the early 1950s—rock and

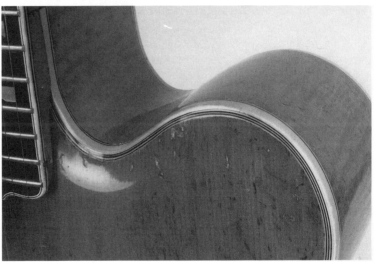

- 1939 Super 400PN(E) body
- 1939 Super 400PN(E) top
- 1939 Super 400PN(E) cutaway

roll—also featured Super 400 guitars on occasion. The most famous rock and roll player of Super 400 guitars was Scotty Moore, who was Elvis Presley's guitarist from Presley's earliest recording days through many years of changes that followed. Moore utilized both an Alnico-equipped Super 400CESN and a later Florentine cutaway Super 400CES, which Presley also used in his 1969 televised "Comeback Special." Also, Bill Haley used a Super 400C with a DeArmond pickup in much of his early stage and movie work as one of rock and roll's first singer-guitarists.

The Super 400CES and L-5CES were the culmination of Gibson's ever-evolving design process with amplified arch-top guitars, and these two instruments remained the top-of-the-line amplified arch-top guitars for Gibson until the Citation was introduced in 1969, though the Citation's overall impact on the Gibson product line was very slight.

One of Gibson's first official attempts at electrifying the Super 400 is illustrated with the 1939 Super 400 Premiere. This instrument was modified at the factory to accept the small slanted P90-style pickup furnished with lesser model arch-top guitars prior to World War II. The guitar was "electrified" by building the instrument first, then routing a small oval hole in the top for the insertion of the pickup and smaller holes for its accompanying controls. This is the same process that was used to amplify the prewar Gibson ES-250 and ES-300 guitars and often resulted in braces being cut at the point the routing was initiated. Though this initial amplification of the Super 400 looks somewhat ungainly compared to the postwar designs, it is clear that the postwar Super 400CES had its origins in this factory attempt, whose originality has been confirmed in writing by Julius Bellson. He stated that this instrument was ordered from the factory equipped exactly as illustrated, and the instrument may well be the first factory-built Super 400 electric guitar ever made.

Materials, Construction, and Assembly

The Super 400CES was made out of the same materials utilized in the prewar Super 400—wood, plastic, mother-of-pearl, and metal. As in its acoustic prewar and early postwar predecessors, the electric Super 400 utilized holly for the headstock overlay and curly maple for the neck, rims, and back of the guitar. Mahogany was used for the internal neck block and end blocks, the kerfing, and the center neck strips. Ebony was used for the fretboard, and apparently ebony has been used from the beginning; no Brazilian rosewood fretboards were utilized on the early Super 400CES guitars. The finest close-grain spruce was used for the top and for the internal top braces. Rosewood was used to make the bridge. The Super 400CES utilized several parts made of plastic, including an ivoroid plastic for the nut and binding, and a tortoise shell–colored plastic for the fingerrest with a mottled plastic overlay as well. The knobs and switch tips were also made of plastic. Mother-of-pearl was used for all of the inlays. The guitar utilized a steel truss rod, nickel-silver frets, and miscellaneous brass parts such as the tailpiece, tuners, and screws. All of the brass parts were gold-plated.

The same manufacturing system used for the acoustic Super 400 guitars was used on the electric Super 400 guitars as well, with some modifications for the routing of the top for the pickups and controls. The same Gibson craftsmen performed the same discrete carved-top assembly tasks that they had been doing so well for so long. Some of the Gibson craftsmen shaped and assembled the necks of the guitars, while others carved and routed the tops and carved the backs. Still other Gibson workers made the various smaller parts such as the pickguards and headstock overlays, while different craftsmen did the actual inlay work. Once again, this division of labor allowed for considerable quality control in the manufacture of the instruments, which resulted in the introduction of a top-quality acoustic-electric guitar from the beginning.

Specific Production Models

Electric Super 400 guitar production can be roughly divided into three models with eight variations. To keep all of the various Super 400 models separate and somewhat distinct, I will continue to utilize the numbering system begun with the first model Super 400 of 1934 and illustrated in Table B-1 in Appendix B. Therefore, the Super 400CES range of models includes the sixth model Venetian cutaway guitar, from 1951–1960; the seventh model Florentine cutaway electric guitar from 1960 through 1969; and the eighth model Venetian cutaway guitar from 1969 up to the present time. Each of these models will be discussed in more detail below, with illustrations of the specific features unique to each model.

Sixth Model Venetian Cutaway Super 400CES, 1951–1960

The sixth model Super 400CES guitar was the first official electric version of the Super 400 introduced to the public. It is a cutaway guitar whose general appearance is similar to the postwar Super 400C guitar in most respects, with the addition of pickups and controls. This model was produced, with minor changes, from 1951 through mid-1960.

Headstock: The headstock of the first version of the Super 400CES (identified here as the sixth model Super 400) was exactly like the corresponding headstock of the Super 400C of the early 1950s. The postwar Gibson slanted logo was inlaid into the blackened holly veneer on the face of the headstock. The headstock

A FAVORITE OF THE LEADING GUITARISTS

One of the finest electric Spanish guitars ever developed, the Super-400 CES has been given enthusiastic approval by the nation's outstanding musicians.

A definite factor in the quality of tone and responsiveness of the Super-400 CES is the carved spruce top, an unusual feature in an electric guitar. The finest spruce, curly maple and ebony add to the beauty of this instrument, available in Natural (as shown), or the Gibson Golden Sunburst finish.

- The two pickups are set close to the bridge and fingerboard for wider contrast in tone color.
- Modern cutaway design and small neck for fast, easy action.
- Gibson Tune-O-Matic bridge and extra large, individually adjustable Alnico No. 5 magnets give greater sustaining power and perfect accuracy from each string.
- Pickups have adjustable pole pieces and separate tone and volume controls which can be pre-set.
- Three-position toggle switch on treble side activates either or both pickups.
- Kluson Sealfast Pegs.
- Professional 20 fret fingerboard and Gibson Adjustable Truss Rod neck construction.
- Body size: 18″ wide and 21¾″ long.
- Decorative accents to the beauty of the Super-400 CES include gold plated metal parts, deluxe pearl inlays and alternate black-white-black ivoroid binding.

Super-400 CES Electric Spanish Cutaway Guitar—Golden Sunburst Finish.
Super-400 CESN Electric Spanish Cutaway Guitar—Natural Finish.
Case for Above Instruments—400 Faultless

Super-400 CESN

● **1956 Gibson catalog, Super 400CESN**

contours followed their Super 400C counterparts. Five-ply binding was used around the face of the headstock, and the headstock had the same pearl split-diamond inlays on the front and back. The truss-rod cover was the same as that utilized on the corresponding Super 400C, and the word "Custom" appeared on the white diagonal in the early 1960s. Tuning machines were identical to those of the Super 400C—the gold-plated Kluson Sealfast units, initially equipped with a plastic button that was pressed onto the tuner post.

These plastic buttons were replaced by gold-plated brass buttons of a similar shape in 1958.

Neck: The neck of the first version of the Super 400CES was exactly like the neck of its Super 400C counterpart. It was a two-piece curly maple neck of book-matched highly flamed wood, with a center mahogany strip. The necks on these first Super 400CES guitars, from 1951 through 1959, were notably rounded and somewhat thick in cross section. All fretboards on the Super 400CES were ebony, and to my knowledge no rosewood fretboards were issued on even the earliest versions of this guitar. Mother-of-pearl split-block inlays were utilized in the same positions on these instruments. The heel cap of the Super 400CES was plain ivoroid plastic like that of the postwar Super 400C.

Body: The body of the sixth model Super 400 appeared identical to the Super 400C body from the same time period except for the addition of the pickups and electronic controls. The body consisted of a carved spruce top, which was slightly thicker than the Super 400C top. There were two long spruce braces or tone bars underneath the top, spaced far enough apart to allow for top routing for the pickup cavities without cutting the braces. There were several smaller spruce or mahogany cross braces placed crossways between the tone bars and smaller "strut" braces touching them at either end. These smaller braces added additional rigidity to the top to dampen vibration when the guitar was played electrically at high volume.

Three distinct types of electric pickups were used on the sixth model Super 400. The very first Super 400CES guitars, from late 1951 through 1953, were equipped with two single-coil P90 pickups, one located close to the end of the fretboard and the other located just forward of the bridge. These P90 pickups had six adjustable gold-plated metal pole pieces, and were covered with black plastic "dog-ear" pickup covers. The P90 pickups themselves were placed in an aluminum frame with a small flange on each end, and these flanges rested on the top of the guitar at either end of the pickup cavity. The black plastic cover was placed over the pickup and attached to the top with two screws that passed through the pickup cover and the flange from the pickup frame, thus securing the whole pickup unit to the top. The height of these pickups was not adjustable, but the pole pieces could be individually raised and lowered. Because of the neck angle of the guitar, the rear pickup was somewhat lower in relation to the guitar strings than the front pickup. Therefore, a small flat plastic riser was placed between the top of the guitar and the underside of the rear pickup frame flange. The pickup cover was attached to this assembly with two screws, one at each end.

From 1954 through mid-1958, the Super 400CES utilized the single-coil Alnico pickups, with six square Alnico-V magnets for pole pieces. These pickups were placed in an aluminum pickup frame that rested on the top of the guitar just as the P90 pickups did. The Alnico pickups used black plastic covers with rectangular slots cut in the top for the pole pieces. A riser was also used to elevate the back pickup somewhat to place it closer to the guitar strings.

The "patent-applied-for" (PAF) humbucking pickup was introduced

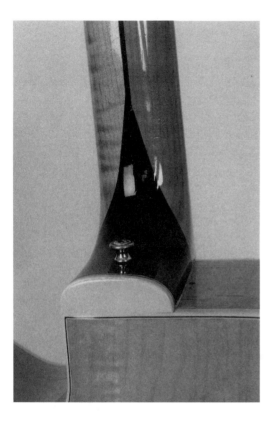

● **1952 Super 400CESN heel cap**

on the Super 400CES #A-26590 in November of 1957. The Alnico pickups were continued until mid-1958 when supplies were exhausted. Approximately midway through 1958, Gibson completed the change over to the PAF humbucking pickup, which replaced the Alnico and P90 pickups on the Super 400CES and

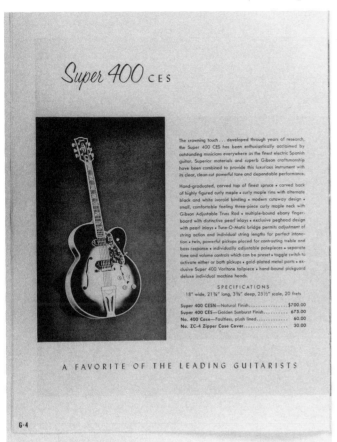

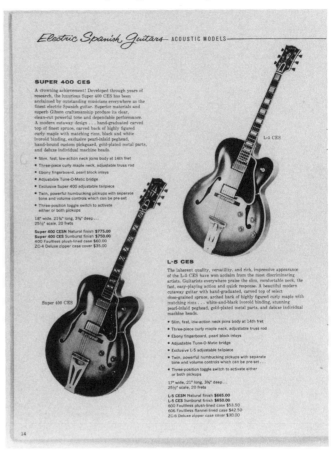

- 1959 Gibson catalog, Super 400CES
- 1960 Gibson catalog, Super 400CES/L-5CES

the L-5CES. The PAF humbucking pickup was a double-coil unit with six adjustable screw-type pole pieces. Pickup covers were gold-plated brass, and the pickups were mounted in rectangular plastic bezels that were screwed onto the guitar's top. The pickups were suspended inside the pickup cavities but attached to the bezels by two slender bolts that passed down through the lateral edges of each pickup bezel to a flange at each end of the pickup frame; the bolt passed through a small spring that was compressed between the bezel and each flange. By turning the bolts, the pickup could be raised or lowered at each edge. Thus the humbucking pickup could be adjusted for overall height, and the pole pieces could be adjusted for individual height as well.

In addition to the graceful Venetian cutaway, the Super 400 body consisted of curly maple rims and a highly figured, two-piece carved and book-matched curly maple back. Interior fittings were made of mahogany except for the spruce tone bars and top braces. The f-holes in the top of the guitar were of the standard length and width, with three-ply white-black-white binding like that of the Super 400C. The first electric Super 400 guitars, from 1951–1954, utilized a solid-base rosewood bridge with a compensated rosewood saddle.

- 1952 Super 400CESN
  body
- 1952 Super 400CESN
  P90 pickups
- 1958 Super 400CES
  body
- 1958 Super 400CES
  Alnico pickups
- 1960 Super 400CES
  body
- 1960 Super 400CES
  PAF pickups

This unit was replaced with the two-footed rosewood bridge base and Tune-O-Matic bridge when the Tune-O-Matic was introduced in approximately 1955. Five controls were placed in the top of the guitar: on either side of the right f-hole were two tone controls and two volume controls, with a pickup selector switch mounted close to the center of the cutaway upper bout. The standard postwar Super 400

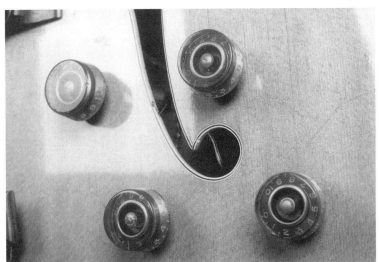

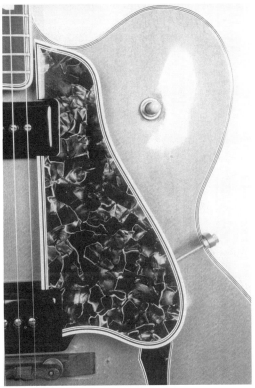

- 1952 Super 400CESN pickguard
- 1952 Super 400CESN "barrel" knobs
- 1958 Super 400CES "top hat" knobs

tailpiece was utilized, made of gold-plated brass with the simpler postwar etching patterns and the larger Varitone control at the end. The sixth model Super 400CES also utilized the beautiful tortoise shell–like plastic pickguard with the mottled plastic overlay, bound profusely and secured to the guitar via a pin at the forward edge that rested in a small hole under the fretboard of the guitar, and the usual threaded bracket and elevated foot assembly that screwed to the side of the guitar rim. The gold-plated input jack was located in the right rim of the guitar near the lower bout, now the standard location.

Finish: The sixth model Super 400CES was officially offered only in the golden sunburst and natural finishes from early 1951 through half of 1960. Both finishes highlighted the spectacular wood in these early electric Super 400s, and it is rare to find a Super 400CES from this time period that has anything but the finest rim and back materials. I have seen an early Super 400CES in a custom red finish (see Tsumura, *Guitars: The Tsumura Collection,* p.73), but such a finish is extremely rare.

Case: The Super 400CES produced from 1951 through 1960 was supplied with a standard Lifton plywood hard-shell case covered in a brown cloth-like material and lined with pink plush velvet. Case covers were offered as an extra-cost option.

Seventh Model Florentine Cutaway Super 400CES, 1960–1969

The biggest single change in the Super 400CES occurred with the introduction of the seventh model in mid-1960. The change involved replacing the graceful, rounded Venetian cutaway with a deep, pointed Florentine cutaway, which was also introduced on the L-5CES and the last of the ES-5 guitars at the same time. Again we see the influence of Ted McCarty and CMI in the decision to radically alter the appearance of the Super 400CES and the L-5CES to present "something new" to guitarists. This model was produced from mid-1960 through mid-1969.

Headstock: The headstock of the very first seventh model Super 400CES guitars was similar to that of the sixth model, but by 1962 the

● **1962 Gibson catalog, Super 400CES**

66

the headstock contours had changed somewhat, with more notable peaks on the ends of the headstock. Otherwise, the headstock is exactly like the sixth model Super 400CES version in all respects, with the same inlays, holly veneer material, and binding. The instrument continued the use of the Kluson Sealfast tuning machines with the gold-plated brass tuning buttons. The truss-rod cover was the same, except for the small word "Custom" etched in the parallelogram on its face.

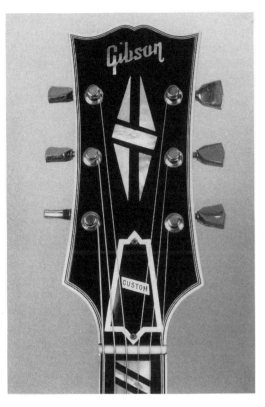

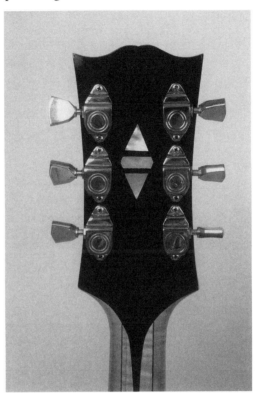

● **1962 Super 400CESN headstock, front**
● **1962 Super 400CESN headstock, back**

Neck: For the Super 400CES, the year 1960 was a time of transition in neck contour as well as body cutaway shape. The necks on the 1960–1962 Super 400CES guitars felt rather wide and flat by comparison to their predecessors, which although retaining the same width were somewhat thicker in circumference, giving the earlier necks a more rounded feel. The fretboard radius remained essentially the same. After 1962, a rounder contour returned to the back of the neck, and that rounded contour continued essentially unchanged from that time through the end of production of the seventh model Super 400CES instruments in mid-1969. The very first seventh model Super 400CES guitars utilized the two-piece book-matched curly maple neck with a center mahogany strip from mid-1960 through possibly early 1961. Very soon thereafter, however, Gibson switched to the three-piece curly maple neck with the slender parallel mahogany strips separating the three pieces. The back of the headstocks were painted black, and on the early natural-finish guitars there is an especially graceful black point that extends down the back of the headstock and the upper part of the neck, as seen in the illustration of the 1962 Super 400CESN here. The fretboards were made of ebony, and the same mother-of-pearl block inlays and inlay patterns were utilized. Five-ply binding was used around the fretboard, and the frets were of the "jumbo" nickel-silver variety.

One further change occurred in the neck of the seventh model Super 400CES, that being the width of the neck at the nut. From mid-1960 through approximately 1965, the neck was $1^{11}/_{16}$ inches wide at the nut. However, sometime in late 1965 the neck width was narrowed to $1^{9}/_{16}$ inches at the nut. This narrower dimension was continued until the end of production of the Florentine Super 400CES in mid-1969. This narrower neck width, combined with the large body size of the guitar, made the guitar seem somewhat awkward to some guitarists. The professional and amateur musicians who owned these instruments, or contemplated owning them, complained at the time about the narrowness of the neck width, so when the eighth model Super 400CES with Venetian cutaway was introduced in late 1969, the neck width reverted to $1^{11}/_{16}$ inches, which has been continued as the standard width to the present day.

Body: The body of the seventh model Super 400CES was the area in which the greatest design changes occurred. The Florentine cutaway was deeper than the earlier Venetian cutaway, and the cutaway extended farther out from the body than the more rounded Venetian cutaway did. Because of the sharp point at the end of the cutaway, the rim could not be bent inward to meet the body, so the rim for the right side of the guitar actually consisted of two pieces. The first piece was secured alongside the neck block and was bent into the cutaway and brought to its outer point. The second piece began here as the outside right rim of the guitar and continued around to the midpoint of the guitar body at the heel block. The two ends of

● **1962 Super 400CESN body**
● **1962 Super 400CESN cutaway detail**

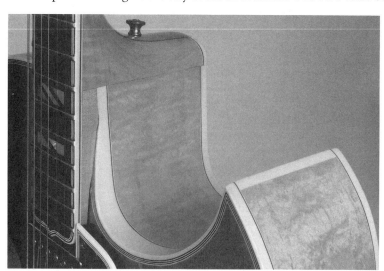

the rim pieces that joined at the point of the cutaway were covered with thick strips of white binding. Because of the depth of the cutaway, a deeper mahogany neck block was utilized on these guitars than on the earlier and subsequent Venetian cutaway models. The pickguard also had to be shortened, giving the appearance that it had been moved back on the guitar body somewhat.

From mid-1960 through 1962, the seventh model Super 400CES

featured PAF-style humbucking pickups with gold-plated pole
pieces and covers. These were encased in black bezels, which
were screwed into the top of the guitar with black screws. The tops
of these guitars were made of carved spruce, and the very early
backs were made of book-matched, carved curly maple. However,
sometime in early 1962 or 1963 Gibson began experimenting with
a pressed plywood back for the electric Super 400s. Most of these
backs are obvious when examined closely, because they have no
center seam and they appear to be one giant piece of highly figured
curly maple. However, the maple that is visible on the back of the
guitars is a laminate, which can be verified if one looks through the
guitar f-holes and notices that the grain pattern on the inside of the
back runs in a different direction from that on the outside. There is
noticeable arching in these pressed backs, and the two-piece carved
curly maple back did not return to the seventh model Super 400CES
until late 1968 or 1969.

The top of the guitar had the standard Super 400 f-holes with their
attendant three-ply binding. The guitar bridge was the standard
gold-plated Tune-O-Matic, with a two-footed rosewood base and
individual adjustable saddles. As on the sixth model, the seventh
model Super 400CES had two volume and two tone controls, one
pair for each pickup, and a pickup selector switch. The selector
switch was mounted in a rubber grommet that was placed in a hole
in the top close to the cutaway on the upper right bout. This rubber
grommet helped isolate the selector switch from the body and
eliminated the loud clicking sound of the switch while the guitar was
amplified. The two pairs of control knobs were mounted on either
side of the right f-hole, down toward the lower bout. The tailpiece

● **1962 Super 400CESN
knobs**

was the same as that used on the earlier Super 400CES guitars,
but the engraving appeared somewhat smaller and simpler. The
shortened pickguard of the seventh model Super 400CES was
mounted with a screw at the front edge directly into the top,
and the usual threaded-rod assembly connected the trailing edge
of the pickguard to the guitar rim. The gold-plated input jack
was located in the right rim of the guitar near the lower bout,

in the standard location.

Finish: The seventh model Super 400CES was offered in the golden sunburst and natural finishes. The sunburst finishes of the early 1960s varied from dark brown at the rims to a golden center, while the sunburst finishes from the mid-1960s had a more reddish tint in the darkened areas. By the time production of the seventh model Super 400CES had ended in mid-1969, the sunburst finish had a glowing cherry hue to its outer edges. Though no other finishes were listed as standard for the Super 400CES, I have observed at least one factory black seventh model Super 400CES that was obviously finished this way when the instrument was made. Gibson often attempted to accommodate the individual tastes of its varied customers, and occasionally one may see such instruments with cherry or other factory custom finishes as well.

Case: Cases for the seventh model Super 400CES from 1960 through 1962 were the brown Lifton case with a pink plush lining. After 1962, the Lifton cases were covered in a black vinyl-like material with an orange plush lining. This case was continued essentially unchanged through the production run of the seventh model Super 400CES guitar. The zipper case cover was also offered as an option.

Eighth Model Super 400CES, 1969–Present

In mid-1969, the Super 400CES was again altered when the cutaway was changed from the Florentine cutaway of the seventh model to the Venetian or rounded cutaway. This "new" cutaway design was very similar to the earlier sixth model Venetian cutaway, except that it was slightly less "open" in its curvature. The Florentine cutaway seventh model Super 400CES was built through mid-1969, when it was phased out and the eighth model Venetian cutaway guitar was introduced. This version of the electric Super 400 has been continued with some minor changes to the present day. Specific details of the eighth model Super 400CES will be discussed in the following sections.

Headstock: The headstock of the eighth model Super 400CES was similar to that of the last of the seventh model cutaway Super 400CES guitars, with notable peaks at its upper end and the same Gibson script and split-diamond inlays. The headstock overlay material was blackened holly until 1970–1971, when Gibson substituted a more coarse-grained overlay of fiber veneer. This overlay was continued throughout the production of all subsequent Super 400CES guitars, with few exceptions. The headstock veneer was bound to the headstock with the same five-ply binding that had been used previously, and the same truss-rod cover was used with the word "Custom" etched across the diagonal parallelogram. The tuning machines were the same gold-plated Kluson Sealfast tuners with gold-plated brass buttons. These tuners were continued on the Super 400CES until the late 1970s, when a similar Schaller tuning machine was substituted that has been continued to the present day. In the early 1980s, special tuning buttons with miniature crank-winders inside were substituted. Beginning in 1970, the words

"Made in USA" were stamped into the back of the headstock of the Super 400CES just below the serial numbers, and that stamping has also continued to the present.

Neck: The very first 1969 Super 400CES guitars with the "new" Venetian cutaway had an extremely slender neck, just like the last of the seventh model Super 400CES guitars. However, this neck width (1⁹⁄₁₆ inches at the nut) was being phased out and was soon replaced in 1969 by the standard neck width of 1¹¹⁄₁₆ inches. The cross section

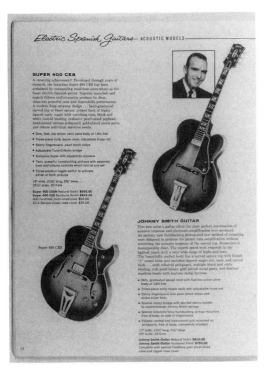

SUPER 400 CES—Cutaway
Many outstanding musicians consider the Super 400 CES to be the finest electric Spanish guitar made. The slim, fast low-action neck joins the extra large, carved top body at the 14th fret. This superb instrument offers a clean, powerful tone and dependable performance.

FEATURES: Carved top of finest spruce, carved back of figured curly maple with matching rims. Five-piece curly maple neck, adjustable truss rod. Ebony fingerboard, pearl block inlays. Adjustable Tune-O-Matic bridge. Exclusive Super 400 tailpiece. Powerful twin humbucking pickups. Separate tone and volume control for each pickup which can be preset. Three position toggle switch to activate either or both pickups. Hand-bound custom pickguard. Gold-plated metal parts. Deluxe individual machine heads. 18" wide, 21½" long, 3¾" deep; 25⅛" scale, 20 frets.

Super 400 CES—Sunburst   Super 400 CESN—Natural
400—Faultless plush-lined case
ZC-4—Deluxe zipper case cover

Super 400CES

- **1962 Gibson catalog, Super 400CES**
- **1970 Gibson catalog, Super 400CES**
- **1978 Gibson catalog, Super 400CES**

of the eighth model Super 400CES neck was also gradually thickened, tapering slightly from where the neck joined the headstock to the opposite end close to the heel. The fretboard continued to be made of ebony, with the same mother-of-pearl inlay patterns as on the previous electric Super 400 guitars. Five-ply binding was also used in the same manner around the fretboard's edge. The neck was constructed of the same three-piece book-matched curly maple sections, with the two narrow mahogany strips separating the three pieces. As on the Super 400C, a major change in the Super 400CES neck occurred when the volute was added to strengthen the neck–headstock joint in approximately 1973–1974. This hump on the back of the neck–headstock joint was almost universally rejected as being ugly and without merit, and was discontinued in approximately 1980–1981. The scale length of the Super 400CES neck was 25½ inches.

Body: The body of the eighth model Super 400CES closely resembled the body of the earlier sixth model Venetian cutaway Super 400CES guitar except for the slight change in the shape of the newer rounded cutaway. The top was made of carved spruce, and the back was made of two pieces of book-matched and carved curly maple. The rims were also made of curly maple. Typically, these first eighth model Super 400CES guitars featured rather spectacular woods in the back, rims, and neck until the early to mid-1970s, when a much plainer variety of maple was substituted.

On the top of the guitar, the instrument continued the twin humbucking pickup arrangement featured on the previous sixth and seventh model Super 400CES guitars. The pickup covers were gold-plated, as were the pickup pole pieces. The guitar had the usual two tone and two volume controls, and a three-way selector switch mounted in the approximate center of the right upper bout. The two pairs of control knobs were mounted on either side of the right f-hole down toward the lower bout. The eighth model Super 400CES continued the use of the basic Tune-O-Matic bridge setup,

● 1969 Super 400CES body
● 1969 Super 400CES knobs

consisting of the two-footed rosewood base and the adjustable brass Tune-O-Matic saddle, which was gold-plated. This bridge was utilized until around 1975, when the ebony adjustable bridge was substituted. As on the Super 400C from the same time period, this bridge utilized a thick ebony base with bow tie–shaped pearl inlays on the ends and a solid ebony saddle that was slightly compensated. This bridge is still used today. The tailpiece continued to be the standard Super 400 design, and the early eighth model Super 400CES guitars had the Varitone control in the tailpiece. However, the Varitone was dropped from the Super 400 tailpiece around 1973–1974 and was never reintroduced.

The Super 400CES tops from this period were braced with two parallel tone bars, along with several cross braces between the parallel tone bars and in between the two pickup cavities. Additional

Plate 9

- **1952 Super 400 CESN, front**
- **1952 Super 400 CESN, back**
- **1958 Super 400 CES, front**
- **1958 Super 400 CES, back**

Plate 10

- 1958 Super 400 CESN, front
- 1958 Super 400 CESN, back
- 1960 Super 400 CES, front
- 1960 Super 400 CES, back

Plate 11

- 1962 Super 400 CESN, front
- 1962 Super 400 CESN, back
- 1964 Super 400 CES, front
- 1964 Super 400 CES, back

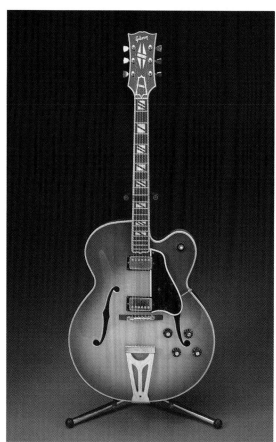
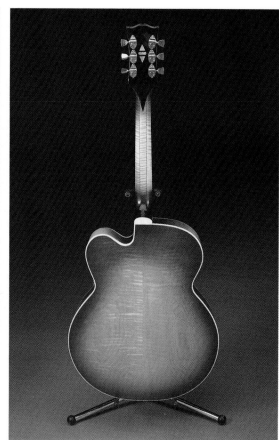
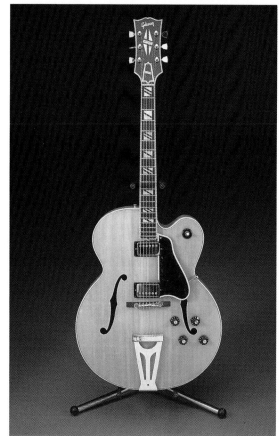
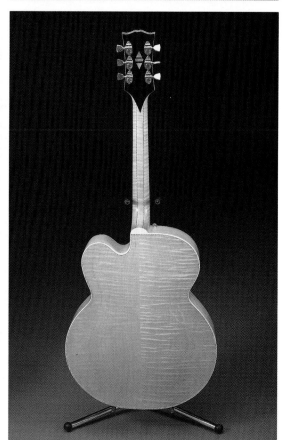

Plate 12

- 1969 Super 400 CES, front
- 1969 Super 400 CES, back
- 1970 Super 400 CESN, front
- 1970 Super 400 CESN, back

Plate 13

- 1978 Super 400 CES-WR, front
- 1978 Super 400 CES-WR, back
- 1939 Super 400 PN(E), built-in pickup
- 1949 Super 400 N, McCarty pickup
- 1949 Super 400 N, DeArmond pickup
- 1967 Super 400C, DeArmond pickup

Plate 14

- 1939 Super 400 PN(E), front
- 1939 Super 400 PN(E), back
- 1984 Super 400 CESN "50th Anniversary," front
- 1984 Super 400 CESN "50th Anniversary," back

Plate 15

- **1939 Super 400 N, with Marty Lanham**
- **1939 Super 400 N, before, showing inside**
- **1939 Super 400 N, before, showing outside**
- **1939 Super 400 N, front**
- **1939 Super 400 N, back**

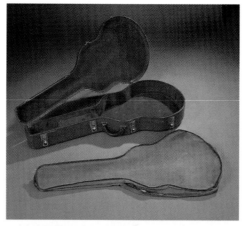
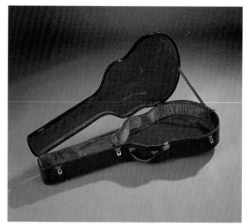

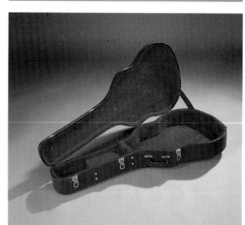

Plate 16
- **1935 Super 400 tan leather case and canvas cover**
- **1939 Super 400 black leather case**
- **1947 Super 400 tan case and vinyl cover**
- **1958 Super 400 brown case**
- **1964 Super 400 black case and canvas cover**
- **1978 Super 400 black case**
- **1984 Super 400 brown case**

- 1969 Super 400CES cutaway and pickguard
- 1969 Super 400CES cutaway detail

smaller braces were attached to the ends of the tone bars near the lower bouts of the guitar. All of this bracing contributed to an inhibition of the acoustic sound of the instrument, but strengthened the top to inhibit production of feedback at moderate volumes. The gold-plated input jack was located in the right rim of the guitar near the lower bout, in the standard location. Body binding was the same seven layers on the top and five layers on the back.

Finish: The eighth model Super 400CES was initially offered only in the golden sunburst and natural finish from 1969 through 1975. In 1976, to use up some of the plainest curly maple back and rim stock, Gibson officially introduced the new ebony and wine red finishes. These finishes were also used to broaden the line somewhat. The ebony and wine red finishes were discontinued in 1980. It should also be noted that the sunburst finish of the Super 400CES from this period ranged from a beautiful, almost cherry sunburst color in 1969–1971 to a darker brown sunburst that had a pronounced triangular-shaped yellow area on the back and top of the guitar, not unlike a large yellow "pick." Gibson changed the shading and labeling of this finish to antique sunburst in the later 1970s, signalling their attempt to return to the dark brown sunburst design of the early Super 400 prewar guitars.

Case: The early eighth model Super 400CES guitars were first supplied with the black Lifton plywood hard-shell case lined with yellow or orange plush velvet, and the black canvas case covers were still offered as an extra-cost option. In the early 1970s, Gibson began to substitute a black vinyl-covered plywood case that seemed somewhat cheaper in design and finish than the fine Lifton cases. This case has a red coarse-velvet lining and was continued in use until the early 1980s when Gibson began purchasing a brown vinyl-covered case with pink plush lining from Canada. These Canadian cases are very sturdy and appear to be a definite improvement over the black cases of the mid- to late 1970s.

● **1978 Super 400CES WR body**

● **1978 Super 400CES WR cutaway detail**

Summary

The electric Super 400 guitar, or Super 400CES, was introduced in late 1951 and evolved through two major body changes, three different pickup designs, and various other minor changes until the present. Essentially, the major change in the instrument's body was in the cutaway, when Gibson switched from the rounded Venetian cutaway in mid-1960 to the pointed Florentine cutaway. The more rounded Venetian cutaway reappeared in mid-1969 and has been continued ever since. The other major change involves the use of different types of pickups on the guitar, beginning with the P90 pickups in late 1951, followed by the Alnico-V single-coil pickups in 1954. These Alnico pickups were utilized until approximately mid-1958, when the PAF humbucking pickup became a standard feature on the instrument. The PAF humbuckers were utilized from mid-1958 through 1962 on both the last Venetian cutaway guitars and the first Florentine cutaway guitars. These PAF humbucking pickups were followed by the almost identical "patent number" humbucking pickups of 1963, which gave way in the early 1970s to humbucking pickups with no patent number markings and possibly different windings that produce a less superior tone than their predecessors.

Other evolutionary trim changes were rather minor in nature. The Super 400CES turned out to be more popular than the acoustic

Super 400, as production totals from the introduction of the guitar up to the present clearly indicate.

Gibson and Norlin upper management made the decision to close the original Kalamazoo factory at the end of August 1984 due to rising labor costs and an uncertainty about the future direction of the guitar market. Coincidentally, 1984 marked the 50th anniversary of the introduction of the Super 400, which made its debut in 1934. Therefore, Gibson decided to finish the last of the Kalamazoo-made Super 400 guitar production by putting their best efforts into some rather spectacular instruments, both aesthetically and musically. Approximately ten Super 400CES guitars were manu-factured and shipped from the factory in 1984, some of which went directly to dealers around the country to fulfill orders while others went to the Nashville factory for later distribution. The distinguishing features of these special Super 400CES guitars are the following:

- The woods in these instruments are highly figured, and appear much superior to the woods used from the mid-1970s up to that time.
- The workmanship and assembly of these instruments are of considerably greater quality than that found on instruments from the mid-1970s up to that time.
- These instruments were all made in 1984, and carry a small inlay at the 17th fret engraved with the words "50th Anniversary." Most of the approximately ten Super 400CES 50th Anniversary guitars were of the natural-finish variation, showing off the woods of these guitars to their best possible advantage.

The Super 400CES was an immediate success in several areas of music, ranging from Country and Western to rhythm and blues to jazz. Country and Western enthusiasts who favored the instrument from the beginning included Merle Travis and Hank Thompson. Jazz artists who favored the Super 400CES included a young George Benson, Eric Gale, Lewis Stewart, and Kenny Burrell, who also enjoyed playing the Super 400C with a detachable DeArmond pickup.

● **1988 Gibson catalog, featuring 1984 Super 400CESN 50th Anniversary**

Outstanding blues and popular guitarist Robben Ford also favored the Florentine cutaway Super 400CES and achieved some outstanding recording and live performances with this instrument, as did his jazz and fusion counterpart Larry Coryell. And of course the legendary Scotty Moore recorded many of Elvis Presley's early hits on his early Super 400CESN, which now reportedly belongs to Nashville record producer and musician Chips Moman. Moore switched to an early 1960s Florentine cutaway Super 400CES, which Presley used on his televised "Comeback Special" in the late 1960s, and this guitar was also featured on the album cover covering the same material. This instrument is presently enshrined at the Hard Rock Cafe in Dallas, Texas.

Though a large guitar, the Super 400CES proved itself to be an exceedingly versatile instrument in many respects. The tone quality of the guitar, unamplified, was less than desirable because of the

● A young Henry Van Wormer, holding his idol Joe Maphis' Super 400 as Joe and Rose Lee Maphis look on

additional bracing under the top, the additional top thickness, and the presence of the pickups and controls mounted in the top. However, such body details were designed to inhibit top vibration and minimize feedback at moderate volumes. When plugged in, the Super 400CES really came into its own, producing a deep tone with much color that was in sharp contrast to other electric guitars available up to that time.

After the 50th Anniversary Super 400CES guitars of 1984 were finished and the Kalamazoo factory was closed, very little Super 400 production was done at the Nashville factory. Of the partial records that are available, it is apparent that only 18 were made in Nashville and shipped from there between 1985 and 1989. The paucity of Super 400CES guitars for this time period is due to the lack of sufficient numbers of trained personnel to make the guitars in Nashville and the increasing difficulties Gibson was having with its old top- and back-carving equipment. Essentially, any Nashville-made Super 400CES is made by hand and usually by one or two very experienced luthiers. These instruments are very seldom encountered, but are well made and very much in the tradition of the the last Super 400CES guitars shipped from Kalamazoo.

76

● Henry Van Wormer today, with his 1960s Super 400CESN

Following is a summary of the number and types of Super 400CES guitars shipped during the time period of 1951 through 1989.

Sixth Model, Sunburst, 1951–1960	140
Sixth Model, Natural, 1951–1960	94
Seventh Model, Sunburst, 1960–1969	320
Seventh Model, Natural, 1960–1969	123
Eighth Model, Sunburst, 1969–Present	848 +
Eighth Model, Natural, 1969–Present	194 +
Eighth Model, Ebony, 1975–1980	?
Eighth Model, Wine Red, 1975–1980	?
Eighth Model, 50th Anniversary, 1984	10
Total, 1951–1989	1729 +

Thus, a total of 1,719 Super 400 guitars were made from 1951–1989, plus the ten or so 50th Anniversary guitars of 1984 and the still incomplete totals for 1980–1984.

Chapter
IV

Restoration
of a 1939
Super 400N

● 1. 1939 Super 400N
back and rim separation
● 2. Rejoining the back's
halves
● 3. Inner surface of
back, with center
reinforcement

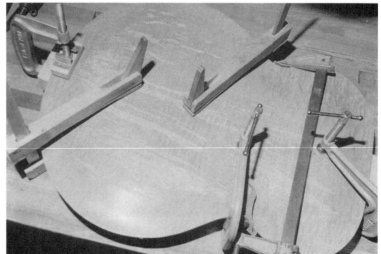

In accounting for all the different Super 400s made by Gibson over the years, it is inevitable that a certain number of these instruments have been played hard, altered, or damaged to a point that they might be considered hopelessly beyond repair. It has been my experience that not many Super 400s are encountered in totally irreparable condition; instead one may find acoustic Super 400s with holes cut in the top for the addition of electric pickups, Super 400s with cracks in the top and/or back that have been repaired with varying degrees of proficiency, and refinished Super 400s.

However, it is rare to find a Super 400 in the initial condition of the instrument described in this chapter. Several years ago Cesar Diaz, a fine amplifier repairman and guitar dealer, contacted me regarding an old Super 400 acoustic guitar that he had recently purchased. The guitar reportedly had been in a flood, and its case had been destroyed. The owner of the guitar had brought the instrument to Diaz's Maryland shop in pieces and sold it to him for a very nominal sum. Diaz knew of my interest in Super 400s and also realized that the instrument would require much effort and expense to restore. Even after such a restoration, there was no guarantee that the instrument would sound good enough to keep. Therefore, Diaz and I agreed on a price for the instrument in truly "as is" condition, and I purchased it sight unseen.

The instrument arrived at my Dallas residence in a shipping carton, without even the benefit of a case to protect its rather fragile condition. After a very thorough inspection, it became obvious that this instrument was essentially complete in every respect and a very significant instrument in the history of the Super 400. No parts were missing from the instrument, and no part of the instrument was cracked or broken. As Diaz had described, the instrument had indeed been in a flood, and the resulting moisture that enveloped the guitar had loosened most of the glue joints, causing the back to separate from the body along with other separations of various materials as well.

What made the instrument truly significant was that it was a 1939 Super 400 in natural finish. As mentioned previously in Chapter 1, only seven natural-finish noncutaway Super 400s were reportedly shipped during the years 1939 to 1941, making this prewar guitar one of the rarest standard versions of the Super 400 ever made. After some deliberation, I decided to proceed with a full-scale restoration project so that the instrument could at least be brought back to playable condition. A truly skilled luthier had to be located to take on the project.

The instrument was photographed in its as-is "before" state by Scott Grey, a medical illustrationist and commercial photographer in Dallas. The restoration of the instrument was photographed by Charmaine Lanham, a professional photographer in Nashville, Tennessee. She was able to illustrate each major step of the restoration process being performed by her husband Marty Lanham, an established and well-recommended Nashville luthier. Finally, the "after" photographs of the instrument were taken by Bill Crump, a commercial photographer in Dallas who took the majority of the photographs for this book.

● 4. Detail, inner back reinforcement and label

Before Restoration

As the photograph in color plate 15 clearly illustrates, the 1939 Super 400N was in rather tattered condition when I first obtained it. The back was completely loose from the guitar, most of the kerfing on the interior of the instrument was either missing or rotten, and many of the glue joints had separated, including those in the top and back seams. The water damage to the guitar's finish was considerable, and much of the finish on the back of the guitar had blistered and was impregnated with pink dye from the interior of the guitar's original case. However, no cracks in any of the guitar materials were discovered. Besides being a rare instrument, this guitar also featured several Gibson options that make it unique in some respects. These options included the natural finish, gold-plated brass tuning buttons instead of the usual amber plastic ones, and the Gibson neck-cord assembly that was attached on the back of the headstock and on the outside end of the tailpiece. Also, this guitar was unique in that its top was X-braced internally, as can be seen in the accompanying photographs. The top also featured the widened f-holes first begun in 1937, with the same length as those of the first model Super 400. The label, though tattered, was also intact.

After the instrument was obtained and evaluated, the first major step in the restoration process was to locate a luthier who had the sufficient skills and motivation to take on such a project. Initially, I shipped the guitar to the Gibson factory in Nashville, where Custom Shop personnel sent a bid on the restoration that included a time estimate as well as the financial cost of all work involved. However, Custom Shop personnel warned me that their time was limited and that they were working very hard on producing new instruments rather than restoring old ones. I then contacted George Gruhn of Gruhn Guitars in Nashville, and Gruhn recommended Marty Lanham to restore the instrument. Lanham is a luthier in Nashville who had worked at Gruhn's shop for approximately eight years before leaving to start his own musical repair business. Gruhn recommended Lanham highly, stating that he was well trained in the art of restoring carved-top guitars and that he was a very dependable and conscientious luthier as well. I contacted Marty Lanham, and after a rather lengthy telephone conversation the "remains" of the instrument were transported across town from the Gibson factory to Lanham's repair shop. After inspecting the instrument, Lanham described in some detail the process that would be involved in its restoration. He gave me an estimate of the time and expenses involved, and Charmaine Lanham began to photograph the various major steps of the restoration process.

● 5. Inside of body

The Restoration

The biggest task involved in restoring this instrument seemed to be the reassembly of the body. Putting the back on the guitar body was the most obvious problem and the most difficult problem to correct, so Lanham began by working with the back while it was off the guitar. The center seam in the back was separated, so it had to be closed up; it was joined at each end but was separated in the middle. Therefore, the center seam on the back had to be rejoined and reinforced with cross-grain maple of about the same density as the back itself, as illustrated in pictures 1, 2, 3, and 4. In picture number 1 the separation of the back from the body can be seen clearly, as can the blistering of the finish on the back. In illustration 2, the joining of the center seam of the back can be observed from the outside

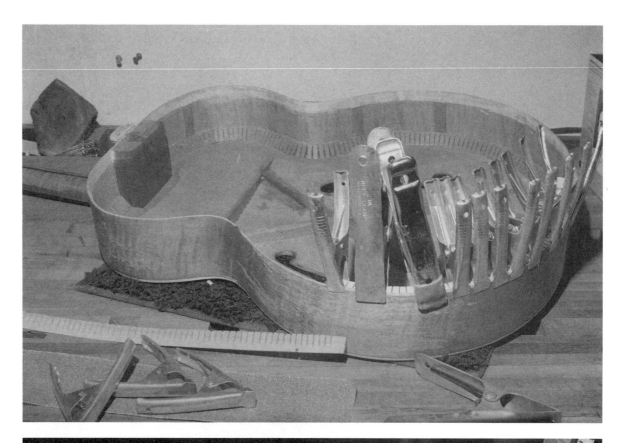

- 6. Inside of body, with new
  kerfing clamped in place
- 7. New kerfing section in place

or finished area of back. In illustration 3, the inner portion of the back can be viewed clearly with the reinforcing strip of cross-grain maple being secured along the inside of the center seam. Illustration 4 shows this reinforcement in more detail, along with the instrument's label.

The next major step involved removing all pieces of the kerfing from around the edge of the back and rims and cleaning the back and rims so that new kerfing could be installed. This area in which the back and rims were joined via the old kerfing can be seen in illustration 5 with the lighter area highlighting the guitar rims. Also, illustration 5 shows the ribs that had to be reglued on the side of the guitar. New kerfing was then made while all the old kerfing was cleaned out down to the rim wood. This condition is illustrated in picture number 7, in which a section of the new kerfing that would eventually join the back to the rims had been installed. New poplar kerfing has been glued and is being held in place by a number of spring clamps, as shown in picture 6.

In this early phase of the guitar's restoration, Lanham was alternately working on the back of the guitar and the kerfing on the rims. Lanham was also working on replacing the binding that would help secure the back of the guitar to the rims. This is illustrated in picture number 8, in which the binding can be seen as it is being joined to the

● 8. New binding joined to rims
● 9. Body braced and clamped to recapture original shape

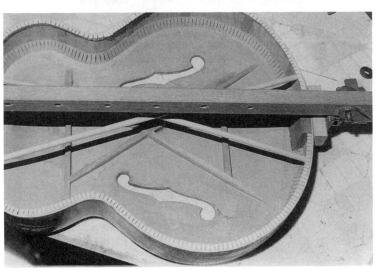

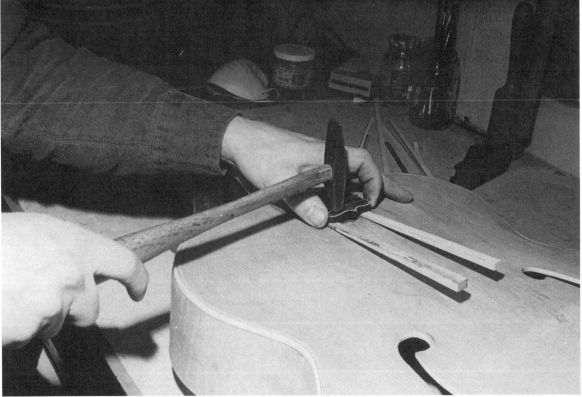

● 10. Clamping the back to the body
● 11. Installing the last new fret

guitar rims. The binding was glued to the rims in order to hold the back in position while it was being glued in place. In addition, picture 8 and picture 9 illustrate the long wooden dowels that were used to reshape the body of the guitar from within to fit the back, because the body had been distorted. An overall shrinkage of approximately ¼ inch had occurred all around the back, necessitating the use of the cross dowels and the long center clamp, which helped press the body of the guitar inwards somewhat from each end.

Once the above steps were completed, the back of the guitar was glued onto the body. Picture number 10 illustrates the actual clamping of the back onto the body and the use of several different kinds of clamps and some strapping to complete this procedure. Because of the shrinkage of the back, Lanham had to perform a rather radical step in fitting the rims to the back. As seen in color plate 15, he is sawing a small section off the end of each rim. By removing approximately ⅛ inch from each guitar rim, he could remove a total of about ¼ inch from the rims, which would then match closely the overall shrinkage of the guitar back. After removing these two rim pieces, he was able to finish the kerfing on the rims and successfully join the back to the rims as shown in illustration number 10. The body of the guitar was left in the illustrated clamped position for approximately two days before the clamps and tape were removed.

The next major step was to refret the entire fretboard, and illustration 11 shows Lanham installing the last fret on the fretboard of the instrument, with two small wedges underneath the end of the fretboard to prevent its being compressed onto the top of the guitar. All of the frets were pulled from the fretboard, and the fretboard was planed so that it would be level from one end to the other. Also, a small maple shim was placed between the fretboard extension and the underside of the fretboard to completely level that portion of the fretboard.

When beginning the refretting process, Lanham discovered that the neck joint was loose and the neck alignment was off-center, so he had to reset the neck later. The fingerboard was planed and the inner binding of black-and-white plastic was installed. The fret slots were cut through the binding, and then the frets were installed. As seen in illustration number 12, the gluing of the inner binding on the end of the fingerboard can be seen where Lanham had to make a special jig to press this binding into place.

Picture number 13 illustrates the installation all along the neck of the large outer white binding. Clamps, masking tape, and strapping were used to hold the binding in place. The binding was trimmed by hand with files and sandpaper to match how it had originally been fitted to the neck. Picture number 14 illustrates the clamping process at the headstock more clearly. Some cosmetic work was done to touch up the headstock, and some of the headstock binding was reglued.

Picture number 15 shows the ends of the outer binding just prior to their reshaping to round off the end of the fretboard. The guitar's label, on the inside of the back, was tattered but was glued together and taped back down inside the body.

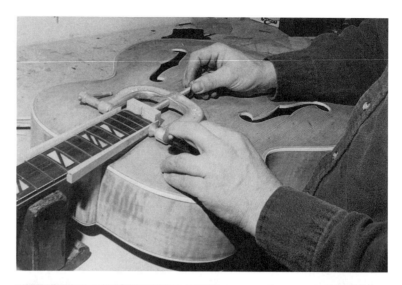

● 12. Pressing binding
onto fretboard tip
● 13. Clamping outer
binding to the neck

The main metal parts on the instrument—the tuning machines and the tailpiece—were buffed until they were cleaned of any remains of previous gold-plating. They were then given a high polish and lacquered.

Refinishing the guitar was one of the last steps in the restoration process. At first Lanham thought he would French polish the top while refinishing the back, sides, and neck of the instrument. However, the top had to be refinished also because of some staining problems from being immersed in water inside the pink plush-lined case. Various parts of the guitar body had to be sanded to remove much of the pink stain, so Lanham used nitrocellulose lacquer with a slight amber tint to match the overall color of the instrument. Since the instrument was originally given a natural finish, the restoration work had to be done extremely carefully because it could not be hidden by sunburst shading.

Once the finish had dried sufficiently, the instrument was strung up and Lanham called me to report that the project was complete. Much to everyone's amazement, the instrument sounded incredibly good, with a very full tone and considerable volume. It had obviously been played a great deal by its previous owner, and the qualitiy of the restoration probably only enhanced the inherent tone qualities in the instrument.

In retrospect, Lanham offered several comments about the construction and nature of carved-top guitars that make them rather complicated instruments requiring considerable skill in restoration (Marty Lanham, personal interview, 1988). In general, carved-top guitars tend to stay structurally stable if no cracks in the instrument develop and/or if no seams or wooden parts become loosened. That is, these are very strong instruments if the complete integrity of the body and neck are maintained. Once a crack or seam separation develops, however, the considerable string tension on the body of the guitar may lead to a rather rapid deterioration of the instrument, advancing cracking and seam separation even further. Lanham also noted that the three-piece laminated neck seemed stronger than either a one-piece neck, such as those used by D'Angelico, or the five-piece neck adopted by Gibson in late 1960. He stated that curly maple is a somewhat unstable wood and that the more highly figured curly maple has a greater tendency to "move a bit" over time and under considerable string tension. Finally, Lanham made a very

● 14. Headstock detail
● 15. Outer binding in place, prior to bending around fretboard tip

interesting point regarding such an extensive restoration project: The luthier never really knows what he or she is going to run into while working through the completion of such a project. Unusual problems crop up that may never have been dealt with before, problems that are unique to that guitar and that require a novel or unique solution at the moment. Certain tools may have to be made to bring certain parts of the guitar together, or additional research may have to be done to ensure that the restoration is being done as accurately and with as much care and forethought as possible.

Completion

As seen in color plate 15, the "finished product" is a truly impressive instrument. What the photos do not convey, however, is the incredible tone and power of this particular guitar. All of us involved in this project were very gratified at the results of the restoration, and the guitar's musical timbre proved to be the most gratifying experience of all. Words cannot really describe my joy and excitement on receiving this instrument approximately one year after the restoration project began. It truly sounded like one of the best orchestra guitars one has ever dreamed of hearing and playing, which is probably a testimony to the many persons involved in this instrument's life—its original builders, its original owner, and its restorer.

Chapter
V

The
Super 400's
Future

~

A number of key events have
occurred during the past 15 years that have dramatically affected the
future of Gibson's Super 400 guitar. These events include the opening
of the Nashville plant in 1976; the closing of the Kalamazoo factory in
1984; the shift of production of the carved-top guitars to Nashville
in 1985; and the sale of Gibson by Norlin, Inc., to the present
independent ownership in 1986. Each of these major events has played
a crucial role in determining the Super 400's future, and changing
demands in the guitar marketplace have also affected its production
to a certain extent.

Opening of
the Nashville Plant

The Nashville, Tennessee, guitar factory was an entirely new
factory built by Norlin, Inc., in 1976, following Norlin's formal
takeover of Gibson from CMI in 1974. The Nashville plant was
designed from the ground up to be an electric guitar manufacturing
facility, with machinery and manufacturing processes that were
considered state-of-the-art at that time. Norlin was betting on the
increasing popularity of the electric guitar as one of the principal
reasons for constructing the Nashville plant; the company also wished
to avoid the escalating costs of utilizing organized labor to make the
instruments, as was the case in Kalamazoo.

Originally, Norlin's plan seemed to be that the Nashville plant
would concentrate on electric guitars and basses, while the Kalamazoo
plant would continue to manufacture flat-top guitars, carved-top
guitars, mandolins, banjos, and various types of custom instruments.
However, short-term market conditions at that time indicated an
ever-increasing interest in the electric guitar with an apparent
diminished interest in acoustic instruments. Norlin operated both
plants simultaneously from 1976 until 1984, when they decided to
close the Kalamazoo factory.

Closing of
the Kalamazoo Factory

The decision to close the Kalamazoo factory was both a financial
and an emotional one. Financially, it seemed to make sense to Norlin
to get out of the acoustic and custom guitar market to a great extent,
since that market seemed rather sluggish and without direction at the
time. By concentrating on production of electric instruments plus
some limited production of acoustic instruments, Norlin hoped to cut
their overhead and direct the company toward their vision of the
future. The emotional part of the decision to close the Kalamazoo
factory may never be completely understood. However, the

Kalamazoo staff made a Super 400C for the Nashville management staff and named this special guitar "Passing the Torch" to symbolize the passing of Gibson craftsmanship from Kalamazoo to Nashville. This guitar was signed inside by all of the craftsmen at the Kalamazoo factory who were associated with it, and it was presented to the Gibson management team in Nashville in a private ceremony prior to the closing of the Kalamazoo factory.

I visited the Kalamazoo factory in May, 1984, approximately three months prior to its closing. During that visit, I observed in the plant an overall emotional tone of sadness that was oddly mated to a growing sense of pride in the tradition of craftsmanship that was about to be terminated. The sadness was apparent when I talked with the dwindling staff of management and production employees at the factory, as they discussed their feelings about the imminent closing of the Kalamazoo factory and its effect on their personal and professional lives. They were also concerned about the effect of the plant's closing on the future of the custom instruments made there, including the Super 400 and L-5 guitars. Despite the sadness, many of the staff stubbornly clung to a real sense of pride in their work. Many of them seemed determined to produce the best instruments possible as a fitting finale to the Gibson company as they knew it. Their craftsmanship is abundantly evident in the production of the 1984 50th Anniversary Gibson Super 400CES and L-5CES guitars, which are featured in other portions of this book. The Kalamazoo factory was formally closed at the end of August or early September of 1984, with plans to transfer production of the Super 400 and L-5 guitars to the Nashville facility.

Shift of Production to Nashville

During the Kalamazoo closing process, much of the machinery used to carve the tops and backs of the Gibson arch-top guitars, as well as rim-bending machines and other tooling, were shipped to the Nashville facility. Unfortunately, when the machinery arrived it was stored outside for a period of time and the elements apparently damaged the machinery to some extent. Thus began a series of problems for the production of the Super 400 guitars that has continued in one form or another up to the present day. Eight electric Super 400s and one acoustic Super 400 were produced in Nashville in 1985, followed by two acoustic and three electric Super 400s in 1986 and one acoustic and one electric Super 400 in 1987. Clearly, the production trend was in a downward direction. Then Norlin decided to sell the Gibson company in November of 1986 to a trio of independent businessmen—Henry Juskiewicz, David Berryman, and Gary Zebrowski. Juskiewicz was subsequently named president and Berryman vice-president of finance and accounting in the newly formed Gibson Guitar Corporation, while Zebrowski did not take an active role in the company. The partners were Harvard Business School graduate students in the late 1970s who had been very successful in turning a failing high-tech company in Oklahoma City

(Phi Technologies) into a thriving multimillion-dollar electronics business. Just as the closing of the Kalamazoo factory had been in part an emotional decision, so the purchase of Gibson by these men was apparently an emotional decision in part as well. Juskiewicz, a Gibson guitar player for many years, was drawn to the company because of the name and the products it represented.

However, the new Gibson Guitar Corporation faced several interrelated problems in trying to get its overall production up to a more acceptable level. There were several problems in producing the Super 400 in particular that have limited the output of these guitars since 1986. These problems began with the design of the Nashville factory, which was not conducive to the labor-intensive assembly of acoustic instruments. The climate in Nashville, Tennessee, was also far more humid than that in Kalamazoo, Michigan, and there were inadequate climate controls built into the plant to offset the Tennessee humidity. Therefore, it became very difficult to make any type of acoustic instruments in the Nashville plant without subsequent problems such as cracked tops and backs on flat-top guitars. Another factor in the dramatic slowdown in Super 400 production was the decreased demand for the instrument during the early and middle 1980s. (Of course, subsequent demand for this guitar has increased so dramatically that the Norlin prediction of dwindling demand for such high-quality instruments was clearly proven incorrect.) In addition, the obsolete and/or worn-out machinery shipped from Kalamazoo was simply not adequate to produce Super 400 and L-5 guitars any longer. Besides being damaged by the elements, the top- and back-carving machinery had simply been used for too long and needed to be replaced. Its accuracy could not be depended on any further. Finally, there were not enough skilled craftsmen to make these instruments at the Nashville facility. Although several Kalamazoo employees were offered the opportunity to move to Nashville, most of them declined both Norlin's and the new Gibson management's offers. The shortage of highly skilled luthiers has severely restricted the output of Super 400 guitars, even with the recent intensive training program underway and the arrival of new and much more accurate top- and back-carving equipment. One key employee in Nashville has been James Hutchins, who did make a few Super 400s essentially by himself in the Nashville facility just to show that it could still be done and to keep alive the barely flickering flame of the art of making such fine guitars.

Current Plans for Super 400 Production

Hutchins, like a few other Gibson staff in Nashville, was a Kalamazoo craftsman who has been very helpful in teaching the newer Nashville employees the fine art of making guitars like the Super 400. Through the acquisition of computer-controlled top- and back-carving machines, as well as other more modern equipment, Hutchins was able to implement a training program with support from other key Gibson management personnel that would teach the

Nashville staff how to make the best carved-top guitars available on a commercial basis. At least, this has been the goal of Gibson's endeavors in recent years. Personnel were trained first to make laminated-body ES-175s and then to carve the top for the L-4CES, essentially an ES-175 with deluxe appointments and a carved spruce top. Eventually, various personnel involved in this project were taught to carve the tops and backs for Byrdland and L-5 guitars as their skills improved. After a brief hiatus, the L-5CES is now back in production, and it was reported that about 150 L-5s would eventually be shipped from the Gibson facility during 1990.

The new Gibson Guitar Corporation purchased the Flatiron Mandolin Company and retained the services of its owner, Steve Carlsen, in 1989. The purpose of this purchase was to utilize the skills of Carlsen and his staff to make the Gibson mandolins and flat-top guitars, which could not be made in the Nashville facility for the reasons noted above. At one time it was rumored that the Super 400 would also be made in the old Flatiron facility in Bozeman, Montana; however, Gibson currently does not envision that as a possibility.

Instead, Gibson has decided to build the Super 400C and Super 400CES in the Nashville plant, using highly skilled Custom Shop staff to personally make each guitar. Most Super 400s made will be electric, although a few acoustics will be crafted also. These instruments will be marketed as Gibson's top-line *production* models, and will be distributed through a small, rather exclusive dealer network. These limited-production instruments will be priced accordingly—reportedly $9,000 for the sunburst version and $12,000 for the natural-finish version. The primary reason given for the high price of the natural-finish Super 400 is the extreme cost and limited availability of suitable spruce tops and curly maple backs that are large enough and beautiful enough for such a fine instrument. The first instruments were to be finished and available for sale in the summer of 1991.

The current high demand for Super 400 guitars began in the vintage instrument arena and has been fueled by an increasing public awareness among collectors and guitar players of the construction and musical qualities of these guitars. Also, the relatively small number of Super 400s and L-5s available on the vintage guitar market has finally caught the attention of those buyers who in the past would have spurned such instruments because they seemed "unpopular" or "slow sellers." At the present time, even the plainest of mid-1970s Super 400 and L-5 guitars will fetch a price around $3000, and those instruments that are either older and/or more highly figured in their body woods may bring considerably more. Current Gibson management has become increasingly aware of the vintage market trend towards higher demand and higher prices for the L-5 and Super 400 guitars, leading to their decision to continue the instruments in Nashville and distribute them through a small dealer network.

Chapter
VI

The
Gibson L–5 Guitar:
Elegant Simplicity

● **1947 L-5, 1948 L-5N,**
   1948 L-5 Premiere:
   "Three to draw to"

The L-5 was designed as an accompaniment instrument for orchestra, small group, and solo settings. At the time of its introduction, there was no other guitar made by any manufacturer that even remotely resembled the L-5 in overall form or function. Soon after its auspicious debut in 1923, the L-5 became one of Gibson's all-time great guitars, a milestone in the evolution of the carved-top instrument and a major contributor to American acoustic and electric music. The L-5 was designed by a special engineering team led by Lloyd Loar and was part of a product line that included the F-5 mandolin, the H-5 mandola, and the K-5 mandocello. Of these four instruments, the L-5 guitar and the F-5 mandolin became outstanding performers and prized instruments valued by players and collectors alike. These two instruments set high standards for corporate instrument manufacturers and individual luthiers—standards that some would argue have yet to be surpassed. The strategy of the simultaneous introduction of a "family" of related instruments was repeated again in 1934 when Gibson introduced the Super 400 and the Advanced line of carved-top guitars that ranged beneath it. This marketing strategy has usually proven valuable to Gibson, and they have repeated it several times since the 1920s with ever-broadening markets and increasing sales.

In compiling a brief history of the L-5 guitar, the reader must keep in mind that a truly complete history is beyond the scope of this book. Therefore, I will present a condensed overview of the evolution and development of the L-5 guitar from its beginnings up to the present, and the reader will notice some parallels between the development of the L-5 and the development of the Super 400, once the Super 400 was introduced. A more complete description of the history and evolution of the L-5 guitar would merit a separate book.

There are four distinct versions of the L-5 guitar. These are the prewar 16-inch L-5, made from 1923–1937; the prewar 17-inch Advanced L-5, made from 1934–1941; the postwar L-5 acoustic guitar, made from 1946–present; and the postwar L-5 electric guitar or L-5CES, made from 1951–present. As with the Super 400, there are differences, both subtle and major, between each of these distinct versions of the L-5. The following description will serve to orient the reader toward the distinctions between these various models and the variations within each broad model category. Production data will also be provided to assist the reader in determining the relative rarity of a particular instrument once it is properly identified. Unfortunately, no production data exist for the majority of the first model 16-inch L-5s made between 1923 and 1934. However, records do exist showing that a small number of 16-inch L-5s were manufactured from 1935–1937; these 16-inch L-5s will be included in the overall L-5 shipping totals and other forms of the L-5 data presented later in this chapter.

● 1934 16-inch L-5, front

The First Model L-5

The first model L-5 guitar was introduced in late 1922. This instrument, with a lower bout width of 16 inches, was essentially produced in three variations before it was substantially altered in 1934 to become the Advanced L-5. These three variations consist of the first L-5 guitars of 1923–1924, which contain two labels inside the body. One of these labels was signed by Lloyd Loar, along with the date, model designation, and serial number. These L-5s are the "Lloyd Loar" L-5s, although the second variation of the 16-inch L-5 is essentially the same in construction, but without Lloyd Loar's signature on one of the two inside labels. The second variation usually does not contain the Virzi tone producer (see Wheeler, *American Guitars,* p.114) that was offered in the first L-5s only in 1924. The third variation of the 16-inch L-5 was introduced in late 1929, when the fretboard inlays were changed from simple pearl dots beginning at the third fret to large rectangular pearloid block inlays. The following information applies to all three variations of the first model L-5, except where specifically noted.

Headstocks: The headstock of the first model L-5 is truly an exercise in elegant simplicity. Beginning where the headstock joins the neck, the contours taper toward the top of the headstock so that the headstock is narrower at the end than it is in the area close to the neck joint. "The Gibson" was written diagonally in the beautiful prewar style across the top of the headstock on the front, and directly underneath that was the now famous torch or flower-pot mother-of-pearl inlay that the L-5 has retained in various forms to the present day. The headstock design remained essentially unchanged for the life of the first model L-5, except that "The Gibson" inlay was changed to a horizontal position for the second and third variations of the guitar. All of the 16-inch L-5s used open-back worm-gear tuners. The Loar L-5s used silver-plated tuners, while the second and third variations used gold-plated tuners, including some that were "three on a plate" with pearl buttons. Through 1925, the tuning gear wheels were above the shaft; then they were moved below the shaft.

Necks: The neck of the first 16-inch L-5s was rather thick in cross section, most noticeably at the neck-headstock joint. The scale length of the guitar was 24¾ inches, and the fretboard was made of ebony and utilized very simple mother-of-pearl dot position markers beginning at the 5th fret. Sometime later during the production of the second variation of the 16-inch L-5, a dot position marker was added at the 3rd fret, and the third variation featured rectangular pearl block inlays beginning at the 3rd fret. The neck on Loar models utilized single-ply white binding, ending in a graceful point over the top of the guitar. This point was dropped during the later production of the second variation and on the third variation of the 16-inch guitar; these guitars had three-ply binding. The fretboard utilized nickel-silver frets. The neck itself was two pieces of book-matched curly maple with a center mahogany strip. The neck joined the body at the 14th fret, and had a narrow heel that was also very graceful in its appearance.

Bodies: One of the most obvious and distinguishing characteristics of the first model L-5 is its body. The bodies of these guitars measured approximately 16 inches across the lower bout, and the noncutaway body design remained essentially unchanged throughout the production of the first model guitar. In fact, it is this body size and configuration that really defines the first model L-5 and separates it from its later relatives. The top was a carved spruce affair, with twin parallel spruce braces underneath. The rims were made of curly maple, while the backs of early Loar-signed guitars were made of birch. Some of the Loar guitars may have had backs made of book-matched curly maple.

The L-5 was Gibson's first carved-top guitar with violin-style sound holes or f-holes as opposed to oval or round sound holes. The f-holes were unbound and were rather small in some respects, especially when compared with later versions of the L-5. The bridge was made of ebony with a solid base and compensated saddle. The tailpiece was a simple hinged trapeze affair, and on the earliest versions the strings passed through and over the top of the tailpiece crossbar before resting on the bridge, while later versions of the 16-inch guitar utilized a similar tailpiece in which the strings passed directly through the tailpiece crossbar rather than wrapping over the top of it.

The pickguard design for the first model L-5 was essentially the same on the Loar and slightly later variations, and was a very graceful tortoise shell-like plastic with white three-ply celluloid binding. The pickguard was fastened under the fretboard with spikes at the forward edge and mounted to the rim of the guitar via the Gibson threaded rod and bracket assembly made either of brass or plastic on loops. On the third variation, the pickguard was approximately on inch longer and screwed directly to the top of the guitar at its forward edge.

Finishes: The only finish offered on the 16-inch L-5, in all three variations, was the cremona sunburst finish, whose overall appearance was a dark brown with subtle shading into slightly lighter tones around the center of the top and back, along certain areas of the rims, and along the sides of the neck. This was a hand-rubbed finish, and had a very nice overall appearance. The finish was done with varnish through mid-1929, then nitrocellulose lacquer.

Cases: I have examined several 16-inch L-5s that were made between 1924–1934, and the original case for these guitars appears to be a small, form-fitting hard-shell case covered in thin black leather-grained cloth and equipped with nickel-silver latches and hinges. The interior of the case is usually lined in green or red (and later purple) plush-velvet material.

For a more detailed description of the various changes that occurred in the 16-inch L-5, the reader is referred to Wheeler, *American Guitars,* pp. 111–115.

The Advanced L-5

Gibson repeated their marketing strategy of 1923–1924 again in 1934, when they introduced the Super 400 guitar and the Advanced line of 17-inch-wide carved-top guitars, including the Advanced L-5. Once Gibson had simultaneously introduced the Super 400 and the Advanced L-5, the evolution of the L-5 and the Super 400 guitars was strikingly similar. Therefore, much of what will be described about the evolution of the Advanced or second model L-5, as well as its postwar relatives and the electric L-5, will be very similar to the evolution of the comparable Super 400 models. The Advanced L-5 was produced from later 1934 through 1941. As with the Super 400, several variations of this instrument appeared with the standard 17-inch width at the lower bout. There are three variations of the prewar 17-inch L-5, and each of these will be discussed briefly, although some overlapping features probably exist that may blur the distinctions between these variations in some respects. The three main variations of the prewar 17-inch L-5 are the X-braced version made from 1935–1939; the later parallel-braced version made from 1939–1941; and the cutaway or Premiere version, also made from 1939–1941. Production data are available on most of these models, and will be discussed later in this chapter.

Headstocks: The headstock of the Advanced L-5 was enlarged somewhat, becoming broader at the top rather than at the bottom where the headstock joined the neck. The shape was essentially unchanged from 1934 through 1941. On the face of the headstock overlay was inlaid the prewar Gibson logo in thick horizontal script.

● **1937 Gibson catalog, the Advanced L-5**

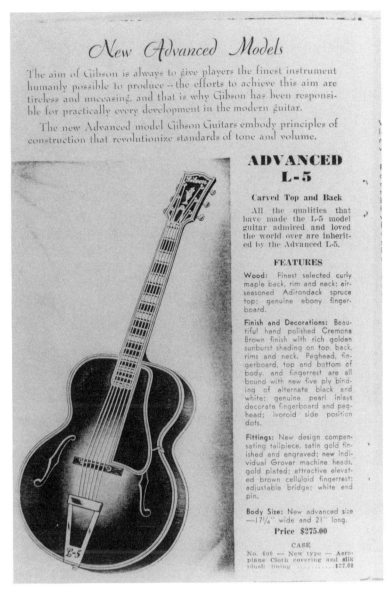

New Advanced Models

The aim of Gibson is always to give players the finest instrument humanly possible to produce — the efforts to achieve this aim are tireless and unceasing, and that is why Gibson has been responsible for practically every development in the modern guitar.

The new Advanced model Gibson Guitars embody principles of construction that revolutionize standards of tone and volume.

ADVANCED L-5

Carved Top and Back

All the qualities that have made the L-5 model guitar admired and loved the world over are inherited by the Advanced L-5.

FEATURES

Wood: Finest selected curly maple back, rim and neck; air-seasoned Adirondack spruce top; genuine ebony fingerboard.

Finish and Decorations: Beautiful hand polished Cremona Brown finish with rich golden sunburst shading on top, back, rims and neck. Peghead, fingerboard, top and bottom of body, and fingerrest are all bound with new five ply binding of alternate black and white; genuine pearl inlays decorate fingerboard and peghead; ivoroid side position dots.

Fittings: New design compensating tailpiece, satin gold finished and engraved; new individual Grover machine heads, gold plated; attractive elevated brown celluloid fingerrest; adjustable bridge; white end pin.

Body Size: New advanced size —17¼" wide and 21" long.
Price $275.00

CASE
No. 600 — New type — Aeroplane Cloth covering and silk plush lining $27.00

The flower-pot inlay was continued, and a bell-shaped truss-rod cover that was bound in white plastic covered the adjustable end of the truss rod. The tuning machines for the first of the Advanced L-5s were gold-plated, open-back Kluson tuners. These were later replaced by the larger Kluson Sealfast machines as utilized on the Super 400 of the same time period. These tuners were also gold-plated.

Necks: The necks continued to be made of two pieces of book-matched curly maple with a mahogany center strip. The fretboard was made of ebony, with small nickel-silver frets and block pearl inlays now beginning at the first fret. The shape of the blocks was somewhat more square than on the last version of the 16-inch L-5. The thickness of the binding around the fretboard was increased, and the point at the end of the fretboard was reinstated. The scale length on the very first Advanced L-5s was kept at 24¾ inches, although this was subsequently lengthened to 25½ inches at about the same time that this changed occurred on the Super 400, in approximately

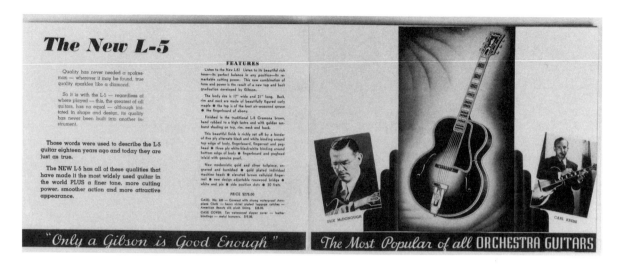

● **1940 Gibson catalog, the new L-5**

1937. The neck joined the body at the 14th fret, and this neck–body juncture would remain standardized. The necks on the very early Advanced L-5s seemed rather thick in cross section, although not as thick as the earlier 16-inch L-5 necks. The necks became somewhat slimmer in width and cross section later in the 1930s, and the guitars subsequently became easier to play as well.

Bodies: As with the earlier 16-inch L-5, the 17-inch body of the Advanced L-5 defines this instrument and separates it from its predecessor. The 17-inch body width at the lower bout was retained for both the noncutaway and cutaway versions of the guitar. The guitar was approximately 3¼ inches deep at the rim. The top was made of carved spruce, and the carved back was made of two pieces of book-matched curly maple. The rims were also made of curly maple. The f-holes on the top of the earliest Advanced models were unbound, with a single layer of white celluloid binding used later. The Advanced L-5 continued to use a slightly altered version of the bridge first introduced on the 16-inch L-5, with a solid rosewood base and a compensated rosewood saddle. The gold-plated brass tailpiece of the L-5 underwent some evolutionary changes during the years of the Advanced model, beginning as a hinged tailpiece that was heavier than the trapeze-type tailpiece of the 16-inch L-5. The crossbar on the tailpiece was definitely heavier, and the very first Advanced L-5s had the designation "L-5" engraved at the end of the tailpiece. These tailpieces were open in the center. Shortly thereafter, the center of the tailpiece was partially filled with a silver-plated metal insert that was pointed at both ends and had some simple engraving patterns on it. The sides of the tailpiece were also indented in several areas, and this shape eventually became the final form of the L-5 tailpiece, which would not vary much from the design introduced in the later 1930s. The Varitone tension-altering device was introduced in 1939, replacing the earlier hinged tailpiece as was done on the Super 400 also.

As noted earlier, the tops of the first Advanced models were X-braced, and parallel bracing was not reintroduced until 1939.

In 1939, Gibson introduced the L-5 Premiere, a cutaway version of the Advanced 17-inch guitar. The Premiere was immediately accepted by professional musicians and sold quite well for Gibson. The single distinguishing characteristic of the L-5 Premiere is the cutaway in the upper right bout of the guitar, and like the Super 400 Premiere, the first L-5 Premieres had a cutaway whose edges seemed somewhat swollen in the curved area. The fretboards on the very first L-5 Premieres rested almost flat on top of the guitar but were later elevated slightly. The Premiere was continued after World War II and was actually called the Premiere during 1947–1948, when it was renamed the L-5C. The prewar L-5 Premiere guitars are among the most prized L-5 acoustic instruments ever made, probably second in popularity only to the signed Lloyd Loar 16-inch L-5s. Bracing on all the L-5 Premieres was parallel, since 1939 marked the return to parallel bracing for both the cutaway and noncutaway versions of the L-5.

Finishes: Like the Super 400, the Advanced L-5 was initially offered only in the cremona or golden sunburst finish. This sunburst finish, first introduced on the Loar-designed 16-inch L-5, gradually changed to include a more expanded area of gold-yellow color in the center of the top and back as well as on the rims and back of the neck. In 1939 the natural or blond finish was offered as an option on the noncutaway L-5 and the L-5 Premiere. For these guitars, the wood had to be even more highly figured than on the sunburst versions, and these natural-finish prewar L-5s are usually very striking in their appearance. Both the natural and sunburst finishes were done in nitrocellulose lacquer, but the hand-rubbed finish was replaced by a sprayed finish on the Advanced guitars.

Cases: With the introduction of the larger-bodied L-5, the cases were changed as well. Several different types of cases were supplied with the Advanced prewar guitars. These included a tweed-style linen-covered Lifton hard-shell case, a black case covered in leather-grained cloth, and an occasional brown cloth-covered Geib hard-shell case as well. It is my impression that most of the prewar Advanced L-5 were equipped with the tweed-covered hard-shell case, with orange and black stripes across the center of the case body. These cases were made of arched plywood, and were lined with either purple or pink plush material. They also utilized nickel-silver hinges, and were very sturdy protectors of the valuable instruments they carried. A zipper case cover was offered as an optional accessory.

Prewar L-5 Acoustic Production Summary

From 1935 to 1941, a total of approximately 1,005 prewar acoustic L-5 guitars were shipped from the Gibson factory. This total includes three basic models and five variations of the guitar, including the final production of the 16-inch guitars from 1935 through 1937; the 17-inch Advanced L-5 noncutaway guitars offered from 1934–1938 in sunburst and from 1939–1941 in sunburst and natural finish; and the cutaway or Premiere L-5s also offered from 1939 through 1941 in sunburst and natural finish. The following totals are approximations based on current available shipping-ledger information provided by Julius Bellson. Additional tables

tables in Appendix B provide more detailed information.

In summary, the following versions of the prewar acoustic L-5 guitar were produced:

First Model (16-inch) L-5, 1935–1937	99
Second Model (17-inch) Advanced L-5, Sunburst, 1935–1941	752
Second Model (17-inch) Advanced L-5, Natural, 1939–1941	36
Third Model Premiere L-5, Sunburst, 1939–1941	65
Third Model Premiere L-5, Natural, 1939–1941	53
Total, 1935–1941	1,005

● **1960 Gibson catalog, the L-5C**

Postwar Acoustic L-5 Guitars

Production of the L-5 acoustic guitars resumed in late 1947, and official shipping ledgers note that shipments of the L-5, L-5N, L-5P, and L-5PN were resumed in 1948. The L-5 and L-5N remained in production through 1958, when their dwindling popularity, coupled with the rise in interest in the cutaway L-5 and the electric L-5, made it no longer economically feasible to manufacture the noncutaway guitar. The first cutaway L-5s produced after World War II (1947 and 1948) often will bear the designation "L-5P" on the label inside the

SUPER 400 C

A superlative instrument, flawless in appearance and performance. Designed with carved top and back in modern cutaway style, its rare beauty, response, and magical tone are the fruits of Gibson's expert craftsmanship.

Features: Carved top of finest close-grained spruce, and carved back of highly figured curly maple with matching rims and white-black-white ivoroid binding. Slim, fast, low-action, three-piece curly maple neck with adjustable truss rod. Ebony fingerboard and peghead with large pearl inlays. Rosewood adjustable bridge. Exclusive Super 400 adjustable tailpiece. Gold-plated metal parts and Sealfast individual machine heads with metal buttons.

18" wide, 21¾" long, 3⅜" deep . . .
25½" scale, 20 frets

Super 400CN Natural finish **$675.00**
Super 400C Sunburst finish **$650.00**
400 Faultless plush-lined case $60.00
ZC-4 Deluxe zipper case cover $35.00

L-5CN

The L-5 has held its enviable position as an exceedingly popular orchestra guitar for many years . . . a wonderfully rich tone, easy playing action, and beautiful cutaway styling are among the reasons.

Features: Carved top of finest close-grained spruce, carved back of highly figured curly maple with matching rims, and white-black-white ivoroid binding. Slim, fast, low-action, three-piece curly maple neck with adjustable truss rod. Ebony fingerboard with black pearl inlays. Rosewood adjustable bridge. Hand bound pickguard. Exclusive adjustable tailpiece. Gold-plated metal parts and Sealfast individual machine heads with metal buttons.

17" wide, 21" long, 3⅜" deep . . .
25½" scale, 20 frets

L-5CN Natural finish **$580.00**
L-5C Sunburst finish **$565.00**
600 Faultless plush-lined case $53.50
606 Faultless, flannel-lined case $42.50
ZC-6 Deluxe zipper case cover $30.00

L-5 CT Thin Body Cutaway

Developed expressly for George Gobel with the same fine features as L-5CN . . . plus thinner body in gleaming cherry-red finish.

17" wide, 21" long, 2⅜" thin . . .
24¾" scale, 20 frets

L-5CT Cherry finish **$565.00**
603 Faultless plush-lined case $53.50
ZC-6 Deluxe zipper case cover $30.00

● 1960 Gibson catalog, the Super 400C, L-5CN, and L-5CT

body. Thus, technically these postwar guitars are also considered L-5 Premieres like their prewar ancestors. Some subtle changes in ornamentation occurred between the prewar and postwar guitars, and these early postwar instruments are usually combined with the L-5C and L-5CN totals beginning in 1949 when one takes an overview of the postwar L-5 cutaway guitar. A brief summary of the evolution of the various features of the postwar acoustic L-5 guitars will be given below.

Headstocks: L-5 acoustic guitars from 1947–1948 usually carry the prewar Gibson thick script logo inlaid diagonally across the face of the headstock. Headstocks continue to feature the holly overlay, with the L-5 flower-pot inlay and the bound, bell-shaped truss-rod cover as well. The tuning machines on the postwar L-5 guitars were the standard Kluson Sealfast gold-plated units, using plastic buttons until approximately 1958, when gold-plated brass buttons were substituted from then on.

The more modern postwar Gibson diagonal logo replaced the prewar script logo in 1949, and has been continued with subtle variations to the present day.

The headstock contours remained the same until the early 1960s, when the end of the headstock seemed more pointed on each of its corners. In the early 1980s, special tuning buttons were utilized on Schaller tuning gears that had miniature cranks inside them that could be pulled out and utilized to tune up the guitar more quickly. Headstock binding continued in the same pattern from the early postwar guitars up to the present day.

Necks: The early postwar L-5 acoustic guitars had a neck that was very similar to their prewar ancestors, made of two pieces of book-matched curly maple with a center mahogany strip. The necks on some of these early postwar guitars of 1947–1949 are rather thick in cross section, but became somewhat thinner in the early 1950s. The neck width was standardized at 1^{11}/$_{16}$ inches at the nut, and this neck width remained standard until the mid-1960s, at which time the neck width was narrowed at the nut to 1^9/$_{16}$ inches. This was not popular with most guitarists at the time, and Gibson returned to the 1^{11}/$_{16}$-inch neck width by late 1969. As on the Super 400, the L-5 neck was changed from a two-piece to a three-piece version in 1961. The three-piece version consisted of three pieces of book-matched curly maple with two slender mahogany strips separating the three pieces. This neck design has continued to the present day. The volute was introduced at the neck–headstock juncture in 1974–1975, and dropped by 1982.

The fretboards of the early postwar L-5s are either ebony, as on some of the earliest 1947 guitars, or Brazilian rosewood, which was utilized on the 1948 and 1949 guitars because of the early postwar ebony shortage. Ebony was again used for the guitar fretboards beginning in approximately late 1950, and utilized from then on. Frets were initially the small nickel-silver variety, and were enlarged somewhat to the "jumbo" nickel-silver frets in approximately 1959. Fretboard binding continued to be the multilayered variety, with a small graceful point at the end of the fretboard. The scale length continued to be 25½ inches except on a special version of the cutaway L-5 called the L-5CT.

The L-5CT was a limited editon L-5C whose chief distinguishing characteristics were its 24¾-inch scale length, its body depth of 2⅛ inches, and its standard finish of cherry red instead of sunburst or natural. When viewed from the front, the instrument appeared identical to the L-5C except for the color of the finish. However, when viewed from the side and especially when played, the guitar took on a distinctive quality all its own. The thinner body and slightly shorter scale were very comfortable for most players. Reportedly a single L-5CT was designed for television star George Gobel (who earlier played a Super 400N), who had requested that Gibson build him a custom L-5 that would be comfortable to play and beautiful to behold on color television. The thin body and shorter scale were designed for Gobel, and the red finish was added to make the guitar more visually appealing. After this initial guitar was completed in 1959, Gibson decided to offer the instrument between 1959–1961. A total of 43 of these instruments were shipped from the factory during those three years. The instrument illustrated in color plate 19 is a slightly later model, custom-ordered from the factory and shipped in 1969. It has the same cherry red finish and

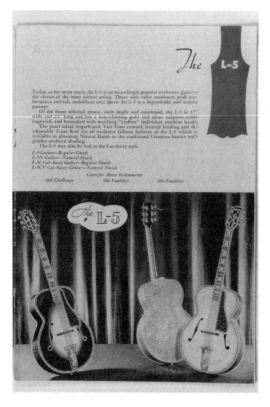

● 1950 Gibson catalog,
the L-5 and L-5N
(shown in prewar
models)

body depth as the earlier L-5CTs, but has the longer 25½-inch scale.

Bodies: The bodies of the postwar noncutaway L-5 and L-5N were similar to those of their prewar relatives. The tops were made of carved spruce with f-holes bound in single-ply white binding, braced internally with two parallel spruce tone bars. The rims and backs were made of curly maple, and the back was a two-piece book-matched carved affair that was often very striking in its appearance, especially on the natural-finish guitars. The body size remained the same, with the 17-inch lower bout that had been used since 1934. The body depth was 3⅛ inches at the rim. The L-5P/L-5C body was the cutaway version of the guitar, and the cutaway remained essentially similar on the instrument from 1948 to the present period. There was a slight alteration in the contour of the

L-5CN

Through the years, the Gibson L-5 has maintained its enviable position as an exceedingly popular orchestra guitar. Available in modern Cutaway Style and traditional body shape (without cutaway).

Attractively bound with alternate white-black-white ivoroid • carved top of finest close-grained spruce and carved back of highly figured curly maple are expertly matched to curly maple rims. Three piece curly maple neck with adjustable Truss Rod construction • multiple bound ebony fingerboard with large block pearl inlays. Gold-plated metal parts, exclusive L-5 Varitone tailpiece, rosewood adjustable bridge, hand bound pickguard, and Sealfast individual machine heads with metal buttons.

SPECIFICATIONS
17″ wide, 21″ long, 3⅜″ deep, 25½″ scale, 20 frets

L-5CN — Natural Finish
L-5C — Golden Sunburst Finish
L-5N — Guitar • Natural Finish
L-5 — Guitar • Golden Sunburst Finish
No. 600 Case — Faultless construction, plush lined
No. 606 Case — Faultless construction, flannel lined
ZC-6 — Zipper Cover for cases No. 600 and No. 606

● **1956 Gibson catalog, the L-5CN**

cutaway during the late 1970s, and the binding in the cutaway was altered from rather narrow binding on the early guitars to wider binding on the later models beginning in the early 1950s.

As mentioned above, the body of the L-5CT was different from the L-5C body in that it was 2⅛ inches deep at the rim, a full inch shallower in depth than the regular L-5C. The same materials were used in the L-5CT bodies as were used in the deeper L-5C bodies— carved spruce top, two-piece book-matched curly maple back, and curly maple rims.

On the acoustic L-5s, the tailpiece continued to be of the same design as that of the late prewar guitars, with the Varitone device installed in the tailpiece until the mid-1970s, when it was finally eliminated. "L-5" was engraved in script at the lower part of the tailpiece, and the tailpiece was manufactured of brass, which was gold-plated with a silver-plated insert in the center. All postwar tailpieces were of the rigid variety and were not hinged as were some of the earlier prewar tailpieces. The early postwar L-5 acoustic guitars continued to use the rosewood bridge base and compensated rosewood saddle. This design was continued until the mid-1970s when an ebony bridge base and saddle were substituted, much like those used on the Johnny Smith and the Super 400 guitars from the same period.

L-5CN
L-5CT Thin Body Cutaway

The L-5C has held its enviable position as an exceedingly popular orchestra guitar for many years . . . a wonderfully rich tone, easy playing action, and beautiful cutaway styling are among the reasons. L-5CT is a thin body (2⅜″ thin) with the same fine features. Developed expressly for George Gobel in gleaming cherry-red finish.

Features: Carved top of finest close-grained spruce, carved back of highly figured curly maple with matching rims, and white-black-white ivoroid binding. Slim, fast, low-action, three-piece curly maple neck with adjustable truss rod. Ebony fingerboard with black pearl inlays. Rosewood adjustable bridge. Hand bound pickguard. Exclusive adjustable tailpiece. Gold-plated metal parts and Seal-fast individual machine heads with metal buttons.

17″ wide, 21″ long, 3⅜″ deep . . . 25½″ scale, 20 frets.

L-5CN Natural finish **$635.00**
L-5C Sunburst finish **$620.00**
600 Faultless plush-lined case $56.00
ZC-6 Deluxe zipper case cover $30.00
L-5CT Cherry finish (24¾″ scale) **$620.00**
603 Faultless plush-lined case $56.00
ZC-3 Zipper case cover $30.00

L-5CN

- 1962 Gibson catalog, the L-5C
- 1970 Gibson catalog, the L-5C

L-5C

The orchestra guitarist will marvel at the wonderfully rich tone, easy playing action and beautiful cutaway styling of the L-5C. This remarkable guitar has held its enviable position as an exceedingly popular carved top acoustic for many years.

FEATURES: Carved top of finest close-grained spruce, carved back of highly figured curly maple with matching rims, and white-black-white ivoroid binding. Slim, fast, low-action, five-piece curly maple neck with adjustable truss rod. Ebony fingerboard with beautiful pearl block inlays. Rosewood adjustable bridge. Hand bound pickguard. Exclusive adjustable tailpiece. Gold-plated metal parts and machine heads with gold buttons. 17 inches wide, 21 inches long, 3⅜ inches deep; 25½ inch scale, 20 frets.

L-5C—Sunburst finish
L-5CN—Natural finish

600—Faultless plush-lined case
ZC-6—Deluxe zipper case cover

Pickguards continued to be made of the bound tortoise shell–like plastic, with the Gibson rod and bracket assembly utilized until the early 1970s, when a simpler bent bracket arrangement was substituted. The binding on the top of the guitar was the same seven-layer arrangement, with a simpler form of binding utilized on the back.

Finishes: The postwar noncutaway and cutaway L-5 acoustic guitars have been offered in both sunburst and natural finishes from

1947–1948 up to the present time. As noted above, the L-5CT was offered in cherry red as its official finish during the short time it was manufactured. The red finish applied to the L-5CT body was thin enough to allow the grain of the body to show through, making for a very handsome appearance. However, I have seen one L-5CT that was equipped with a natural finish and set up at the factory as an L-5CES with twin humbucking pickups and the accompanying controls. I have also observed an early 1960s sunburst-finish L-5CES

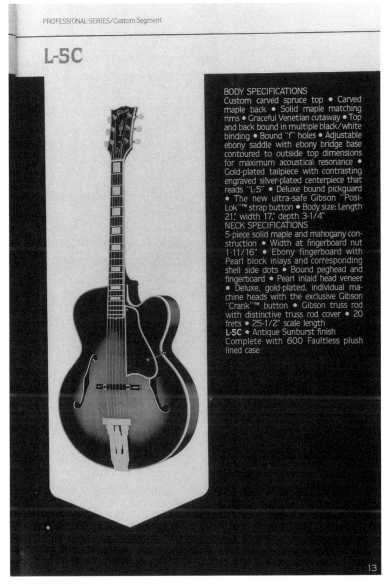

PROFESSIONAL SERIES/Custom Segment

L-5C

BODY SPECIFICATIONS
Custom carved spruce top • Carved maple back • Solid maple matching rims • Graceful Venetian cutaway • Top and back bound in multiple black/white binding • Bound "f" holes • Adjustable ebony saddle with ebony bridge base contoured to outside top dimensions for maximum acoustical resonance • Gold-plated tailpiece with contrasting engraved silver-plated centerpiece that reads "L-5" • Deluxe bound pickguard • The new ultra-safe Gibson "Posi-Lok"™ strap button • Body size: Length 21", width 17", depth 3-1/4"
NECK SPECIFICATIONS
5-piece solid maple and mahogany construction • Width at fingerboard nut 1-11/16" • Ebony fingerboard with Pearl block inlays and corresponding shell side dots • Bound peghead and fingerboard • Pearl inlaid head veneer • Deluxe, gold-plated, individual machine heads with the exclusive Gibson "Crank"™ button • Gibson truss rod with distinctive truss rod cover • 20 frets • 25-1/2" scale length
L-5C • Antique Sunburst finish Complete with 600 Faultless plush lined case

13

• **1980 Gibson catalog, the L-5C**

Florentine cutaway with a thin body and shorter scale arrangement. One could arguably classify these guitars as L-5CES models with a thin body or as electrified L-5CT models. Perhaps the distinction should be based on how they are actually labeled inside the guitar body.

The additional finishes of ebony and wine red were offered as an option on the L-5C beginning in 1976 to utilize some of the plainer woods Gibson had on hand for tops, backs, and rims.

Cases: The postwar L-5 acoustic guitars, from 1948 through approximately 1960, utilized the Lifton hard-shell plywood case covered in a brown fabric and lined with a pink plush interior. Occasionally, a case of a different color combination may be encountered. In the early 1960s, a Lifton hard-shell case with a black vinyl covering and yellow or orange lining was substituted, and this case was continued until the early 1970s when a somewhat cheaper hard-shell case with a red lining was introduced. This case was used until Gibson began importing a new version of the old Lifton brown case from Canada, beginning in 1984 and continuing up to the present day. Case covers were offered as an option with the L-5 until the 1980s.

Postwar Acoustic L-5 Production Summary

From 1948 through 1989, a total of approximately 1,364 postwar acoustic L-5 guitars were shipped from the Gibson factory. This total includes three basic models and five variations of the guitar: the last production of the noncutaway L-5 guitar in both sunburst and natural finish, the L-5C and L-5CN guitars, and the L-5CT or "George Gobel" thin-bodied acoustic cutaway guitar. From 1980 through 1984, Gibson's recordkeeping was much less exact regarding production and shipping data. Therefore, totals for those years are incomplete and are presented as such. It is safe to estimate that the total production of L-5 and L-5CN guitars will be somewhat higher than that listed for 1948–1989, since those guitars were manufactured from 1980 through 1984 in very small quantities. Also, it is known that Gibson made one L-5 and one L-5N in 1978, both noncutaway guitars that were intended for trade-show use only. These guitars were subsequently sold and found their way into the vintage market at a later time.

In summary, the following versions of the postwar acoustic L-5 guitar were produced (Appendix B provides more detailed production information):

Fourth Model L-5, Sunburst, 1948–1958	193
Fourth Model L-5, Natural, 1948–1958	95
Fifth Model L-5C, Sunburst, 1948–1989	681 +
Fifth Model L-5C, Natural, 1948–1989	352 +
Sixth Model L-5CT, Cherry Red, 1959–1961	43
Total 1948–1989	1,364

The L-5CES Guitar

The L-5CES, or electric L-5, was introduced in late 1951 when 31 sunburst and 8 natural-finish guitars were shipped from the Kalamazoo factory. The L-5CES was introduced slightly before the Super 400CES, but both models were shown together at trade shows just prior to the L-5CES introduction. Like the Super 400CES, the L-5CES evolved through a series of changes in pickups, body cutaways, and neck contours as the instrument became more an electric guitar and less an acoustic guitar. The evolutionary changes of the L-5CES will be summarized in some detail below.

● 1960 Gibson catalog,
the L-5CESN

The new electric L-5 guitar was designed to incorporate a combination of features from the L-5C and the ES-5, Gibson's premier electric guitar from 1948 through 1950. From the L-5C, the L-5CES took its neck and body design and also incorporated the carved spruce top and carved, book-matched curly maple back. From the ES-5, the L-5CES utilized the more rigid internal bracing under the top, which was routed to accommodate two P90 single-coil pickups and fitted with two tone and volume controls and a pickup selector switch (slightly different from that of the ES-5, which sported three P90 pickups, three volume controls and one tone control, and no selector switch.) Thus, the L-5CES emerged as an ingenious blending of features from two very fine but different instruments, and quickly assumed a personality of its own.

The evolutionary changes of the L-5CES include the following models: the seventh model L-5CES and L-5CESN, which were made from 1951 through the first half of 1960; the eighth model L-5CES and L-5CESN with the Florentine cutaway, which were produced from mid-1960 through 1969; and finally the ninth model L-5CES and L-5CESN (plus the additional ebony and wine red finishes), which were manufactured from the latter part of 1969 to the present day. These time periods correspond with the most dramatic change in the L-5CES—the alteration of the body cutaway from the rounded Venetian cutaway to the sharp Florentine cutaway, then back again to the Venetian cutaway. An additional tenth model L-5CES, which became the precursor to the Super V-CES guitar, was manufactured from 1973 to 1976. This guitar utilized the L-5CES body and appointments mated to the Super 400CES neck. Determination of the difference between the tenth model L-5CES and a Super V must be made on the basis of the label and the year of manufacture, since the guitars are vitually identical in other respects.

Headstocks: The headstock of the seventh model L-5CES was shaped exactly like that of its acoustic counterpart, the fifth model

TONE AND BEAUTY FOR ARTIST PERFORMANCE

The depth and mellowness of the L-5 CES is winning acclaim for this fine guitar from the most discriminating artists. The tonal quality of the acoustic guitar and the advantages of an electric instrument are combined in this one superlative instrument.

Guitarists are singing the praises of the narrow, thin neck, the fast, easy action and the rich beauty of the carved spruce top, the curly maple back and rim, the pearl inlaid ebony fingerboard and beautiful ivoroid binding. Available in Natural Finish (as shown) or with Gibson Golden Sunburst Finish.

- Pickups are close to the bridge and fingerboard.
- Greater sustaining power and perfect accuracy of each string are achieved through the Gibson Tune-O-Matic Bridge and extra large, individually adjustable Alnico No. 5 magnets.
- Pickups have adjustable pole pieces and separate tone and volume controls which can be pre-set.
- Three-position toggle switch on treble side activates either or both pickups.
- Kluson Sealfast Pegs.
- Professional 20 fret fingerboard and Gibson Adjustable Truss Rod neck construction.
- Body size: 17″ wide and 21″ long.
- All metal parts are gold plated.

L-5 CES Electric Spanish Cutaway Guitar—Golden Sunburst Finish
L-5 CESN Electric Spanish Cutaway Guitar—Natural Finish
Cases for Above Instruments
606 Faultless   600 Faultless

L-5 CESN

● **1956 Gibson catalog, the L-5CESN**

L-5C from the same period of 1951 through the first half of 1960. The headstock utilized the postwar Gibson slanted logo, the trademark L-5 flower-pot inlay, and the bound bell-shaped truss-rod cover. The same binding pattern was used as on the L-5C of the same time period, and Kluson Sealfast machines were utilized as tuners with plastic buttons. These plastic buttons were replaced with gold-plated buttons in approximately 1958. On the eighth model L-5CES with Florentine cutaway, 1960–1969, the headstock appeared more pointed at its upper corners, but otherwise all appointments were the same as those on the seventh model L-5CES. On the ninth model L-5CES, made from the latter half of 1969 through the present, some subtle changes were made in the headstock design. The Gibson script logo was slightly altered in several respects and the dreaded volute was added to the headstock–neck joint in approximately 1974–1975. Eventually the volute was removed around 1982, and the Kluson Sealfast tuners were replaced by Schaller units in the early

1980s. Some of these had mini-crank winder buttons on them as well.

Necks: On the seventh model L-5CES, the neck also followed its fifth model L-5 counterpart exactly. All fretboards were ebony, all binding patterns were the same, and all inlay patterns were the same. The neck changed from a two-piece, book-matched curly maple design with a mahogany center strip to a three-piece, book-matched maple neck with two thin mahogany strips in 1961. Scale length remained unchanged at 25½ inches. For the eighth model L-5CES with Florentine cutaway, the necks became somewhat slimmer and more rounded in cross section in the early to mid-1960s. In the later 1960s, the neck was narrowed at the nut to 1⁹⁄₁₆ inches, which most players did not find appealing. The neck width returned to the standard 1¹¹⁄₁₆ inches in the latter half of 1969. The ninth model L-5CES, again with the rounded Venetian cutaway (1969–present), followed its companion L-5C acoustic from the same time period. The neck width was standardized, and the volute noted earlier was added in 1974–1975 and deleted around 1982.

Bodies: It is in the body of the L-5CES, as on the corresponding Super 400CES guitars, that the most dramatic changes were made during its long and successful production. The seventh model L-5CES (1951 through mid-1960) utilized the rounded Venetian cutaway exclusively. The top was carved, close-grained spruce and the back was a two-piece book-matched curly maple assembly. The rims were also curly maple. The top was braced internally somewhat stiffer than on corresponding L-5C guitars, and the tops were also carved a little thicker. Both of these features were designed to inhibit top vibration caused by the addition of the pickups. Three distinct versions of the seventh model L-5CES were produced, and they were distinguished by the type of pickups that the guitars utilize. From 1951 through approximately 1953, the L-5CES was equipped with twin P90 single-coil pickups with adjustable pole pieces. From 1954 through approximately the first half of 1958, the L-5CES was equipped with twin Alnico pickups with large rectangular nonadjustable pole pieces. Finally, for the latter half of 1958 through the first half of 1960, the L-5CES was equipped with PAF humbucking pickups.

Typically, the 1951–1953 L-5CES guitars were also equipped with a solid-base rosewood bridge with a compensated rosewood saddle. These guitars were also equipped with tone and volume controls that were capped with the typical Gibson "barrel" plastic knobs of the period. All metal parts were gold-plated. Beginning roughly in 1954, the Tune-O-Matic bridge saddle was also available and the Alnico pickup–equipped versions of the L-5CES were subsequently equipped with the two-footed rosewood bridge base and the Tune-O-Matic bridge saddle. This same bridge base and bridge saddle were used with the PAF-equipped Venetian cutaway L-5CES guitars as well. Around 1955–1956, the "top-hat"–shaped control knobs replaced the earlier barrel-shaped knobs on the L-5CES guitars, and this control knob was continued through the first half of 1960. The L-5CES tailpiece was the same as that on the L-5C from the same time period, utilizing the rigid design with the Varitone control at the end.

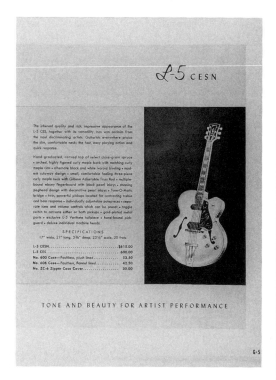

- 1959 Gibson catalog, the L-5CESN
- 1960 Gibson catalog, the L-5CES
- 1966 Gibson catalog, the L-5CES

The eighth model L-5CES (later 1960 through mid-1969) was equipped with the sharp Florentine body cutaway. It was bound at the pointed edge of the cutaway with celluloid material, much like that used to bind the top and back except that it was made of a single piece of plastic. These guitars were braced internally the same as the earlier L-5CES guitars, but they utilized a somewhat longer neck block because the cutaway was so deep and ran parallel to the neck for a longer distance. Otherwise, most appointments for the guitar body remained the same as those in the L-5CES guitars from 1958 though 1960. The top-hat knobs of 1958–1960 were replaced in 1961 with the "dished-top" knobs with the metal insert in the tops. These knobs were utilized for tone and volume controls until about 1967, when the black top-hat knobs were introduced. (The reader is referred to Duchossoir, *Gibson Guitars,* Vol. I, page 167, for a discussion of the sequential variation on these Gibson knobs.) The pickups in these guitars were initially PAF humbuckers, which were replaced by the patent-number humbuckers in approximately 1963. Although all L-5CES guitars from 1960–1969 were listed as Florentine cutaways, a few L-5CES guitars were manufactured in the mid-1960s

116

● **1980 Gibson catalog, the L-5CES**

PROFESSIONAL SERIES/Custom Segment

L-5CES

BODY SPECIFICATIONS
Custom carved spruce top ● Carved maple back ● Solid maple matching rims ● Graceful Venetian cutaway ● Top and back bound in multiple black/white binding ● Bound "f" holes ● Adjustable ebony saddle with Pearl inlaid ebony bridge base contoured to outside top dimensions for maximum acoustical resonance ● Gold-plated tailpiece with contrasting engraved silver-plated centerpiece that reads "L-5" ● Deluxe bound pickguard ● Two Gibson Humbucking pickups with individual volume and tone controls ● 3-position toggle switch for pickup selection (individual or both pickups simultaneously) ● The new ultra-safe Gibson "Posi-Lok"™ strap button ● Body size: Length 21", width 17", depth 3-1/4"
NECK SPECIFICATIONS
5-piece solid maple and mahogany construction ● Width at fingerboard nut 1-11/16" ● Ebony fingerboard with Pearl block inlays and corresponding shell side dots ● Bound peghead and fingerboard ● Pearl inlaid head veneer ● Deluxe gold-plated, individual machine heads with the exclusive Gibson "Crank"™ button ● Gibson truss rod with distinctive truss rod cover ● 20 frets ● 25-1/2" scale length
L-5CES ● Natural or Antique Sunburst finish
Complete with 600 Faultless plush lined case

9

with a Venetian cutaway and a single humbucking pickup in the neck position. These guitars utilized a single tone and volume control, with no pickup selector switch, and were patterned after the two custom L-5CES guitars manufactured especially for the late Wes Montgomery. It is not known how many of these guitars were manufactured, and great care must be taken to determine if a guitar of this configuration is actually an L-5CES or a converted L-5C. This can easily be decided, however, by removing the pickup from the top of the guitar and observing whether the braces have been spaced apart far enough to accommodate the pickup, or whether the braces have been cut to accommodate the pickup. If the braces have been cut, the guitar was originally an L-5C. Also, internal bracing on these one-pickup L-5CES guitars should be the same as that on the two-pickup version; that is, there should be two parallel tone bars, plus cross braces and additional small struts at the very end of the tone bars going towards the end of the body of the guitar.

The ninth model L-5CES was phased in in mid-1969, and its body again featured the rounded Venetian cutaway. This guitar has been continued with some minor changes up to the present day. The shape of this cutaway was changed subtly in the mid-1970s but remained rounded nonetheless. The guitar continued to use Gibson humbucking pickups and the standard tone and volume control setups with pickup selector switch. The pickguards were moved back some from the cutaway and were somewhat shorter than those on the early L-5CES guitars. However, they were the same bound tortoise-like plastic material affixed to the top initially with a forward screw and the Gibson threaded rod and bracket assembly at the rim. However, in the early 1970s the simpler bent bracket was substituted for the threaded rod and bracket assembly, and this bent bracket continues to the present day. The Tune-O-Matic bridge saddle and two-footed bridge base were discontinued in the mid-1970s and were replaced by the Johnny Smith–style ebony bridge base and compensated ebony saddle. The tailpiece remained the same, but it lost the Varitone control in the early 1970s, which resulted in a simplified and more reliable tailpiece in an overall sense.

Finishes: The seventh model L-5CES was offered in the golden sunburst and natural finishes. The eighth model L-5CES was also offered in the golden sunburst and natural finishes. The sunburst on the Florentine cutaway L-5CES guitar changed subtly from a dark brown sunburst to a more reddish sunburst towards the end of the 1960s. The finishes offered on the ninth model L-5CES were initially a cherry sunburst and the natural finish. However, two additional finishes were offered from 1976 through 1979. These were the wine red and ebony finishes, and these finishes were utilized to cover up the rather plain grain patterns of many L-5CES bodies and necks that were available during the mid-1970s. These finishes were discontinued in approximately 1979, but have been available on a special-order basis at various times throughout the history of the L-5CES guitar.

Cases: The seventh model L-5CES guitar utilized the brown Lifton hard-shell case. The eighth model L-5CES guitar utilized the brown Lifton case until 1961–1962 or so, when it was replaced by the black Lifton hard case with the orange lining. This case was continued through the range of the eighth model L-5CES and into the early years of the ninth model L-5CES, when it was finally replaced with a cheaper hard-shell case of indeterminate manufacture, with a red lining and less sturdy construction. Finally, the Gibson company began utilizing a Canadian reproduction of the brown Lifton case in the mid-1980s, which proved to be a sturdier affair than the Gibson case that it replaced.

Postwar L-5CES Production Summary

The production summary of the L-5CES guitars is more complicated than that of the L-5C guitar because of the changes in body styles and pickups. Therefore, the reader is referred to Tables B-20 through B-22 in Appendix B, which summarize all the

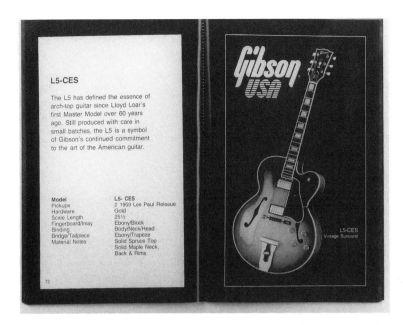

1988 Gibson catalog, the L-5CES

variations and the shipping totals for sunburst and natural finishes and the estimates of production totals of the early pickup variations of the seventh model L-5CES, from 1951 through half of 1960. Please note that these production totals are incomplete, because the data from 1980 through 1989 is spotty at best. Therefore, a slightly higher estimate should be made regarding the total number of L-5CES and L-5CESN guitars manufactured from 1969 to the present.

In summary, the following versions of the L-5CES guitar were produced from 1951–1989.

Seventh Model L-5CES, Sunburst, 1951–1960	248
Seventh Model L-5CES, Natural, 1951–1960	188
Eighth Model L-5CES, Sunburst, 1960–1969	601
Eighth Model L-5CES, Natural, 1960–1969	118
Ninth Model L-5CES, Sunburst, 1969–Present	1,499 +
Ninth Model L-5CES, Natural, 1969–Present	535 +
Tenth Model L-5CES, 1973–1976	17
Total, 1951–1989	3,206

Plate 17
- 1934 L-5, front
- 1934 L-5, back
- 1940 L-5P, front
- 1948 L-5P, front

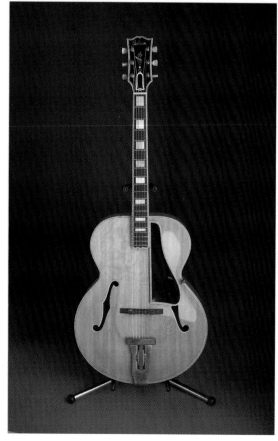

Plate 18

- **1947 L-5, front**
- **1947 L-5, back**
- **1948 L-5N, front**
- **1948 L-5N, back**

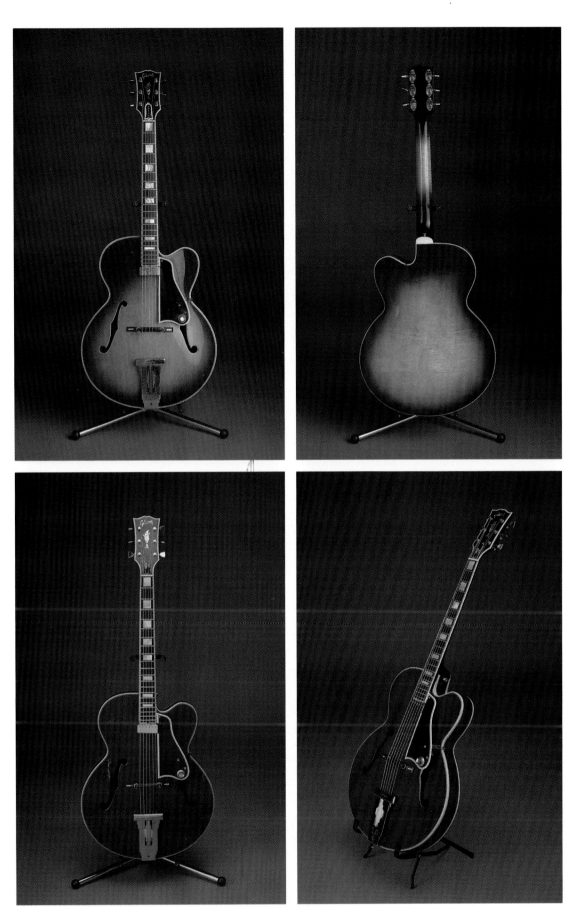

Plate 19

- 1969 L-5C Special, front
- 1969 L-5C Special, back
- 1969 L-5CT, front
- 1969 L-5CT, angled front (side)

Plate 20
- **1970 L-5CES, front**
- **1970 L-5CES, back**
- **1989 L-5CES, front**
- **1989 L-5CES, back**

Plate 21

- **1984 L-5CESN and Super 400 CESN "50th Anniv.," front**
- **1984 L-5CESN "50th Anniv.," front**
- **1960 D'Angelico Excel, front**
- **1960 D'Angelico Excel, back**

Plate 22

- **1946 Epiphone Emperor, front**
- **1953 Epiphone Zephyr Emperor Regent, front**
- **1947 D'Angelico New Yorker, front**
- **1947 Stromberg Master 400, front**

Plate 23

- **1989 Heritage Super Eagle (elec.), front**
- **1990 Heritage Super Eagle (acoustic), front**
- **1989 Benedetto Fratello, front**
- **1990 Benedetto Cremona, front**

Plate 24

- 1990 D'Aquisto New Yorker, front
- 1990 D'Aquisto Classic, front
- 1990 D'Aquisto Avant-Garde, front
- 1990 D'Aquisto Excel, front

Chapter VII

Competitors of the Super 400

Early
Acoustic Competitors

Although the variety of carved-top acoustic guitars in the mid-1930s was increasing, the Super 400 was the first carved-top acoustic guitar to measure a full 18 inches across its lower bout. Apparently this was considered a radical departure from accepted carved-top guitar design of the times, not only because of the increased body size but also the corresponding increase in ornateness of appointments. Other guitar makers, both corporate and individual, soon followed Gibson's lead in this particular area of the carved-top guitar market with designs of their own that resembled the Super 400 in certain respects. The earliest and most notable competitors to emerge shortly after the Super 400's introduction were the Epiphone Emperor, the Gretsch 400 Synchromatic, the D'Angelico New Yorker, and the Stromberg Master 400. Of these four instruments, only the Gretsch 400 Synchromatic failed to make a lasting impression on the market, and details about its production are very sketchy.

However, the Epiphone Emperor, the D'Angelico New Yorker, and the Stromberg Master 400 all proved to be worthy competitors to the Gibson Super 400 in various ways. Since these instruments' resemblance to the Super 400 varies, an example of each instrument will be described in detail below with appropriate references. A 1941 Gibson Super 400N will be used to provide a baseline for comparison purposes. Finally, a table later in the chapter will summarize major features of each instrument for a quick comparison.

The Epiphone Emperor

The Epiphone Emperor was perhaps the first direct corporate challenge to the Gibson Super 400. Epiphone and Gibson were extremely competitive guitar manufacturers, especially during the 1930s. Both companies offered almost identical instruments, and when the Super 400 was introduced Epiphone felt compelled to follow suit with a large-bodied carved-top guitar of their own. According to Herb Sunshine, an employee of the Epiphone Company for approximately six or seven years beginning in the 1930s, the name Emperor was selected because of the current furor over the Duke of Windsor renouncing his throne in England to marry an American commoner (Wheeler, *American Guitars,* pp. 30–31). Sunshine came up with a promotional idea called "The Emperor and the Maid" for Epiphone's new large-bodied guitar. A nude model was photographed posing with the Emperor guitar in front of her, and the photographic display was brought to a New York Hotel for a trade show in 1936. Apparently the display was the hit of the show and Epiphone decided to stick with the name Emperor. The price of the Epiphone Emperor was $400, including case and cover, exactly the same price as the Gibson Super 400 at that time. Most of the features of the instrument were similar to those of the Super 400, but there were some minor variations in body dimensions that gave the instrument a slightly different feel. For example, the upper bouts were about an inch narrower than those of the second model Super 400 (1937–1941), and these small upper bouts tended to emphasize the width of the lower bout like the first model Super 400 of 1934. At the time of the Emperor's introduction, Gibson was finishing out production of the first model Super 400 with the smaller upper bouts during 1936, and at the beginning of 1937 would go to the larger upper-bout width of 13¾ inches. Epiphone chose to retain the slightly smaller upper bouts on the Emperor until the guitar was discontinued.

The instruments shared a great deal in terms of the types of materials they were made with and the manner in which the guitars were manufactured. The Emperor's neck was made of curly maple laminated with mahogany strips. The fretboard was rosewood (instead of the Super 400's ebony), and the headstock overlay was holly. Fretboard inlays were both mother-of-pearl and abalone. Headstock inlays were mother-of-pearl. The top was a two-piece carved plate of fine spruce, while the back was a two-piece carved and book-matched plate of curly maple. The rims were curly maple also. The bridge was rosewood, the pickguard was bound tortoise shell–like plastic, and all the metal parts were gold-plated.

The instrument illustrated in color plate 22 is a 1946 Emperor in natural finish. This instrument is in near-mint condition and is a very good example of an Emperor as originally manufactured. In viewing the Emperor from the front, some differences between its design and the design of the Super 400 are obvious. First, the headstock design is somewhat different and perhaps more elaborate in its own way. Also, the fretboard is made of rosewood instead of ebony. The fretboard inlays appear to be blocks, but they are actually segmented inlays in which the center portion is abalone while the right and left portions are mother-of-pearl. There are other such differences in various parts of the guitar, such as the slightly longer pickguard that is made of a different material, the bridge with its unique reverse contour on the saddle, and the unique Frequensator tailpiece, which was also reportedly designed by Herb Sunshine. Sunshine's notion was that a heavy tailpiece "muted the sound," so he devised two separate partial tailpieces to function as a "frequency compensator." This design, while interesting visually, does have a serious weakness at the angled portion where the base plate joins the body of the guitar. Perhaps because the two tailpiece arms pull separately, rather than a single arm pulling across the top, the metal base plate that attaches to the rim of the guitar often splits or cracks right where the plate touches the top of the guitar. Replacing these cracked tailpiece plates is extremely difficult since such parts are very scarce.

Another interesting aspect of the neck of this particular guitar is that the truss rod adjusts under the end of the fretboard rather than in font of the nut as on the Super 400. This design was utilized because the truss-rod design Gibson used at the time was patented. (The earliest Emperors had no truss rod.) The Emperor subsequently used the Gibson-styled truss-rod adjustment scheme in the 1950s when Gibson's patent expired. When viewed from the rear, the neck is also notable for its construction of seven pieces—three mahogany strips and four pieces of curly maple including two center strips. It was thought that such a lamination procedure would make the neck more resistant to warpage.

The body of the Emperor, as mention above, had a general shape similar to the first model Super 400 with the smaller upper bouts and an 18½ inch lower bout. Such a difference in the upper and lower bout sizes produced a rather narrow waist where the sides curve in towards the center of the body. This made the guitar very comfortable to play in a sitting position, and also presented a rather striking visual appearance. The body was constructed of a two-piece carved spruce top, and a two-piece carved curly maple back. The rims were also made of curly maple. The top and back utilized elaborate eight-ply binding to help attach them to the rim. The f-holes on the instrument were shaped like those of a cello, different in appearance from those of the Super 400. Other body accessories such as the pickguard, the tailpiece, and the bridge were much plainer than those of the Super 400. Nevertheless, each part (except the tailpiece as noted above) seemed very functional and helped the instrument produce a very powerful acoustic tone when played vigorously.

The Emperor was offered in both a sunburst and natural finish, but records are not available regarding production of the noncutaway Emperor or any other such data as presently exists for the Super 400. The Emperor was briefly offered in a cutaway style, which Gibson continued after they purchased the Epiphone Company until all Epiphone production was halted.

The D'Angelico New Yorker

One of the most famous carved-top guitars of all time is the D'Angelico New Yorker, created by luthier John D'Angelico in 1936 and continued by him in various forms until his death in 1964. The New Yorker was introduced after the Super 400 had made its initial appearance, and the first recorded production of a New Yorker was number 1208, delivered October 14, 1936 (Tsumura, *Guitars: The Tsumura Collection,* p. 178). John D'Angelico made a total of 1,164 instruments. According to Tsumura's transcriptions of John D'Angelico's ledgers, a total of 215 New Yorkers were made, including a few instruments labeled Special New Yorker or New Yorker Special. It is not known whether these instruments were 17-inch New Yorkers or whether they had special ornamentation. In any event, the 215 New Yorkers represent 18.5 percent of D'Angelico's total production of 1,164 instruments. Thus, any New Yorker should be considered a rare instrument when comparing it to any other type of arch-top guitar. Of course, there were some D'Angelico guitar models that were produced in fewer numbers than the New Yorker. However, the New Yorker has always been considered D'Angelico's crowning achievement and is the instrument in which he invested the most labor and materials.

The New Yorker illustrated in color plate 22 was completed by D'Angelico in 1947 and shipped to Gravois Music in St. Louis, Missouri. Gravois Music Company was apparently a steady customer of D'Angelico's, since numerous instruments of his were sold to them over the years. This particular New Yorker is comparable to the 1941 Super 400N guitar in almost all body dimensions. There are some obvious ornamentation differences between the two instruments, however. The New Yorker headstock has nine-ply binding around its border, which is much more elaborate than the comparable Super 400 headstock. The inlays on the ebony fretboard alternate in a manner opposite from the Super 400 inlays. The neck is very different from the Super 400's neck in that the D'Angelico neck is made of one piece of curly maple with a nonadjustable truss rod placed in a channel inlet into the face of the neck underneath the fretboard. Like Epiphone, D'Angelico had to devise a different type of truss-rod system because of Gibson's existing patent on the adjustable truss rod. Although D'Angelico's truss rod was nonadjustable, it is well known for remaining in adjustment throughout the lifetime of the instrument.

This New Yorker body consists of a two-piece carved spruce top, a two-piece carved bird's-eye maple back, and bird's-eye maple rims. D'Angelico tended to use curly maple most of the time, but bird's-eye back are bound to the rims with nine-ply plastic binding. The f-holes are of a traditional design with three-ply plastic binding. The are of a traditional design with three-ply ivoroid binding. The pickguard and the tailpiece, like the headstock, appear very dramatic in their ornateness of detail and execution. Such details make the New Yorker more ornate than the Super 400. The pickguard is made of a very thick celluloid material and is intricately bound with nine-ply binding. It is firmly fixed to the top with a single screw through the top corner of the pickguard into the top of the guitar, and it rests on a thick, bent brass bracket with a single screw through the top of the pickguard into the bracket itself. The bracket is screwed onto the rim of the guitar with a single screw. The hinged tailpiece also is a unique design, which was manufactured for D'Angelico outside of his shop. It is made of brass and is gold-plated, with the name D'Angelico nicely engraved, as well as much detailing. It matches the other ornamentation on the guitar very well.

One final difference between this New Yorker and the 1941 Super 400 is the method of bracing the top. This New Yorker, like most if not all of D'Angelico's guitars, is X-braced underneath the top. By 1939 Gibson had changed to the parallel bracing system on the Super 400, never to return to the X-braced method again on this particular instrument.

The Stromberg Master 400

Of all the Super 400's competitors, the Stromberg Master 400 must be considered the boldest in some respects. Conceived and built by Elmer Stromberg, the Master 400 was actually the largest carved-top guitar built at the time of its introduction (late 1930s or early 1940s). The instrument was 19 inches wide across the lower bout, a full inch wider than the Super 400 and the New Yorker. Charles and Elmer Stromberg reportedly built approximately 685 instruments in all, but no exact number of Master 400s is currently available. Charles Stromberg built banjos from 1910, and Elmer built guitars from the mid-1930s, until both men died in 1955. The Stromberg Guitar Shop was then closed and the company was dissolved, and no further instruments were built. Although the early smaller Strombergs were reportedly somewhat mediocre in quality, the Master 400 guitars and others built in the 1940s and 1950s were top-quality instruments that possessed an extremely powerful tone and volume that was suitable for rhythm guitar work in any large orchestra. The Stromberg guitars were endorsed by many famous rhythm guitarists from the 1930s through the 1950s, including Irving Ashby, Mundell Lowe, Barry Galbraith, Freddie Green, Fred Guy, and Bobby Gibbons (Stromberg brochure, late 1930s–early 1940s).

The instrument illustrated in color plate 22 was made in 1947 by Elmer Stromberg for Steve Hester, then a rhythm guitarist for the Larry Clinton Orchestra in New York. Hester relocated to San Antonio, Texas, some years ago, and he sold the instrument to Danny McKnight, another professional guitarist who used the instrument continuously in both solo and ensemble settings until I purchased it in 1989.

The neck on the Master 400 is a five-piece arrangement, with two very narrow center strips of mahogany, one slightly wider center strip of maple, and two large outside strips of maple. Interestingly, the width of the neck at the nut is 1¾ inches, which together with its thickness makes it feel considerably larger than the other instruments used in this comparison. The fretboard is made of ebony, with mother-of-pearl split-block inlays that are divided at an opposite angle from those of the Super 400. Five-ply binding is used on the fretboard, and the fretboard extension ends in a graceful point somewhat similar to that of the Super 400. The headstock is very unusual in that it is wider at the area closer to the nut than at the tip of the headstock, somewhat like the early 16-inch Gibson L-5s. However, this headstock is very wide at the lower end, and consists of a three-layer overlay on the face whose edges are beveled rather than bound. The Stromberg name, the model, and the city of origin are all engraved and painted on the face of the overlay rather than inlaid into it. The tuning keys on this particular instrument are Grover Imperials, although Kluson Sealfast tuners have been used on these guitars as well. The truss-rod adjustment on this instrument is most unusual in that it terminates beneath the nut of the instrument. To adjust the truss rod, one must loosen all of the strings of the instrument and remove the nut, under which a slot can be seen in which narrow-nose pliers can be inserted to twist the truss-rod nut back and forth. This arrangement is yet another attempt at providing an adjustable truss rod without directly infringing on Gibson's patent. On the back of the headstock there is a two-layer overlay, which blends nicely into the neck–headstock joint.

The 19-inch body of the Master 400 consists of a two-piece carved spruce top, a two-piece carved curly maple back, and curly maple rims. Seven-ply binding is used to secure the top of the guitar to the rims, and four-ply binding is used to secure the back of the guitar to the rims. The f-holes are of a traditional design with a slightly larger opening at the lower end, with two-ply ivoroid binding. This instrument is missing its pickguard, so the reader is referred to Tsumura, *Guitars: The Tsumura Collection,* pp. 350–351, to see an original pickguard for the guitar. The pickguard is made of celluloid plastic with multiple layers of ivoroid binding with a simple bent brass bracket that helps secure it to the rim of the guitar. The tailpiece is of a traditional hinged design and is gold-plated, as are the other metal parts on the guitar. One of the most notable features of the Master 400 is its single diagonal top brace, which is not encountered in any other type of carved-top instruments such as these. The bridge has a rosewood base with two triangular inlays and a compensated rosewood saddle made in a very traditional manner.

The Gretsch 400 Synchromatic

Although the Gretsch 400 Synchromatic was not a commercial success, it is an important instrument to consider in relation to the Super 400 for several reasons. Gretsch introduced the 400 in the late 1930s (Wheeler, *American Guitars,* p. 204). It was introduced with a companion line of lesser-priced instruments whose model designations corresponded with their price, much as Gibson had done in the past. Besides the 18-inch Gretsch 400 ($400), the new models included the Gretsch 300 ($300), the Gretsch 200 ($200), and the Gretsch 160 ($160), all of which were 17-inch bodied guitars with varying degrees of ornamentation. But of these four, the Gretsch 400 was clearly designed to be a direct competitor with the Gibson Super 400 in every respect. The 400 Synchromatic had a carved spruce top and a carved and book-matched two-piece maple back, with maple body rims. The five-piece laminated neck was also made of curly maple, with an ebony fretboard. The 400 was 17 ½ to 18 inches wide across the lower bout and was initially introduced as a noncutaway guitar. In 1948 a cutaway option was offered, and the guitar could be ordered in either the sunburst or natural finish in either body style. Scale length of the guitar was 26 inches.

The 400 Synchromatic was unique-looking in several respects. Its sound holes were shaped like elongated teardrops or "cat's eyes," the name often given to them by collectors. The headstock on the original Gretsch 400 was also rather unusual in appearance, approximating somewhat the headstock designs of earlier prewar Epiphone guitars with a somewhat rounded or elongated appearance that was reminiscent of an enlarged banjo headstock. The guitar had a newly designed tailpiece with six brass "barrels" through which each string was individually threaded. The tailpiece and the tuning keys were gold-plated. The guitar also featured a rather unusual asymmetrical rosewood compensated bridge, whose base was thicker and more elongated on the bass side than on the treble side.

Finally, a most unusual design feature was the contour of the back of the neck. Instead of the neck contour being symmetrical with a centered ridge, the ridge down the back of the neck was offset to the left, toward the right-handed player's thumb. Gretsch advertised this design feature as making the guitar more comfortable to play for long periods of time. In 1952–1953, the Gretsch 400 Synchromatic's name was changed to Eldorado, and its headstock design was changed to match that of the other Gretsch models available at that time. The reader is referred to Tsumura, *Guitars: The Tsumura Collection,* pp. 110-111, for pictures of the Gretsch 400 Synchromatic and an unusual natural-finish Gretsch that bears a striking resemblance to the Super 400, but whose model name is not available.

Competitors of the Super 400—Style and Dimensions

Features:	1941 Gibson Super 400N	1946–1947 Epiphone Emperor	1947 D'Angelico New Yorker	1947 Stromberg Master 400
Style	Noncutaway	Noncutaway	Noncutaway	Noncutaway
Finish	Natural	Natural	Natural	Natural
Weight	6½ lb.	6 lb.	8 lb.	7 lb.
Case	Geib hard case, leather covered	Lifton hard case	Geib hard case	Lifton hard case
Body Data:				
Length	21¾"	21½"	21½"	21¾"
Depth at rim	3¼"	3¼"	3¼"	3½"
Width, upper bout	13¾"	12¾"	13⅞"	13"
Width, lower bout	18"	18⅜"	18⅜"	19"
F-hole length	7⅝"	7"	7"	7"
F-hole width	1³⁄₁₆"	1¼"	1½"	1⅞"
Bracing	Parallel	Parallel	X	Single diagonal
Neck Data:				
Width at nut	1¹¹⁄₁₆"	1¹¹⁄₁₆"	1¹¹⁄₁₆"	1¾"
Width at 12th fret	2¹⁄₁₆"	2⅛"	2¹⁄₁₆"	2⅛"
Scale Length:	25½"	25½"	25½"	25"
Price when new	$426	$400	$400	Unknown

Early Electric Competitors: The Epiphone Emperor

Unlike the variety of carved-top acoustic guitars designed to compete with the acoustic Super 400, only one 18-inch guitar was ever designed and produced to compete with the early Super 400CES. The guitar is the Epiphone Emperor, first produced in the early 1950s by the Epiphone Company until production ceased between 1955 and 1957. During that time Gibson bought the Epiphone Company, and later in the 1950s Gibson began to produce the Epiphone Emperor once again. The Gibson version of the Epiphone Emperor initially utilized all of the remaining genuine Epiphone parts, eventually substituting more modern Gibson parts such as tuning gears, pickups, and other types of hardware before the production of the Gibson-made Emperor was discontinued in the late 1960s.

The original electric Epiphone was called the Zephyr Emperor, or Zephyr Emperor Regent, interchangeably. Epiphone utilized the term *Zephyr* to designate an electric guitar, while the word *Regent* referred to a cutaway body style. The original Epiphone Zephyr Emperor Regents were different from their acoustic counterparts in two major respects. First, all of the Zephyr Emperors were cutaway guitars. Second, the Zephyr Emperors utilized a laminated spruce top and a laminated one-piece maple back instead of the carved spruce top and carved, book-matched maple back panel on the acoustic Emperor guitars. Apparently this laminated top and back design was utilized to increase the strength of the instrument and to cut down on vibration resulting in unwanted feedback. The original electric Emperors utilized three single-coil pickups, a single tone and volume control, and a unique six-way pickup selector switch called the Varitone. This selector switch allowed for six different combinations of tones and was quite versatile, though its appearance was somewhat ungainly on the top of the guitar. These instruments used the standard Epiphone solid-base rosewood bridge and saddle, and all other appointments were exactly like those on the acoustic Epiphone Emperor of the same time period.

When Gibson began to remanufacture the Epiphone Zephyr Emperor Regent, the guitar was initially almost exactly like the original Epiphone Zephyr Emperor in every respect. However, once the original pickup stock was used up, Gibson began to feature their mini-humbuckers on the Emperor and on their other electric guitars as well. These pickups were of a superior design to the original Epiphone single-coil pickups, and were used on Gibson-made Epiphones from the early 1960s until the Epiphone line was discontinued in the late 1960s. Gibson also dispensed with the Varitone selector switch, opting for a simpler toggle switch arrangement and additional tone and volume controls.

The original Epiphones were offered in either sunburst or natural finish. The Gibson-made Epiphone Emperors were originally offered in sunburst and natural finish, but were also occasionally seen in either a cherry or ebony finish as well. In addition, Gibson produced most of the Zephyr Emperor Regents as a thinline version that had a body depth of about 2 inches instead of the normal 3⅛-inch body depth of both the original and full-size Epiphone Emperors. The thinline Epiphone Emperor was not a big seller, and very few of these instruments are encountered today. The instrument illustrated in color plate 22 is an original 1953 Epiphone Zephyr Emperor which belonged to the late J. B. Brinkley of Fort Worth, Texas. Brinkley was a guitarist for the Light Crust Doughboys, and also was a staff guitarist for WBAP radio in the Dallas–Fort Worth area. Brinkley was reportedly given this guitar by the Epiphone Company, and he can be seen playing the guitar in various Epiphone catalog illustrations from the late 1950s or early 1960s. The instrument originally was equipped with a standard Epiphone Frequensator tailpiece, but Brinkley replaced this with a Bigsby tailpiece at a later date. The guitar exhibits considerable signs of playing wear, yet has an undeniable appeal because of its rich golden sunburst finish and its musical history. The instrument is supplied with a brown Lifton hard-shell case, embossed with the large letter *E* on the underside of the case lid.

It originally came with a zipper case cover, which deteriorated, so Brinkley utilized a hybrid case cover for the rest of the time that he owned the guitar. The appointments on the guitar are like those of the acoustic Emperor in all other respects, with a Brazilian rosewood fretboard with split-block pearl and abalone inlays, curly maple seven-piece neck, and curly maple rims with multiple top and back binding. The Epiphone "tree of life" inlay on the headstock was done in mother-of-pearl, and all metal parts were gold-plated.

It is not known how many original or Gibson-produced electric Emperors were manufactured. It is known that the Zephyr Emperor Regent was produced between 1952 and 1953 or possibly slightly later, while the Gibson-made Zephyr Emperor Regent was produced perhaps as early as 1957 and throughout its various minor trim evolutions until the late 1960s.

Modern Acoustic and Electric Competitors

When the early competitors of the Super 400 first appeared—the Gretsch 400, the D'Angelico New Yorker, the Epiphone Emperor, the Stromberg Master 400—most of these instruments were made to order for guitar players. Of the 1,164 guitars that John D'Angelico made during his lifetime, about 215 were New Yorkers. The vast majority of these instruments were made to order for guitar players, although occasionally certain East Coast and Midwestern dealers ordered a New Yorker for stock. John D'Angelico died in 1964, and no more D'Angelico guitars were made. Charles and Elmer Stromberg made a total of about 685 guitars, and when father and son both died in 1955 no more of their instruments were made. Most of their instruments were made to order for guitar players, and it is not known if some were made to order for dealer stock. The Epiphone Emperors were discontinued by Gibson during the late 1960s. Although an exact count is not available, the original Epiphone Company and Gibson both made far fewer Emperors than Gibson made Super 400s. Finally, as mentioned earlier, the Gretsch 400 (later renamed Eldorado) was never a popular instrument in terms of sales, and its impact on the guitar-playing market was minimal.

Many of these early competitors of the Super 400 are still being used to make music today, but more of them are being sought by collectors than musicians, so they "compete" with the Super 400 in the vintage/collectible guitar market instead. Of course, a vintage guitar market did not exist when these guitars were being introduced, but a fledgling vintage market began to take shape in the mid-1960s. The emergence of the carved-top guitar as a collectible instrument began to occur by the mid-1970s. So in a sense, the market for the Super 400 and its early competitors has expanded somewhat from a market of strictly guitar players to one composed of players, player/collectors, collector/players, and strictly collectors. Despite the discontinuation of the above early competitors with the Super 400, there are newer competitors which, though traditional in appearance, are actually more modern in design than any of the models noted above.

Modern Luthier-Made Competitors

The D'Aquisto New Yorker: James D'Aquisto began his career in luthiery as an apprentice to John D'Angelico for approximately 15 years prior to D'Angelico's death in 1964. In 1965, D'Aquisto continued the craft that D'Angelico had taught him when he began making carved-top guitars under his own name. In that year, D'Aquisto made his first D'Aquisto New Yorker, and he has continued to make the New Yorker in relatively small numbers up to the present day. Between 1965 and 1987, D'Aquisto made approximately 61 New Yorkers, an average of almost three a year. These guitars have been made only on a to-order basis for guitar players and collectors. The D'Aquisto New Yorker has been made as a cutaway acoustic guitar, though many have been fitted with a floating pickup of some kind either by D'Aquisto or as an add-on device. The D'Aquisto New Yorker has gradually evolved into a very distinct instrument over the years, with numerous changes that have resulted in a highly refined and very versatile guitar. D'Aquisto enlarged and reshaped the f-holes after he had made his first few New Yorkers in the more traditional D'Angelico design. D'Aquisto also abandoned the D'Angelico-style hinged brass tailpiece when he perfected an adjustable ebony tailpiece. He also widened the base of the ebony bridge.

Over the years, D'Aquisto has continued to refine the New Yorker, making it lighter in weight as he carves the tops and backs somewhat thinner to achieve a fuller, more modern sound. The pickguards have also become narrower, and have been made of ebony for a number of years. These instruments, as seen in color plate 24, represent the pinnacle of carved-top guitar design as we know it today, and they command top prices on the vintage/collectible market when they make a rare appearance there. The instruments are X-braced, with a 25½-inch scale length, and are made of only the finest materials including Austrian spruce tops, a one-piece carved curly maple neck, and book-matched carved curly maple back and sides. Fretboards are made of ebony, with split-block pearl inlays similar to those of the Super 400. The headstocks are D'Aquisto's unique design, serving as a crown on a truly royal instrument of considerable versatility.

The D'Aquisto Avant-Garde: Even more versatile than the New Yorker is D'Aquisto's new guitar, the Avant-Garde. This guitar is designed to be an all-around acoustic instrument, with great tone, sustaining quality, depth, and volume. It represents both the culmination of D'Aquisto's 39 years of experience at building fine guitars and his fervent attempt to move away from narrow traditional thinking of what a carved-top guitar should look like and sound like. This instrument's design and construction—its twin oval sound holes, wood binding, and slotted headstock—clearly point the way to a bright future for the carved-top acoustic guitar.

D'Aquisto puts his all into these guitars, and the 18-inch Avant-Garde (see color plate 24) may be the ultimate Super 400 competitor. His vision of what a fine guitar should sound like and look like is far-reaching, and unsettling to those who restrict the carved-top guitar to a jazz-guitar role or a rhythm-guitar role. Instead, he has made the Avant-Garde with perfect intonation, even acoustic response across the fretboard, and incredible volume and tone color. What comes out of it—musically speaking—is then up to the individual guitarist. With the Avant-Garde and his more recent Solo and Centura models, D'Aquisto is pointing to the future of acoustic music just as Gibson did with the Super 400 in 1934.

The Benedetto Supreme: Robert Benedetto began making carved-top guitars in 1968 and had offered the 18-inch Supreme model as a worthy competitor to the Super 400. The Supreme was a cutaway acoustic guitar since its beginning and has only been made to order. Most of these instruments were supplied with a DeArmond #1100 floating pickup. Benedetto continued to evolve his design ideas, and by 1980 Benedetto had five models: the 18-inch Supreme, 17-inch Cremona, 17-inch 7-String, 16-inch Limelite and the new Fratello model. In 1983, he discontinued the 18-inch Supreme and in 1981 discontinued the 16-inch Limelite (a different model using the same Limelite name was introduced in 1990). All models were now available in 18-inch, 17-inch and 16-inch body sizes (the body size no longer designated the model). In 1989 the popular Manhattan model was introduced, followed by the LaVanezia and Americana in 1993. Benedetto continues to advance archtop evolution with his distinct solid ebony tailpiece uniquely fastened to the instrument with cello tailgut, and his original honey blonde finish. He uses both American and European woods, parallel or X-braced tops, 25-inch fingerboard scale length, and solid ebony fingerboard, fingerrest and bridge. Benedetto guitars are currently popular with both guitar players and collectors alike and have achieved real acceptance as instruments of true value. A standard Cremona (s/n 19790) is illustrated in color plate 23. The 17-inch Fratello (s/n 18589) also found in color plate 23 was made for the author in 1989.

Modern Commercially Made Competitors

The Heritage Super Eagle: The only current manufacturer of an 18-inch guitar that competes with the Gibson Super 400 is Heritage Guitar, Inc., of Kalamazoo, Michigan. To understand the nature of the Heritage Super Eagle, a brief discussion of the company's development might be helpful. When Gibson decided to close its Kalamazoo factory in 1984, several of the supervisory and assembly-line staff were offered positions with Gibson in Nashville. For various reasons, most of the Kalamazoo employees declined Gibson's offer and subsequently found themselves out of work once the Gibson factory was closed in the fall of 1984. Gibson's decision to close the Kalamazoo factory was a protracted and painful one for many people involved, but several of the Kalamazoo staff were determined to carry on the tradition of making fine guitars that was part of their association with Gibson. In early 1985, Heritage Guitar, Inc., was formed by five former Gibson staffers of the Kalamazoo plant—James Deurloo, Mark Lamb, J. P. Moats, Michael Korpak, and William Paige. These gentlemen seized an opportunity to use an 11,000-square-foot section of the old Gibson Kalamazoo factory in order to continue making the kind of guitars they had made with great pride during their employment with Gibson. With seven other Heritage employees who were also Gibson alumni, the cumulative experience of Heritage was described as exceeding 250 years.

Heritage did not immediately introduce the Super Eagle but concentrated their initial efforts on launching a variety of electric guitars of various solid-body configurations, as well as thinline ES-335–style guitars and basses. However, they did offer a single carved-top instrument called the Golden Eagle, a 17-inch-wide guitar of superlative craftsmanship that incorporated design elements of the L-5C and the Johnny Smith guitars by Gibson. The Golden Eagle was apparently well received, and it was made as a strictly acoustic instrument with a floating pickup available through the factory. The success of this instrument led to the creation of several similar 17-inch carved-top and laminated-body guitars of various configurations as well.

The Heritage Super Eagle made its official debut in 1988 as an electric guitar only. This instrument resembles the Super 400CES in many ways, although its headstock design is noticeably different. The Super Eagle is made with a parallel-braced, carved spruce top, carved and book-matched curly maple back, curly maple rims, and a five-piece curly maple neck with an ebony fretboard. The guitar utilizes twin Schaller humbucking pickups, gold-plated metal parts, and an ebony adjustable bridge with pearl inlays somewhat similar to the Johnny Smith–style bridge offered by Gibson. The bound pickguard is made of curly maple and uses the bent bracket common to the current Gibson Super 400 guitars. These instruments are of very high quality, and their list price in 1989 was $3,150 in sunburst finish and $3,350 in a natural finish.

In late 1988 Peter Wagener of LaVonne Wagener Music in Savage, Minnesota, heard that Heritage *might* be offering an acoustic version of the Super Eagle guitar for sale. He ordered, sight unseen, an acoustic cutaway Super Eagle in natural finish with select woods for me. I communicated directly with James Deurloo and Bill Paige of Heritage on certain aspects of the guitar's design. Deurloo stated that they were going to make the acoustic Super Eagle in very limited quantities, and that my particular guitar would have an X-braced top of select spruce, with a select, book-matched curly maple back and curly maple rims. The top and back would be tap-tuned to achieve further acoustic resonance and balance. When this instrument was completed, it was delivered to me with a Gibson BJB floating pickup with tone and volume control fixed to the pickguard as noted in the accompanying illustration (see color plate 23). This particular instrument has an exceptional acoustic tone and is a very light-weight guitar for an instrument of its size.

Taken together, the Heritage Super Eagle electric and acoustic guitars are the only direct competitors with the Super 400CES and the Super 400C currently being manufactured by any guitar-making company. These instruments have been readily accepted by guitar players and to a certain extent by guitar collectors as well. Interestingly, the Heritage Company can operate as essentially a custom shop for the production of custom-order instruments. They are able to do this because of their collective guitar-making experience and because the core personnel in the Heritage Company were in fact the Custom Shop for Gibson until the Kalamazoo plant closed in 1984. The quality of these instruments is the equal of Gibson's current efforts in the Super 400, and the competition between the two companies for purchasers of their 18-inch carved-top guitars should be rather spirited in the years to come.

Chapter VIII

Musical Instrument Collecting and the Gibson Super 400

● **Greater Southwest
Guitar Show, Dallas,
1985. Photo © 1985
M. Pollock.**

In evaluating the relative worth of a Gibson Super 400 guitar or any other fine vintage instrument, many factors must be taken into consideration. The attachment of monetary value to a specific musical instrument is an extremely complex process, and the purpose of this chapter is to explain some of the principles involved in arriving at the "worth" of a particular instrument. In reviewing the popular literature related to musical instrument collecting (and especially guitar collecting), I encountered a surprising diversity of viewpoints. I propose an integration of these different viewpoints to facilitate understanding the process of determining the worth of various vintage instruments. The review of many articles and opinions produced four primary areas of information regarding the principles for valuation of vintage instruments. These source areas include articles on the principles of vintage instrument collecting, the vintage instrument market, guitar shows as a particular segment of the vintage instrument market, and specific comments about the Super 400 guitar as an example of collectible vintage instruments.

Vintage Instrument Collecting Principles

To my knowledge, the first serious review of vintage instrument collecting principles appeared in Willcut and Ball's book titled *The Musical Instrument Collector* (New York: The Bold Strummer Ltd., 1978). The authors wrote a good general text on collecting principles and the unique state of the vintage instrument market in 1978. The authors also summarized information from interviews with well-known persons involved in musical instrument collecting at that time. Many of the authors' conclusions focused on the nature of the collectors of musical instruments. Willcut and Ball noted that collectors take diverse approaches in their collecting efforts, ranging from the eclectic to the specifically focused. Collectors also share certain common values about the musical instruments they are interested in. Among these values are the notion that instruments should be played, not hoarded. However, preservation of valuable instruments should and does occur naturally as a result of collecting. Collectors feel that older instruments have workmanship and acoustical properties superior to their newer counterparts, whether this is in fact the case or not. Most collectors agree that the originality of vintage instruments should be preserved and rate this factor as a very high priority in their pursuit of instruments of their own interest.

However, Willcut and Ball noted that collectors often don't build their collections systematically, but change their holdings on a rather pragmatic basis. The changing of a collector's holdings may reflect several factors, such as the particular desirability of certain instruments

139

at particular points in time, the collector's increasing sophistication and knowledge base about certain instruments, and a certain maturational process occurring within collectors that may lead them from a rather eclectic or broad-based collection to something much more refined and focused. Willcut and Ball recommended that collectors should receive some positive recognition for their role in preserving vintage instruments. The authors also noted that part of the reward for vintage instrument collecting is in the hunt and "making good deals" along the way. Finally, the authors recommended that instruments should be made available to others if others are willing to pay the price to take care of the instruments they are purchasing.

In my opinion, the next significant body of information about collecting musical instruments was a group of articles published in the February 1985 issue of *Frets* magazine, some of which accurately reflected the state of the vintage instrument market in 1985. The articles touch on a wide variety of subjects ranging from predictions by well-known dealers regarding the investment or appreciation potential for certain musical instruments to the process of learning about collecting guitars. Used postwar Martin guitars, selected Gibson acoustic guitars—prewar J-200s, J-185s, J-45s, and J-50s from the 1950s and 1960s—and certain Gibson arch-top guitars were all described as instruments with good future appreciation potential. However, in one specific article investigating the relative investment merits of vintage guitars (Gartner, p. 17), it was noted that as an investment, vintage instruments lack liquidity, resulting in a time-consuming and expensive selling process; vintage guitars have little intrinsic value compared to other collectible items such as gold coins; and the collector of vintage instruments must at least love them, play them, and buy them below market value to realize any potential gain. Prewar and postwar Martin guitars were compared with five other investment vehicles (stocks, diamonds, gold, silver, and rare coins) plus the Consumer Price Index (CPI), and a hypothetical investment of $500 in each category produced some rather interesting results for the time period 1973–1983. Among the conclusions drawn, it was noted that the prewar Martin guitars yielded approximately $1500, beating postwar Martin guitars, stocks, the CPI, and diamonds as an investment during that time period. However, rare coins were the best overall investment, with an almost 5000% increase over the ten-year period reviewed.

In a similar article (Hood, p. 18), several dealers were asked about their predictions, and the conclusion seemed to be that although no vintage instruments were "home runs," solid performances by D-size Martin guitars of the 1950s and 1960s and the prewar Gibson rosewood J-200s were registered.

In an important contrasting article (Hutto, pp. 28–30, 60), the process of dealing in Stradivarius violins was compared with the process of dealing in vintage fretted instruments. Hutto noted that by comparison to guitars, very early violins are still played and highly prized for their playability. There is, of course, a world demand for classical music and a ready market associated with these instruments, while the market for antique guitars—those made before the turn of the century—is relatively small and the vintage guitar market in general is still evolving.

The acquisition of knowledge about vintage instruments is one of the most important factors an aspiring or well-established collector can develop as he or she matures and participates more fully in the vintage instrument market. Fake and forged vintage instruments are becoming increasingly commonplace, although such unfortunate events happen more often with violins than with guitars. For violins, various faking techniques include finish faking, fake labels, and label substitution. However, similar forgeries can be done with vintage fretted instruments if there are luthiers willing to do such work and new or used parts are readily available (Humphrey, pp. 32–40).

As an example of some particular musical instrument collections, George Gruhn (*Guitar Player,* March 1985, pp. 16–23) and Rick Turner (*Frets,* June 1987, pp. 34–37) offer two views of different types of vintage instrument collections that share some similar values. Gruhn notes that collectability of the 1958–1960 Les Paul sunburst guitar seems to be based on originality, condition, sound, and playability, with the amount of curl featured in the curly maple top of the guitar being the most important factor. Gruhn added that the numbers of such Les Paul guitars for sale in very fine original condition "aren't nearly so plentiful as potential buyers." Also, he noted that some Les Paul sunburst guitars have been forged from 1958 Les Paul gold-top guitars, whose finish was stripped to reveal a rather stunning curly maple cap that was then "re-sunbursted." In addition, Gibson has also offered recent reissue versions of these vintage guitars that are very nice instruments, and these can occasionally be faked to look like old instruments as well. Again, Gruhn echoes earlier sentiments in demanding that the potential vintage instrument collector develop his or her knowledge to a high level to avoid being seduced by a beautiful forgery.

In reviewing the Silber collection, Turner noted that the collecting of vintage fretted instruments is still in its infancy and that the prices for collectible instruments seemed low compared to other types of American collectible items. Turner singled out utility as a factor that tends to hold down the price of instruments, but then seemingly reversed himself by saying the popularity of a certain style of music may increase the value of instruments associated with that type of music, implying that utility plus popularity may increase the value of the instrument. Turner did mention a rather interesting factor regarding rarity of vintage instruments: The absolute rarity of a single instrument, such as a one-of-a-kind piece, seems less important than in other collectible areas. (I can substantiate that statement, because well-known makers and models of instruments are usually sought, and often the instruments that tend to bring the highest prices are those that are the most perfect examples of standard catalog offerings.) Finally, Turner noted that historic or sociological associations also are important regarding certain types of musical instruments, as well as their craftsmanship.

Regarding the formation of a musical instrument collection, Richard Smith noted (*Guitar Player,* July 1989, pp. 26–29) that John

Sprung's collection of early Fender lap steel guitars and amplifiers has a definite focus (the earliest Fender electric guitars in general plus the earliest instruments from any given company) and that such a collection is the product of patience, education, attendance at vintage guitar shows, and not paying exorbitant prices unless absolutely necessary.

To determine the factors behind vintage instrument collecting, Dr. Bill Blackburn surveyed several vintage instrument collectors and dealers asking *why* people collect guitars. His survey suggested five main reasons why people collect guitars: that the instrument collected is one's "dream guitar"; that there is a certain addictive/compulsive nature to the collecting process for certain people; that there are certain recreational/social components to the collecting process that many collectors value; that many instruments have a nostalgic appeal to collectors; and finally, that many collectors derive a sense of personal accomplishment from an outstanding collection of certain types of instruments (Blackburn, *Guitar World,* July 1987, pp. 62–64, 72). Thus, Blackburn focuses on the factors within the collector that often drive him or her to enter and participate in the vintage instrument market as opposed to the more traditional motives noted above, which focus on the instruments themselves.

A debate that occurs with increasing frequency seems to reflect the rather polarized positions of those favoring the qualities of old instruments versus new ones. Wade Miller and George Gruhn (*Frets,* December 1988, pp. 12 , 17, 32) staked out opposing positions in this argument with clarity. Miller favored new instruments over old, citing improvements in instrument materials, manufacturing processes, cost control, playability, and tuning accuracy as factors in favor of newer instruments. Gruhn favored older instruments over new (with some exceptions), stating that older materials and manufacturing were often superior to the newer materials and manufacturing processes. In particular, Gruhn noted that some materials present in vintage instruments, such as the fine woods utilized in acoustic guitars, are often no longer available. He also noted that new wood is often quickly cut and then kiln-dried, rather than air-dried for five or ten years, producing wood for guitar bodies and necks that is not as stable as the older wood. In a followup article (*Frets,* February 1989, p. 11), Gruhn reiterated his beliefs that factory-made guitars by the better makers during the pre–World War II era were better made when new and are better now than factory-made guitars currently being produced. He also stated that new instuments will not take away from the historical significance of vintage ones and will not diminish the artistic appeal, rarity, and investment potential of collectible vintage models.

Not all collectors, vintage instrument dealers, and writers agree with the above summarized vintage instrument collecting principles. In fact, some individual dealers and writers are rather negative and critical of vintage instrument prices and the purchasers of such instruments. For example, some dealers state that they will not knowingly sell instruments to those who would export them overseas, because to export fine American vintage instruments seems somehow un-American to them. Also, some dealers and writers seem outraged that instrument buyers, both foreign and domestic, would pay such high prices for certain instruments, as though they are depriving musical instrument players of their chance to own some of these instruments.

The Vintage Instrument Market

More recently, articles have appeared that describe the current vintage instrument market. George Gruhn has written a series of articles that provide a unique perspective on the development of this market. He discusses certain factors that influence or determine the desirability of instruments, the price of such instruments, and so forth. Although Gruhn is not the only authority who has written or spoken about the vintage instrument market, his ongoing analysis of this market has resulted in an increasingly lucid and perceptive evaluation of the many factors that influence the marketing of vintage instruments, and vintage guitars in particular. In 1986 (*Guitar Player,* July 1986, pp. 102–130), Gruhn identified vintage instrument customers as persons who are more mature than new instrument customers, and also as "baby boomers" (from 30 to 40 years of age) who have more security, sophistication, and purchasing power than their younger counterparts, who tend to purchase new instruments. Gruhn noted that these more mature customers tended to lend more stability to the vintage instrument market. Other factors he identified as influencing the vintage instrument market included the expansion of the market from a domestic to a worldwide market with emphasis on the increasing sophistication of overseas buyers as an emerging factor in the market. He also noted that the price of a vintage instrument at any point in time seemed to be a function of supply, demand, and prior precedent or price. He noted in 1986 that there was an increasing interest both in quality and in the investment potential of certain vintage instruments that had not been perceived as valuable in prior years. An increase in demand for fine vintage instruments, coupled with a decline in the dollar's value, also led to increased sales and higher prices in Gruhn's opinion. Of course, part of the increase in sales has been due to purchases by overseas buyers who have taken advantage of the dollar's decline in value. When the dollar becomes stronger, sales to overseas buyers often diminish. Gruhn was rather optimistic about the vintage instrument market in 1986, and stated that "high-quality arch-top acoustic jazz guitars are selling better than any time in the past 20 years." This was one of the first instances in which high-quality arch-top guitars were singled out as a category of instruments whose sales had begun to increase after many years of a rather undervalued pricing structure.

In his next article (*Frets,* May 1988, pp. 9, 55–56), Gruhn noted that the vintage instrument market in 1988 was "unstable," with rapidly rising prices occurring for many instruments. He described the forces driving the market at that time as fads, musical imprinting (the identification of certain instruments with certain musical styles or periods), an increasingly sophisticated clientele, the rather fixed or slightly falling supply of vintage instruments, and the interaction between the increasing demand for certain instruments and the number of such instruments that may subsequently appear on the market. He also cited world economic forces, such as the rise and fall of the dollar, as affecting the market especially in a global sense, and he noted that rising interest rates tended to affect the market as well. However, when interest rates fall, collectibles seemingly become a liability. Interestingly, he predicted that the prices on instruments that were "hot" at the moment—Fender Stratocaster guitars—would go down because the number of such collectible instruments on the market had increased dramatically since prices had begun to escalate. Such a market response is apparently highly predictable if enough examples of a particular collectible instrument exist to depress prices when they enter the market. (If the absolute number of examples of a certain vintage instrument is very small, however, the absolute number of similar instruments appearing on the market will also be rather small even as prices increase, thus perhaps insulating that particular instrument from a too-rapid run-up in prices, which is often followed by a peak and then a drop-off in demand and moderate decline in price.)

Gruhn goes on to state that precedent is critically important in establishing current vintage instrument values, with *precedent* defined as prices paid for similar instruments in the recent past. Gruhn described the 1988 vintage market as unstable, because prices for some instruments were increasing so rapidly that precedent was at times being ignored as prices tended to surpass one another in an upward direction. Additional factors influencing the 1988 vintage instrument market were the small overall market size; the "rather minimal" role of dealers in the market; and the emerging differences between different examples of the same instrument in differing grades of condition. Differentiation between grades of condition for the same musical instrument category is an important factor in determining the true worth of an individual instrument, especially if the overall number of such instruments potentially available is relatively small. Finally, Gruhn described the future market for vintage instrument collectors as one dominated by baby boomers, overseas buyers, and a market whose continuing upward spiral seems somewhat dependent on the fall of the dollar.

Gruhn also took on the challenge of attempting to describe vintage instruments as potential investment vehicles, stating that in the broadest sense vintage guitars can be viewed as either instruments for collecting purposes or for utility purposes. For utility purposes, instrument sound and playability were the most important factors considered by purchasers. For collecting purposes, many more factors seemed to be important, such as the maker, age, and model of the instrument, and its historic significance, condition, degree of originality, rarity, and aesthetic appeal. Gruhn cautioned that prospective buyers should not consider the current cash value of an instrument as an investment factor, noting that the best investments tended to be instruments in excellent, fully original condition.

In an interesting comparison of original prices of past with current instruments, Gruhn (*Frets,* November 1988, pp. 57, 70) noted that many different variables exist that make older and newer versions of the same instrument either a greater or lesser value to the current purchaser, depending on one's perspective. For example, in comparing the list price of the 1940 L-5 Premiere with the 1988 L-5C, he noted that the guitar sold for $290 in 1940 and $3,487 in 1988. This would seem to imply that the 1940 L-5 is a better value. However, when the list price is refigured in 1986 dollars, the 1940 price jumps to $2,260 while the 1988 price remains $3,487. In looking at the cost of the instrument in terms of the number of hours one would have to work to pay for such an instrument, he noted that an average wage earner would have to work 460 hours to pay for a 1940 L-5 Premiere, while the same wage earner would have to work only 280 hours at 1988 wage levels to pay for a comparable L-5C.

In 1989, Gruhn wrote a pair of articles about the vintage instrument market in which he explored factors that dealers consider in pricing guitars and factors that seem to influence the demand on certain types of vintage instruments. In the first article (*Guitar Player,* June 1989, pp. 22, 161) Gruhn elaborated on the factors dealers consider in pricing a vintage instrument. These factors include the following:

- *Intrinsic Value*—The intrinsic value is the cost of producing an exact replica of a vintage instrument in all respects.
- *Condition*—The overall structural integrity, originality of parts, and the presence or absence of repairs and/or modification greatly affect the price.
- *Original Price*—Though not often related to current prices of vintage instruments, the original price can help determine if today's instruments reflect true intrinsic value or a premium based on association with the past.
- *Precedent*—The current market price of a particular vintage instrument is usually based on the price that the last one like it sold for.
- *Rarity*—This factor is not quite as important in vintage instruments as is the "pristine" original condition of a standard instrument; Gruhn predicted that the rare or one-of-a-kind guitar may become more valued as the absolute number of available vintage instruments declines, especially for certain instruments with low past production and little or no current production.
- *Supply*—This factor is important in pricing because the absolute number of vintage instruments is fixed, with the number available rising and falling over time; if prices continually increase and supply does not meet demand, prices will increase even further.

Extreme rarity thus becomes a problem, as are such other factors as the rise or decline in the strength of the dollar and changing trends in the vintage instrument marketplace.

In his second article (*Guitar Player,* July 1989, pp. 8, 177) Gruhn noted that demand was the ultimate market factor in determining the price of any vintage instrument. Factors influencing demand included the following:

- *Domestic Collectors*—These people protect the instruments, generate research and information on instruments, and actually put more instruments into circulation because of their relentless search for the perfect example of a particular instrument. In view of the artistry involved in making a fine guitar, collectors also pay a relatively low price.
- *Overseas Collectors*—Gruhn again noted that the market is now an international one, and overseas collectors are just as deserving of fine instruments as domestic collectors. I agree wholeheartedly; negative statements made about overseas collectors reflect the biases of the persons making them.
- *Fads*—Gruhn noted that fads based on who is playing (or has played) what instrument affect the demand of certain vintage instruments to some extent. (I'd also add that demand is somewhat influenced by the related fad of what dealers are buying and selling at the present time.) Gruhn cites "Stratmania"—the almost maniacal increase in the buying and selling of pre-CBS Fender Stratocasters between 1986 and 1988—as a particular example of a fad that peaked and actually harmed many dealers' businesses to some extent.
- *Dealers*—Gruhn described dealers as the least influential of the factors affecting demand, but "the most maligned." I differ somewhat on this statement, concluding separately that dealers do influence demand to some extent by the price precedents they set, the manner in which they market certain types of instruments, and the manner in which they market themselves as purveyors of certain instruments as well.
- *The Buyer*—Gruhn believes this factor is the ultimate influence on the market and the ultimate influence on the demand for certain types of instruments. (I couldn't agree more.)

In a somewhat different vein, Dan Forte noted more recently (*Guitar Player's Guide*, 1989–90, pp. 137, 141) that the decline in Stratocaster prices seemed to be the result of too many Stratocasters suddenly appearing for sale following the rapid increase in their prices. He also described the recent increase in the price of Les Paul guitars as due to the popularity of such rock and roll groups as Guns 'n' Roses. (However, Guns 'n' Roses did not play vintage Les Paul guitars, and it is my opinion that other factors are at work in the recent increase in vintage Les Paul prices, such as dissatisfaction with Stratocaster pricing, renewed interest in the historical and aesthetic appeal of these instruments, and precedent.) Forte also noted that geography seems to play a role in the pricing of vintage instruments, since certain instruments seem to sell better in certain areas than others. A portion of his article was devoted to brief interviews with certain vintage instrument authorities, some of whom noted a definite increase in prices for carved-top guitars of the highest quality. The prices of these instruments had escalated recently but still seemed undervalued relative to the much higher prices commanded by Stratocasters and Les Pauls, leading one to assume that carved-top guitars were severely underpriced. Although one dealer noted directly that guitars should not be bought for investment, three of the seven dealers surveyed expressed the opinion that carved-top guitars would be one of the best investments of the instruments surveyed at the time.

Finally, Ben Sandmel (*Spirit,* May 1990, pp.42–56) quoted various vintage guitar authorities in his pricing summary, noting that prewar D28 Herringbones were selling for approximately $28,000, prewar D45 Martin guitars for approximately $50,000, 1958–1960 Les Paul Standards for an "average" of $25,000 with a $60,000 peak price, and Fender Stratocasters "for as high as" $15,000. Though these prices could not be verified, it was stated that prices do seem to depend on condition, the colors and wood patterns of the instruments, their sound, their look, and their historic significance. Sandmel also paraphrased George Gruhn's summary of the virtues of collectors—they preserve instruments, generate information that educates the public, and turn up more instruments for sale in their search for items for their collections. Finally, Sandmel noted that some famous musicians, such as Lonnie Mack, the late Stevie Ray Vaughan, and Rodney Crowell, actually use or play their vintage instruments regularly.

Sources of Vintage Guitars

There are a limited number of sources for vintage or collectible guitars. Among these are guitar dealers, including those who specialize in vintage and rare instruments; regular musical instrument dealers who occasionally purchase or take vintage instruments in trade; individuals, both collectors and those desiring to dispose of their vintage instruments; auctions; and vintage guitar shows. Of these sources of vintage instruments, only vintage instrument dealers and vintage guitar shows offer the prospective purchaser the opportunity to compare different versions of the same instrument or different types of instruments prior to purchase. Vintage instrument dealers may often have a wide variety of collectible guitars but not have instruments in every category. However, some basis for comparison of different types of guitars, such as electric L–5s and Super 400s, may be made with some of the larger vintage instrument dealers in the United States if one is willing either to travel to the dealer's showroom or to discuss the merits of the instruments over the telephone with the dealer and begin the bargaining process accordingly. The latter approach leaves much to be desired, although it is often the only way that many persons can purchase a vintage instrument because of their location, demands for a particular type of instrument, and the availability of such instruments in the vintage instrument marketplace.

The vintage instrument show is often the best place for a person to find a particular type of vintage guitar or other fretted vintage instrument. These specialized events, which began as early as 1978, offer prospective purchasers an often unparalleled opportunity to compare many types of the same instrument brought to the show for sale by different dealers from around the country. The instruments can be compared in terms of originality, rarity, sound and playability, price, and other important factors all in the same place at the same time. Finally, serious bargaining can often help a person obtain a truly desirable instrument at one of these events, since dealers may seldom bargain with an individual purchaser over the telephone or by letter but will certainly bargain when several other dealers have similar instruments for sale at the same time in the same place.

Reviews of the vintage guitar show phenomenon are also relatively new, and most reviews I examined tend to be rather unfocused commentaries on various types of instruments available for sale at a particular guitar show. Such commentaries also include critical and caustic remarks reflecting the particular author's biases against certain instruments or trends in the vintage instrument market. However, certain common themes emerge concerning the nature and appeal of vintage instrument shows. First, vintage guitar shows offer a wide variety of instruments for sale. This is especially true at the largest vintage instrument shows in the United States, located in Texas and sponsored by Charley's Guitar Shop of Dallas, Texas, and Texas Guitar Shows, Inc., of Tulsa, Oklahoma. Second, vintage guitar shows have a rather frenetic pace of trading, buying, and selling that may be somewhat intimidating to the uninitiated visitor to such events. Third, much of the business that occurs at vintage guitar shows takes place between the attending dealers who either have booths or who come to buy instruments for their customers back home. Fourth, the presence and impact of the overseas buyers cannot be overstated or overestimated. Increasingly, buyers from Europe and Japan are attending the larger vintage instrument shows in notable numbers, and with considerable cash in hand, to purchase instruments for their native customers or for their own private collections. If, as noted earlier among the factors influencing pricing, the value of the dollar is relatively lower than that of certain foreign currencies, then a great deal of buying by overseas customers may occur.

One key factor emerging among vintage instrument dealers, collectors, and overseas buyers and collectors is an increasing sophistication and knowledge about the various vintage instruments offered for sale at vintage guitar shows. This increase in knowledge and sophistication sometimes goes to extremes, as when certain desirable Stratocaster and Telecaster guitars are disassembled on the spot to determine the exact originality of all the parts contained therein. Even after such a process, there are often several levels of disagreement about the relative originality of such an instrument. This does not necessarily reflect badly on the instrument, but rather on the opinions and knowledge base of the different persons assessing it. However, detailed knowledge of one's favorite or desired vintage instruments is absolutely essential. One's knowledge base can often be expanded by talking with dealers at guitar shows and also by examining, playing, and associating with the many types of vintage instruments available at the shows.

Finally, the vintage guitar show phenomenon usually gives very detailed insights into the current state of the vintage guitar market.

Thus, the relative worth of certain items at a particular show may often determine their worth at subsequent shows. Categories of items that are selling rather rapidly are duly noted, and an increase in sales of these items usually occurs right after the shows as well. Often dealers will continue to do business "off the show" for several months after the show date, as "suddenly" decisive persons contact them regarding pieces displayed at the show that were not sold. Pricing trends can be examined at vintage guitar shows and tracked by comparison to prices of similar items at previous events.

The zest and joy that permeates these shows cannot be overstated. Quite simply put, the larger vintage guitar shows are exciting events that bring together many different types of buyers and sellers of vintage instruments in an atmosphere highly conducive to playing music, establishing and maintaining friendships, and buying or trading musical instruments that certainly possess more intrinsic and indefinable values than certain other types of collectible objects.

The Super 400 in Particular

After reviewing the above information regarding the collecting of musical instruments, the vintage instrument market, and the vintage guitar show phenomenon, we now come to the question of whether the Super 400 guitar is a collectible, desirable, utilitarian, and investment-worthy instrument. The answer to all of these factors is a definite *yes!* First, the instrument meets Gruhn's 1988 criteria for an investment as both a collectible instrument and a utility instrument. Any Super 400 possesses several of the collectible instrument qualities such as famous maker, famous model, rarity, historic significance, and aesthetic appeal. In addition, most Super 400s also meet his criteria for an excellent utility instrument—good sound and playability. The current state of the vintage arch-top guitar market reflects rising prices for top-of-the-line guitars such as the Super 400, the L-5, the Epiphone Emperor and Deluxe, and many Stromberg and D'Angelico guitars. These instruments are now commanding much higher prices relative to their position in the market. In 1985 they were described as being a good buy, but seriously undervalued. However, prices have risen dramatically during the years 1988–1990, as collectors, players, and dealers have all realized the intrinsic, utilitarian, collectible, and resale values of such instruments.

How does the Super 400 compare to other collectible guitars at the current time? While no current prices are available regarding sales of other instruments, notice the difference in production between the selected Gibson Super 400s illustrated below and certain other Martin and Gibson guitars produced during the same time period.

Prewar Acoustic Guitars

	Number Produced
Martin D28 Herringbone, 14-fret neck, 1934–1944	1,410
Martin D45, 1933–1942	91
Gibson Super 400, 1934–1941	455

Postwar Electric Guitars

	Number Produced
Gibson Les Paul Standard, Sunburst, 1958–1960	1,712
Gibson ES-335 Dot, All Finishes, 1958–1961	2,309
Gibson Super 400CES, All Finishes, 1958–1961	136

When comparing production tables, it becomes obvious that the Super 400 is at least as collectible as each of the Martin and Gibson guitars noted above, and in terms of rarity, certainly more collectible than all but the D45. (Appendix B-13, "Table of Relative Rarity of the Super 400," indicates the true scarcity of many Super 400 models.) Certainly, collectors' individual tastes vary, and there are many other forces at work that determine the ultimate collectability and investment potential of the above instruments. However, the production numbers should serve as one kind of guideline when considering the purchase of the Super 400 for collectible or investment purposes.

By contrast, for the pre-CBS Fender Telecasters (1950–1965) and Stratocasters (1954–1965), no production data is available. Despite the fact that many of these instruments fetch extremely high prices, some in excess of $10,000 per instrument, they are essentially mass-produced guitars for which there is no production data to determine their relative rarity. Similarly, the Gretsch 6120, White Falcon, and White Penguin guitars are also considered rare and highly desirable in today's collectible and investment guitar market, but no production data is available for these models either. Some of these Gretsch instruments also fetch prices in excess of $10,000, and yet there is no data to substantiate how rare they really are or to compare them with other types of collectible instruments whose production data is definitely established.

Besides having a collectible or investment potential, the Super 400 guitar, in all its variations, has definite utility value in terms of its sound and playability. Many people are drawn to the instrument for these two factors. Depending on the taste, skill, and ear of the listener and potential purchaser, different Super 400 guitars will strike different people in different ways. To help one decide about the possible purchase of a Super 400 guitar, the following discussion illustrates the conscious factors influencing the purchase of a guitar as well as the individual's personal reasons for purchasing the instrument.

By reviewing the articles discussed earlier in this chapter regarding collectability, desirability, utility, and personal reasons for purchasing instruments, I have devised a working model that also incorporates individual factors often cited by purchasers as reasons for buying a particular musical instrument. These individual factors have been arbitrarily organized into factor groups relating to the instrument itself, the instrument plus certain personal reasons, personal reasons alone, and instrument market factors related to purchase. These four factor groups seem to cover most if not all the reasons that a particular vintage instrument is purchased by an

Prewar Serial Numbers and Factory Order Numbers

The Gibson Corporation has used six different numbering systems to identify its instruments for both internal (factory) as well as for external (dealer) reasons. It is beyond the scope of this book to discuss in great detail all of the various serial number and factory order number variations that Gibson utilized over the course of the manufacture of the Super 400. The following is a brief summary of the serial number and factory order number system for the prewar Super 400s from A. R. Duchossoir's book, *Guitar Identification* (Hal Leonard Publishing Corporation, 1983). The reader is referred to Duchossoir's book for an excellent in-depth discussion of the Gibson serial number and factory order numbering systems, as well as many other details that aid in properly identifying and dating the many instruments of Gibson, Inc.

Briefly, from 1934 through 1941 Gibson utilized a *serial number,* which was written on the label that was pasted inside the guitar body beneath the left f-hole. These serial numbers ran in numerical sequence from approximately 91,400 to 97,400 at the end of 1941. The serial numbers were assigned to each instrument as they were completed, although different types of Gibson instruments often had their own serial number sequences.

The *factory order number* was an internal numbering system used by Gibson to denote batches or racks of instruments of approximately 40 units of the same model within the factory. The factory order numbers were usually found ink-stamped on the inside of the back of the body, beneath the right f-hole. Factory order numbers typically consisted of a three- to five-digit number that identified the batch of the guitars being made plus a one- or two-digit suffix to rank each instrument within that particular batch. In the mid-1930s Gibson also utilized a *code letter,* which was inserted between the batch number and the rank of the instrument within a particular batch. These letters corresponded to the year that the batch was being assembled within the factory, beginning with the letter A for 1935, B for 1936, and so forth, through G for 1941.

In general, prewar Super 400s will have both a serial number, written on the label inside the guitar body under the left f-hole, and a factory order number ink-stamped inside the guitar under the right f-hole. Occasionally, Super 400s made between 1939 and 1940 may have a different serial number that resembles a factory order number stamped on the back of the headstock as well as written on the label inside the guitar body. Usually these numbers will take the form of *EA* plus a four-digit number. The following information is designed to assist the reader in properly identifying a prewar Super 400 by its serial number and factory order number. Of course, the reader should also consult Chapter 1 to note other details of the guitar, such as the headstock logo, design of the f-holes, scale length, upper bout width, and so forth.

TABLE A-1
Prewar Gibson Instrument Numbering System

Year	Approximate First Serial Number	Factory Order Number Code Letter
1934	91400	—
1935	92300	A
1936	92800	B
1937	94100	C
1938	95200	D
1939	95750	E
1940	96050	F
1941	96600	G
1942	97400	—
1943	97700	—
1944	97850	—
1945	98250	—

Source: Courtesy A. R. Duchossoir.

Postwar Serial Numbers and Factory Order Numbers

In the postwar years, Gibson experimented with five major different numbering systems for their guitars. The reader is again referred to *Guitar Identification* by A. R. Duchossoir for a more detailed discussion of this topic. However, the following brief discussion will at least assist the reader in the identification of various postwar Super 400 guitars.

1947–1961
Gibson first used both a *serial number* and *factory order number* to identify instruments from 1947 through early 1961. The serial number consisted of the large letter *A* followed by a three- to five-digit number written or imprinted on the label, glued to the inside surface of the guitar back, and usually visible through the left f-hole of the guitar. A factory order number code letter was usually ink-stamped, along with the appropriate factory order numbers, on the inside of the back under the right f-hole from 1952 through 1961. This two-part numbering scheme is fairly accurate

and consistent, and it is unfortunate that it was abandoned in early 1961. (See Table A-3.)

1961–1969

A confusing sequence of five- to six-digit *serial numbers* without letter prefixes were used, and certain series of numbers within these years were used repeatedly. It is sometimes difficult to date a Super 400 (or any other Gibson guitar) during this time period by utilizing the serial number alone. (Factory order numbers were discontinued in 1961, so that doesn't help much either.) The reader is referred to Table F of *Guitar Identification* (Duchossoir, page 20) for an excellent explanation of these various numbering schemes, reprinted in this book as Table A-5 with permission of Duchossoir.

For Super 400s made between 1961 and1969, there exist at least 25 serial number series in Duchossoir's Table F where possible repetition of serial numbers within the particular series may occur. These repetitions occurred during the production years of 1965–1969 and are illustrated in Table A-2.

TABLE A-2
Gibson's Repeated Use of Selected Serial Numbers

Year of Production						
1963	1964	1965	1966	1967	1968	1969
X				R		
	X	R				
		X		R		
		X		R	R	
		X	R	R	R	
		X	R		R	R
		X			R	
			X		R	R
			X	R		
			X			R
			X	R	R	R
					X	R

X = First year of serial number series
R = Repeated use of serial number series
(Compiled from Table F, A. Duchossoir, *Guitar Identification*, p. 20)

The first year of serial number repetition was 1965, when some numbers in the 174223–176643 range of 1964 were used again. In 1966, two sets of serial number ranges evidenced repetition from their first one in 1965. The years 1967, 1968, and 1969 saw the heaviest reuse of serial number series, and some series were repeated three times during this three-year period. Duchossoir's Table F shows each serial number range that was repeated, with its first year of use and subsequent year(s) of repetition. The clustering of repeated serial number ranges in 1967–1969 makes exact Super 400 dating difficult, but not impossible, for this time period. To help the reader further pinpoint the year of manufacture of a Super 400 between 1963 and 1969, the following general guidelines are offered. (For a more detailed discussion of this topic, please refer to Duchossoir's *Gibson Electrics Volume 1* [Paris: Mediapresse, 1981].)

Additional differentiating factors:
- Neck width at nut (with very few exceptions)
  1949–1964: 1^{11}/$_{16}$ inches
  1965–first half of 1969: 1^9/$_{16}$ inches
- Orange label
  1968: "Union Made" added
- Headstock pitch
  1949–late 1965: 17 degrees
  Late 1965 on: 14 degrees
- Headstock logo
  1968: Began using pantograph-style lettering with a square-cut pattern, closed letters *b* and *o*, and no dotted *i*
- Sunburst finish
  1965–1969: More reddish at borders, with very few exceptions

Note that the above features and changes are integral to the guitar, rather than parts that can be replaced or substituted.

1970–1975

Gibson again repeated several series of serial number sequences during this time period. Proper identification of instruments during this period is difficult, but can be done by using Duchossoir's Table H (included in this book as Table A-6) plus the following additional differentiating factors:
- Neck width at nut: 1^{11}/$_{16}$ inches
- Orange label: 1970–1971
  Purple and white label: 1971–1981
- Headstock pitch: 14 degrees
- Headstock logo: Pantograph-style, square-cut with closed *b* and *o* and no dotted *i*
- Headstock veneer: 1971—holly replaced with black fiber (plastic)
- "Made in U.S.A." stamp: 1970—on back of headstock just below serial number
- Volute: Added to Super 400 and L-5 about 1974—discontinued about 1981
- Sunburst finish: Light yellow center area on top and back shaped like huge triangle or guitar pick—the "pick finish"

All of the above factors, plus the serial number, must be considered when dating a guitar in this time period. The reader is also advised to refer back to the appropriate sections of this book for more information regarding parts and body appointments.

1975–1977

Gibson switched to a two-digit prefix followed by a six-digit serial number in the 100,000 and 200,000 ranges. These numbers were applied with a decal to the back of the headstock instead of being impressed into the headstock. Additional factors present during 1975–1977 also include those listed in the previous section on 1970–1975 instruments.

1977–Present

Finally, in 1977 Gibson settled on a very systematic numbering system that provides a very reliable and foolproof method of identifying the date of manufacture of the guitar. This eight-digit system utilizes the first and fifth digit in a sequence of eight numbers to identify the year the guitar was made, while the second, third, and fourth digits indicate the day of the year and the sixth, seventh, and eighth digits indicate the instrument's rank that day and that the guitar was either manufactured in Kalamazoo (001–499) or Nashville (500–999). No numbering table is needed for this system, but the following examples should help the reader understand and become familiar with it.

Example 1: 8 **2 2 9** 4 **3 6 2**

1st and 5th digits = year 1984

bold digits **229** = 229th day

bold digits **362** = number 362 in Kalamazoo that day

Example 2: 9 **2 4 3** 0 **9 9 9**

1st and 5th digits = year 1990

bold digits **243** = 243rd day

bold digits **999** = number 999 in Nashville that day

TABLE A-3
Postwar Gibson Numbering System, 1947–1961

Year	Approximate First Number	Factory Order Number Code Letter
1947	A-100	—
1948	A-1305	—
1949	A-2666	—
1950	A-4414	—
1951	A-6598	—
1952	A-9420	Z
1953	A-12463	Y
1954	A-16102	X
1955	A-18668	W
1956	A-21910	V
1957	A-24756	U
1958	A-26820	T
1959	A-28881	S
1960	A-32285	R
1961	A-35646	Q

Source: Courtesy A. R. Duchossoir.

TABLE A-4
Shipping Dates for Selected Serial Numbers, 1947–1961

1947		1951	
A-150	May 1, 1947	A-6598	January 4, 1951
A-253	June 3, 1947	A-6890	February 1, 1951
A-411	July 2, 1947	A-7056	March 1, 1951
A-493	August 4, 1947	A-7237	April 3, 1951
A-596	September 2, 1947	A-7542	May 4, 1951
A-813	October 1, 1947	A-7808	June 1, 1951
A-1021	November 3, 1947	A-8030	July 2, 1951
A-1146	December 1, 1947	A-8357	August 13, 1951
		A-8532	September 5, 1951
1948		A-8705	October 1, 1951
A-1305	January 8, 1948	A-8932	November 1, 1951
A-1410	February 4, 1948	A-9194	December 3, 1951
A-1460	March 5, 1948		
A-1540	April 1, 1948	**1952**	
A-1630	May 3, 1948	A-9420	January 2, 1952
A-1713	June 1, 1948	A-9691	February 1, 1952
A-1849	July 2, 1948	A-9931	March 3, 1952
A-1968	August 4, 1948	A-10111	April 2, 1952
A-2158	September 3, 1948	A-10443	May 1, 1952
A-2369	October 6, 1948	A-10772	June 2, 1952
A-2481	November 1, 1948	A-11057	July 1, 1952
A-2613	December 8, 1948	A-11330	August 1, 1952
		A-11486	September 2, 1952
1949		A-11680	October 2, 1952
A-2666	January 5, 1949	A-11897	November 4, 1952
A-2716	February 4, 1949	A-12202	December 1, 1952
A-2852	March 7, 1949		
A-2999	April 1, 1949	**1953**	
A-3145	May 2, 1949	A-12463	January 8, 1953
A-3202	June 1, 1949	A-12662	February 3, 1953
A-3353	July 1, 1949	A-12861	March 6, 1953
A-3512	August 15, 1949	A-13213	April 1, 1953
A-3592	September 1, 1949	A-13566	May 1, 1953
A-3749	October 3, 1949	A-13912	June 4, 1953
A-3953	November 1, 1949	A-14332	July 1, 1953
A-4209	December 1, 1949	A-14706	August 3, 1953
		A-15130	September 2, 1953
1950		A-15432	October 1, 1953
A-4414	January 3, 1950	A-15684	November 2, 1953
A-4589	February 1, 1950	A-15883	December 2, 1953
A-4785	March 1, 1950		
A-5012	April 3, 1950	**1954**	
A-5226	May 1, 1950	A-16102	January 5, 1954
A-5366	June 1, 1950	A-16309	February 3, 1954
A-5456	July 3, 1950	A-16561	March 1, 1954
A-5543	August 2, 1950	A-16761	April 5, 1954
A-5678	September 1, 1950	A-16941	May 5, 1954
A-5833	October 2, 1950	A-17161	June 1, 1954
A-6014	November 1, 1950	A-17435	July 1, 1954
A-6312	December 4, 1950	A-17582	August 3, 1954
		A-17861	September 1, 1954
		A-18149	October 4, 1954
		A-18370	November 2, 1954
		A-18496	December 1, 1954

TABLE A-4
Shipping Dates for Selected Serial Numbers, 1947–1961 continued

1955		**1959**	
A-18668	January 6, 1955	A-28881	January 9, 1959
A-20099	February 2, 1955	A-29010	February 2, 1959
A-20286	March 3, 1955	A-29287	March 3, 1959
A-20468	April 4, 1955	A-29532	April 1, 1959
A-20716	May 5, 1955	A-29826	May 1, 1959
A-20898	June 2, 1955	A-30233	June 1, 1959
A-20991	July 1, 1955	A-30569	July 13, 1959
A-21129	August 8, 1955	A-30696	August 3, 1959
A-21226	September 2, 1955	A-30977	September 3, 1959
A-21356	October 5, 1955	A-31281	October 1, 1959
A-21540	November 1, 1955	A-31532	November 3, 1959
A-21745	December 1, 1955	A-31844	December 2, 1959

1956		**1960**	
A-21910	January 6, 1956	A-32285	January 4, 1960
A-22074	February 1, 1956	A-32527	February 2, 1960
A-22273	March 1, 1956	A-32881	March 2, 1960
A-22556	April 4, 1956	A-33140	April 4, 1960
A-22729	May 1, 1956	A-33340	May 5, 1960
A-23070	June 5, 1956	A-33758	June 2, 1960
A-23387	July 3, 1956	A-34068	July 1, 1960
A-23554	August 6, 1956	A-34237	August 2, 1960
A-23913	September 4, 1956	A-34479	September 1, 1960
A-24135	October 2, 1956	A-34659	October 3, 1960
A-24453	November 1, 1956	A-34905	November 3, 1960
A-24567	December 1, 1956	A-35252	December 1, 1960

1957		**1961**	
A-24756	January 3, 1957	A-35646	January 3, 1961
A-24893	February 1, 1957	A-35943	February 1, 1961
A-25192	March 1, 1957		
A-25368	April 4, 1957		
A-25512	May 3, 1957		
A-25661	June 4, 1957		
A-25899	July 3, 1957		
A-25960	August 7, 1957		
A-26188	September 3, 1957		
A-26381	October 4, 1957		
A-26547	November 5, 1957		
A-26695	December 3, 1957		

1958

A-26820	January 6, 1958
A-27026	February 5, 1958
A-27258	March 5, 1958
A-27361	April 2, 1958
A-27552	May 5, 1958
A-27685	June 2, 1958
A-27816	July 1, 1958
A-27987	August 12, 1958
A-28042	September 2, 1958
A-28282	October 3, 1958
A-28387	November 5, 1958
A-28576	December 1, 1958

Source: Courtesy A. R. Duchossoir.
First serial number, A-100, registered on April 28, 1947.
Last serial number, A-36147, registered on February 21, 1961.

TABLE A-5
Serial Numbers—1961–1969, Selected Series

Series	Year	Series	Year
100–42440	1961	370000–370999	1967
42441–61180	1962	380000–385309	1966
61450–64222	1963	390000–390998	1967
64240–64455	1964	400001–400999	1965, 1966, 1967, 1968
64601–64709	1964	401000–407985	1966
65000–70501	1964	408000–408688	1966
71180–96600	1962	408800–409250	1966
96601–99999	1963	420000–426088	1966
000001–008009	1967	427000–429180	1966
010000–042899	1967	430004–438530	1966
044000–044100	1967	438800–438922	1966
050000–054400	1967	500000–500999	1965, 1966, 1968, 1969
055000–063999	1967	501009–501600	1965
064000–066008	1967	501601–501702	1968
067000–070909	1967	501703–502706	1965, 1968
090000–099999	1967	503010–503109	1968
100000–106099	1963, 1967	503405–520955	1965, 1968
106100–108999	1963	520956–530056	1968
109000–109999	1963, 1967	530061–530850	1966, 1968, 1969
110000–111549	1963	530851–530993	1968, 1969
111550–115799	1963, 1967	530994–539999	1969
115800–118299	1963	540000–540795	1966, 1969
118300–120999	1963, 1967	540796–545009	1969
121000–139999	1963	550000–556909	1966
140000–140100	1963, 1967	558012–567400	1969
140101–144304	1963	570099–570755	1966
144305–144380	1964	580000–580999	1969
144381–145000	1963	600000–600999	1966, 1967, 1968, 1969
147009–149864	1963	601000–601090	1969
149865–149891	1964	605901–606090	1969
149892–152989	1963	700000–700799	1966, 1967
152990–174222	1964	750000–750999	1968, 1969
174223–176643	1964, 1965	800000–800999	1966, 1967, 1968, 1969
176644–199999	1964	801000–812838	1966, 1969
200000–250335	1964	812900–814999	1969
250336–290998	1965	817000–819999	1969
301755–302100	1965	820000–820087	1966, 1969
302754–305983	1965	820088–823830	1966
306000–306099	1965, 1967	824000–824999	1969
307000–307984	1965, 1967	828002–847488	1966, 1969
309848–310999	1965, 1967	847499–858999	1966
311000–320149	1965	859001–880089	1967
320150–320699	1967	893401–895038	1967
320700–321100	1965	895039–896999	1968
322000–326600	1965	897000–898999	1967
328000–328500	1965	899000–899999	1968
328700–329179	1965	900000–902250	1968
329180–330199	1965, 1967	903000–920899	1968
330200–332240	1965, 1967, 1968	940000–941009	1968
332241–347089	1965	942001–943000	1968
348000–348092	1965	945000–945450	1968
348093–349100	1966	947415–956000	1968
349121–368638	1965	959000–960909	1968
368640–369890	1966	970000–972864	1968

Source: A. R. Duchossoir, *Guitar Identification* (Milwaukee: Hal Leonard Publishing Corporation, 1983), p. 20, Table F.

TABLE A-6
Serial Numbers—1970–1975, General Series

Year	Series
1970	
1971	100000, 600000, 700000, and 900000 series
1972	
1973	000001, 100000, 200000, and 800000 series; a few numbers with A plus 6 digits
1974	100000, 200000, 300000, 400000, 500000, 600000, and 800000 series;
1975	a few numbers with A, B, C, D, E, or F plus 6 digits

Source: A. R. Duchossoir, 1983, p. 20, Table H.

TABLE A-7
Serial Numbers—1975–1977, Two-Digit Prefix

Prefix	Year
99	1975
00	1976
06	1977

Source: A. R. Duchossoir, 1983, p. 20, Table I.

Appendix
B

Production
and Shipping
Totals

The numbers contained in the following tables are derived from Gibson's actual shipping ledgers, as recorded by Julius Bellson. However, the data reported here is a slight underestimate of the absolute total production for both the Super 400 and L-5 from 1935 through 1979. Records apparently do not exist for guitars shipped before 1935. From 1980 through 1984, most of the production data was logged into Norlin's computer system and access to this data is not possible. From 1985 through 1987 some data is available and has been included in the overall production tables. Second, there have always been a few Super 400s and L-5s that have not been logged as shipped, but nevertheless find their way into the vintage guitar market. Such guitars may include special-order instruments for trade shows, customized instruments, and instruments for Gibson's own internal use. The only guitar model whose production may be seriously underestimated is the 16-inch L-5, first introduced in 1923, because there is no data for the years 1923–1934.

In addition, certain custom finishes and the 1976–1980 wine red and ebony optional finishes are not listed because there is no separate data available for them. It is not known if these finishes were coded as sunburst or if they were listed elsewhere and lost.

TABLE B-1
Author's Super 400 Classification System

Model	Gibson Name	Defining Features	Variations	Years Made	Number Made
First	Super 400	Smaller upper bouts	None	1934–1936	92
Second	Super 400	Larger upper bouts	Sunburst	1937–1941	309
	Super 400	Same	Natural	1939–1941	7
Third	Super 400 Premiere	Cutaway	Sunburst	1939–1941	29
	Super 400 Premiere	Same	Natural	1939–1941	18
Fourth	Super 400	Noncutaway	Sunburst	1947–1955	154
	Super 400N	Same	Natural	1947–1955	86
Fifth	Super 400C	Cutaway	Sunburst	1947–1979	355
				1985–1989	3
	Super 400CN	Same	Natural	1947–1979	194
				1985–1989	1
	Super 400C-WR	Same	Wine red	1976–1980	?
	Super 400C-E	Same	Ebony	1976–1980	?
Sixth	Super 400CES	Venetian cutaway Electric	Sunburst, P90/ Alnico pickups	1951–1958	98
	Super 400CESN	Same	Natural, P90/ Alnico pickups	1951–1958	75
	Super 400CES	Same	Sunburst, PAFs	1958–1960	42
	Super 400CESN	Same	Natural, PAFs	1958–1960	19
Seventh	Super 400CES	Florentine cutaway Electric	Sunburst	1960–1969	320
	Super 400CESN	Same	Natural	1960–1969	122
Eighth	Super 400CES	Venetian cutaway Electric	Sunburst	1969–1979	832
				1985–1989	16
	Super 400CESN	Same	Natural	1969–1979	193
				1985–1989	2
	Super 400CES-WR	Same	Wine red	1976–1980	?
	Super 400CES-E	Same	Ebony	1976–1980	?

TABLE B-2
Total Super 400 Production Shipping Totals

Instrument	Years of Shipment								
	1935	**1936**	**1937**	**1938**	**1939**	**1940**	**1941**	**1948**	**1949**
Super 400	63	29	104	78	66	30	31	64	31
Super 400N	—	—	—	—	—	7	—	27	13
Super 400P	—	—	—	—	6	10	13	—	—
Super 400PN	—	—	—	—	—	13	5	—	—
	1950	**1951**	**1952**	**1953**	**1954**	**1955**	**1956**	**1957**	**1958**	**1959**
Super 400	12	10	19	10	6	2	—	—	—	—
Super 400N	13	8	17	1	6	1	—	—	—	—
Super 400C	14	5	10	5	17	6	11	11	11	11
Super 400CN	7	7	7	—	7	6	3	14	9	5
Super 400CES	—	2	7	16	17	5	20	24	15	22
Super 400CESN	—	—	11	11	6	6	19	15	15	8
	1960	**1961**	**1962**	**1963**	**1964**	**1965**	**1966**	**1967**	**1968**	**1969**
Super 400C	12	13	16	14	12	16	3	25	24	33
Super 400CN	7	6	5	9	2	4	2	3	3	22
Super 400CES	24	30	24	29	29	31	25	28	52	120
Super 400CESN	7	15	16	14	13	1	4	22	11	45
	1970	**1971**	**1972**	**1973**	**1974**	**1975**	**1976**	**1977**	**1978**	**1979**
Super 400C	5	4	5	3	2	14	15	21	12	5
Super 400CN	2	5	10	—	—	18	13	13	5	—
Super 400CES	31	53	69	93	97	48	29	64	43	245
Super 400CESN	15	9	33	17	3	32	21	24	14	2
	1980	**1981**	**1982**	**1983**	**1984**	**1985**	**1986**	**1987**	**1988**	**1989**
Super 400C	★	★	★	★	★	1	2	—	—	—
Super 400CN	★	★	★	★	★	—	—	1	—	—
Super 400CES	★	★	★	★	★	7	2	1	4	1
Super 400CESN	★	★	★	★	★	1	—	—	1	—

★Note: No production data available for the years 1980–1984.

TABLE B-3
Prewar Acoustic Super 400 Production

Model	Instrument	Years of Shipment							
		1934	**1935**	**1936**	**1937**	**1938**	**1939**	**1940**	**1941**
First	Super 400	★	63	29	—	—	—	—	—
Second	Super 400	—	—	—	104	78	66	30	31
Second	Super 400N	—	—	—	—	—	—	7	—
Third	Super 400P	—	—	—	—	—	6	10	13
Third	Super 400PN	—	—	—	—	—	—	13	5
	Totals by Year	★	63	29	104	78	72	60	49

★Note: No production data available for 1934.

TABLE B-4
Prewar Acoustic Super 400 Production Summary

Model	Instrument	Variation	Number Shipped
First	Super 400	Noncutaway, sunburst, small upper bout	92
Second	Super 400	Noncutaway, sunburst, larger upper bout	309
Second	Super 400N	Noncutaway, natural, larger upper bout	7
Third	Super 400P	Cutaway, sunburst, larger upper bout	29
Third	Super 400PN	Cutaway, natural, larger upper bout	18
		Total, all models, 1934–1941	455

TABLE B-5
Postwar Acoustic Super 400 Production

Model	Instrument	Years of Shipment	
		1948	1949
Fourth	Super 400	64	31
Fourth	Super 400N	27	13
Fifth	Super 400C	—	—
Fifth	Super 400CN	—	—
	Totals by Year	91	44

Model	Instrument	1950	1951	1952	1953	1954	1955	1956	1957	1958	1959
Fourth	Super 400	12	10	19	10	6	2	—	—	—	—
Fourth	Super 400N	13	8	17	1	6	1	—	—	—	—
Fifth	Super 400C	14	5	10	5	17	6	11	11	11	11
Fifth	Super 400N	7	7	7	—	7	6	3	14	9	5
	Totals by Year	46	30	53	16	36	15	14	25	20	16

Model	Instrument	1960	1961	1962	1963	1964	1965	1966	1967	1968	1969
Fifth	Super 400C	12	13	16	14	12	16	3	25	24	33
Fifth	Super 400N	7	6	5	9	2	4	2	3	3	22
	Totals by Year	19	19	21	23	14	20	5	28	27	55

Model	Instrument	1970	1971	1972	1973	1974	1975	1976	1977	1978	1979
Fifth	Super 400C	5	4	5	3	2	14	15	21	12	5
Fifth	Super 400CN	2	5	10	—	—	18	13	13	5	—
	Totals by Year	7	9	15	3	2	32	28	34	17	5

Model	Instrument	1980	1981	1982	1983	1984	1985	1986	1987	1988	1989
Fifth	Super 400C	★	★	★	★	★	1	2	—	—	—
Fifth	Super 400CN	★	★	★	★	★	—	—	1	—	—
	Totals by Year						1	2	1	0	0

★No data available for 1980–1984.

TABLE B-6
Postwar Acoustic Super 400 Production Summary

Model	Instrument	Variation	Number Shipped	
			1948–1979	1985–1989
Fourth	Super 400	Noncutaway, sunburst	154	0
Fourth	Super 400N	Noncutaway, natural	86	0
Fifth	Super 400C	Cutaway, sunburst	355	3
Fifth	Super 400CN	Cutaway, natural	194	1
		Totals, all models	789	4
		Grand Total★	793	

★Plus 1980–1984 missing data.

TABLE B-7
Total Acoustic Super 400 Production, Selected Summary Data

Model	Instrument	Variation	Number Shipped		
			Prewar	Postwar	Total
First	Super 400	Noncutaway body, sunburst finish, smaller upper bout	92	0	92
Second, fourth	Super 400	Noncutaway body, sunburst finish	309	154	463
Second, fourth	Super 400N	Noncutaway body, natural finish	7	86	93
Third, fifth	Super 400P/C	Cutaway body, sunburst finish	29	358	387
Third, fifth	Super 400PN/CN	Cutaway body, natural finish	18	195	213
		Totals, all models	455	793	1248

TABLE B-8
Postwar Electric Super 400 Production

Model	Instrument	Years of Shipment									
		1950	1951	1952	1953	1954	1955	1956	1957	1958	1959
Sixth	Super 400CES	—	2	7	16	17	5	20	24	15	22
Sixth	Super 400CESN	—	—	11	11	6	6	19	15	15	8
	Totals by Year	0	2	18	27	23	11	39	39	30	30
		1960	1961	1962	1963	1964	1965	1966	1967	1968	1969
Sixth	Super 400CES	24	30	24	29	29	31	25	28	52	120
Sixth	Super 400CESN	7	15	16	14	13	1	4	22	11	45
	Totals by Year	31	45	40	43	42	32	29	50	63	165
		1970	1971	1972	1973	1974	1975	1976	1977	1978	1979
Sixth	Super 400CES	31	53	69	93	97	48	29	64	43	245
Sixth	Super 400CESN	15	9	33	17	3	32	21	24	14	2
	Totals by Year	46	62	102	110	100	80	50	88	57	247
		1980	1981	1982	1983	1984	1985	1986	1987	1988	1989
Sixth	Super 400CES	★	★	★	★	★	7	3	1	4	1
Sixth	Super 400CESN	★	★	★	★	★	1	—	—	1	
	Totals by Year	★	★	★	★	★	8	3	1	5	1

★No data available for 1980–1984.

TABLE B-9
Postwar Electric Super 400 Production Summary

Model	Instrument	Variation	Number Shipped			
			1951–First Half of 1960	Second Half of 1960–First Half of 1969	Second Half of 1969–1979	1985–1989
Sixth	Super 400CES	Venetian cutaway Sunburst	140	—	—	—
Sixth	Super 400CESN	Venetian cutaway Natural	94	—	—	—
Seventh	Super 400CES	Florentine cutaway Sunburst	—	320	—	—
Seventh	Super 400CESN	Florentine cutaway Natural	—	123	—	—
Eighth	Super 400CES	Venetian cutaway Sunburst	—	—	832	16
Eighth	Super 400CESN	Venetian cutaway Natural	—	—	192	2
		Totals, all models	234	443	1024	18

Grand Total: 1719 (plus 1980–1984, missing data)

TABLE B-10
Postwar Electric Super 400 Production, Early Pickup Variations

Instrument	Variation	Pickup Configuration Subtotals		
		P90 (1951–1953)	Alnico (1954–First Half of 1958)	PAF (Second Half of 1958–First Half of 1960)
Super 400CES	Venetian cutaway Sunburst	25	73	42
Super 400CESN	Venetian cutaway Natural	22	53	19
	Totals	47	126	61

Note: The above subtotals are approximations, based on observation and Gibson archival and anecdotal information.

TABLE B-11
Prewar Super 400 Prices

Guitar	1934	1935	1936	1937	1938	1939	1940	1941	1942
Super 400	400.00	400.00	400.00	400.00	400.00	400.00	400.00	325.50	325.50
Case	Inc.	Inc.	Inc.	Inc.	Inc.	Inc.	Inc.	90.00	100.00
Cover	Inc.	Inc.	Inc.	Inc.	Inc.	Inc.	Inc.	Inc.	Inc.
Total	400.00	400.00	400.00	400.00	400.00	400.00	400.00	415.50	425.50
Super 400N	—	—	—	—	—	400.00	410.00	336.00	336.00
Case						Inc.	Inc.	90.00	100.00
Cover						Inc.	Inc.	Inc.	Inc.
Total						400.00	410.00	426.00	436.00
Super 400P	—	—	—	—	—	425.00	415.00	351.25	351.25
Case						Inc.	Inc.	90.00	100.00
Cover						Inc.	Inc.	Inc.	Inc.
Total						425.00	415.00	441.25	451.25
Super 400PN	—	—	—	—	—	425.00	425.00	362.25	362.25
Case						Inc.	Inc.	90.00	100.00
Cover						Inc.	Inc.	Inc.	Inc.
Total						425.00	425.00	452.25	462.25

Note: 1943–1946, no production

TABLE B-12
Postwar Super 400 Prices

Guitar	1946	1947	1948	1949
Super 400	No	425.00		425.00
Case	Production	65.00		60.00
Cover		35.00		30.00
Total		525.00		515.00
Super 400N		440.00		450.00
Case		65.00		60.00
Cover		35.00		30.00
Total		540.00		540.00
Super 400C				475.00
Case				60.00
Cover				30.00
Total				565.00
Super 400CN				490.00
Case				60.00
Cover				30.00
Total				580.00

Guitar	1950	1951	1952	1953	1954	1955	1956	1957	1958	1959
Super 400	450.00		475.00		N/L	N/L				
Case	60.00		60.00							
Cover	30.00		30.00							
Total	540.00		565.00							
Super 400N	475.00		500.00		N/L	N/L				
Case	60.00		60.00							
Cover	30.00		30.00							
Total	565.00		590.00							
Super 400C	500.00		525.00		550.00	550.00	575.00	600.00	600.00	600.00
Case	60.00		60.00		60.00	60.00	60.00	60.00	60.00	60.00
Cover	30.00		30.00		30.00	30.00	30.00	30.00	30.00	30.00
Total	590.00		615.00		640.00	640.00	665.00	690.00	690.00	690.00
Super 400CN	525.00		550.00		575.00	575.00	600.00	625.00	625.00	625.00
Case	60.00		60.00		60.00	60.00	60.00	60.00	60.00	60.00
Cover	30.00		30.00		30.00	30.00	30.00	30.00	30.00	30.00
Total	615.00		640.00		665.00	665.00	690.00	715.00	715.00	715.00
Super 400CES	—		595.00		625.00	625.00	650.00	675.00	675.00	675.00
Case			60.00		60.00	60.00	60.00	60.00	60.00	60.00
Cover			30.00		30.00	30.00	30.00	30.00	30.00	30.00
Total			685.00		715.00	715.00	740.00	765.00	765.00	765.00
Super 400CESN	—		620.00		650.00	650.00	675.00	700.00	700.00	700.00
Case			60.00		60.00	60.00	60.00	60.00	60.00	60.00
Cover			30.00		30.00	30.00	30.00	30.00	30.00	30.00
Total			710.00		740.00	740.00	765.00	790.00	790.00	790.00

Guitar	1960	1961	1962	1963	1964	1965	1966	1967	1968	1969
Super 400C	650.00	715.00	715.00	760.00	810.00	810.00	850.00	895.00	975.00	1,035.00
Case	60.00	60.00	60.00	60.00	72.00	72.00	77.00	80.00	92.00	85.00
Cover	35.00	35.00	35.00	35.00	35.00	35.00	35.00	40.00	43.00	43.00
Total	745.00	810.00	810.00	855.00	917.00	917.00	962.00	1,015.00	1,110.00	1,163.00
Super 400CN	675.00	740.00	740.00	785.00	835.00	835.00	875.00	920.00	1,025.00	1,085.00
Case	60.00	60.00	60.00	60.00	72.00	72.00	77.00	80.00	92.00	85.00
Cover	35.00	35.00	35.00	35.00	35.00	35.00	35.00	40.00	43.00	43.00
Total	770.00	835.00	835.00	880.00	942.00	942.00	987.00	1,040.00	1,160.00	1,213.00

TABLE B-12, continued
Postwar Super 400 Prices

Guitar	1960	1961	1962	1963	1964	1965	1966	1967	1968	1969
Super 400CES	750.00	825.00	825.00	875.00	935.00	935.00	1,000.00	1,050.00	1,145.00	1,225.00
Case	60.00	60.00	60.00	60.00	72.00	72.00	77.00	80.00	92.00	85.00
Cover	35.00	35.00	35.00	35.00	35.00	35.00	35.00	40.00	43.00	43.00
Total	845.00	920.00	920.00	970.00	1,042.00	1,042.00	1,112.00	1,170.00	1,280.00	1,353.00
Super 400CESN	775.00	850.00	850.00	900.00	960.00	960.00	1,025.00	1,075.00	1,195.00	1,275.00
Case	60.00	60.00	60.00	60.00	72.00	72.00	77.00	80.00	92.00	85.00
Cover	35.00	35.00	35.00	35.00	35.00	35.00	35.00	40.00	43.00	43.00
Total	870.00	945.00	945.00	995.00	1,067.00	1,067.00	1,137.00	1,195.00	1,330.00	1,403.00

Guitar	1970	1971	1972	1973	1974	1975	1976	1977	1978	1979
Super 400C	1,035.00	1,035.00	1,070.00	1,120.00	1,235.00	1,235.00	1,235.00	1,399.00	1,499.00	1,599.00
Case	85.00	99.00	99.00	110.00	120.00	Inc.	Inc.	Inc.	Inc.	Inc.
Cover	43.00	43.00	43.00	60.00	66.00	66.00	66.00	66.00	66.00	75.00
Total	1,163.00	1,177.00	1,212.00	1,290.00	1,421.00	1,301.00	1,301.00	1,465.00	1,565.00	1,674.00
Super 400CN	1,085.00	1,035.00	1,070.00	1,120.00	1,235.00	1,235.00	1,235.00	1,399.00	1,499.00	1,599.00
Case	85.00	99.00	99.00	110.00	120.00	Inc.	Inc.	Inc.	Inc.	Inc.
Cover	43.00	43.00	43.00	60.00	66.00	66.00	66.00	66.00	66.00	75.00
Total	1,213.00	1,177.00	1,212.00	1,290.00	1,421.00	1,301.00	1,301.00	1,465.00	1,565.00	1,674.00
Super 400CES	1,225.00	1,295.00	1,330.00	1,360.00	1,499.00	1,499.00	1,499.00	1,599.00	1,599.00	1,699.00
Case	85.00	99.00	99.00	110.00	120.00	Inc.	Inc.	Inc.	Inc.	Inc.
Cover	43.00	43.00	43.00	60.00	66.00	66.00	66.00	66.00	66.00	75.00
Total	1,353.00	1,437.00	1,472.00	1,530.00	1,685.00	1,565.00	1,565.00	1,665.00	1,665.00	1,774.00
Super 400CESN	1,275.00	1,295.00	1,330.00	1,360.00	1,499.00	1,499.00	1,499.00	1,599.00	1,599.00	1,799.00
Case	85.00	99.00	99.00	110.00	120.00	Inc.	Inc.	Inc.	Inc.	Inc.
Cover	43.00	43.00	43.00	60.00	66.00	66.00	66.00	66.00	66.00	75.00
Total	1,403.00	1,437.00	1,472.00	1,530.00	1,685.00	1,565.00	1,565.00	1,665.00	1,665.00	1,874.00

Guitar	1980	1981	1982	1983	1984	1985	1986	1987	1988	1989
Super 400C			2,499.00	2,499.00	2,499.00	2,499.00		N/L	N/L	
Case			Inc.	Inc.	Inc.	Inc.				
Cover			—	—	—	—				
Total			2,499.00	2,499.00	2,499.00	2,499.00				
Super 400CN			2,599.00	2,599.00	2,599.00	2,599.00		N/L	N/L	
Case			Inc.	Inc.	Inc.	Inc.				
Cover			—	—	—	—				
Total			2,599.00	2,599.00	2,599.00	2,599.00				
Super 400CES			2,499.00	2,599.00	2,599.00	2,599.00		2,666.00	3,985.00	
Case			Inc.	Inc.	Inc.	Inc.		Inc.	Inc.	
Cover			—	—	—	—		—	—	
Total			2,499.00	2,599.00	2,599.00	2,599.00		2,666.00	3,985.00	
Super 400CESN			2,599.00	2,599.00	2,599.00	2,599.00		2,666.00	3,985.00	
Case			Inc.	Inc.	Inc.	Inc.		Inc.	Inc.	
Cover			—	—	—	—		—	—	
Total			2,599.00	2,599.00	2,599.00	2,599.00		2,666.00	3,985.00	

N/L: Not Listed

TABLE B-13
Table of Relative Rarity of the Super 400

Rank	Model	Instrument	Variation	Years Shipped	Number Shipped	Percent of Total
1	Second	Super 400N	Noncutaway, natural	1939–1941	7	.2%
2	Third	Super 400PN	Cutaway, natural	1939–1941	18	.6%
3	Sixth	Super 400CESN	PAF pickups, natural	Second half of 1958–first half 1960	19	.6%
4	Third	Super 400P	Cutaway, sunburst	1939–1941	29	1.0%
5	Sixth	Super 400CES	PAF pickups, sunburst	Second half of 1958–first half of 1960	42	1.4%
6	Sixth	Super 400CESN	P90/Alnico pickups, natural	1951–first half of 1958	75	2.5%
7	Fourth	Super 400N	Noncutaway, natural	1947–1955	86	2.9%
8	First	Super 400	Smaller upper bouts, sunburst	1934–1936	92	3.1%
9	Sixth	Super 400CES	P90/Alnico pickups, sunburst	1951–first half of 1958	98	3.3%
10	Seventh	Super 400CESN	Florentine cutaway, natural	Second half of 1960–first half of 1969	122	4.1%
11	Fourth	Super 400	Noncutaway, sunburst	1947–1955	154	5.2%
12	Eighth	Super 400CESN	Venetian cutaway, natural	Second half of 1969–1979, 1985–1989	194★	6.5%★
13	Fifth	Super 400CN	Cutaway, natural	1947–1979, 1985–1989	195★	6.6%★
14	Second	Super 400	Noncutaway, sunburst	1937–1941	309	10.4%
15	Seventh	Super 400CES	Florentine cutaway, sunburst	Second half of 1960–first half of 1969	320	10.8%
16	Fifth	Super 400C	Cutaway, sunburst	1947–1979, 1985–1989	358★	12.1%★
17	Eighth	Super 400CES	Venetian cutaway, sunburst	Second half of 1969–1979, 1985–1989	848★	28.6%★
			Totals		2,966	100%

★1980–1984 totals not available.

TABLE B-14
Total L-5 Production Shipping Totals

Instrument	1935	1936	1937	1938	1939	1940	1941	1948	1949
L-5 Small	70	6	23	—	—	—	—	—	—
L-5	30	19	251	197	152	52	51	49	29
L-5N	—	—	—	—	—	—	36	38	17
L-5P	—	—	—	—	40	11	14	—	—
L-5PN	—	—	—	—	—	40	13	—	—
L-5C	—	—	—	—	—	—	—	23	23
L-5CN	—	—	—	—	—	—	—	21	22

Instrument	1950	1951	1952	1953	1954	1955	1956	1957	1958	1959
L-5	17	29	20	15	12	5	7	7	3	—
L-5N	4	11	7	1	3	8	—	4	2	—
L-5C	18	17	17	19	26	11	9	16	15	33
L-5CN	23	9	15	4	13	25	11	16	3	22
L-5CES	—	31	29	25	30	19	23	22	21	26
L-5CESN	—	8	17	18	20	31	32	15	27	12
L-5CT★★	—	—	—	—	—	—	—	—	—	23

Instrument	1960	1961	1962	1963	1964	1965	1966	1967	1968	1969
L-5C	26	19	21	41	23	15	25	10	36	70
L-5CN	13	5	12	4	9	1	9	—	3	19
L-5CES	45	22	30	51	42	34	23	102	189	170
L-5CESN	17	13	11	21	10	10	1	5	11	55
L-5CT★★	9	11	—	—	—	—	—	—	—	—

Instrument	1970	1971	1972	1973	1974	1975	1976	1977	1978	1979
L-5C	8	10	6	2	—	40	34	39	13	12
L-5CN	2	2	6	1	1	4	29	23	19	3
L-5CES	71	101	128	138	208	137	139	147	117	45
L-5CESN	24	26	65	18	17	36	103	100	38	15
L-5CES†	—	—	—	6	6	2	3	—	—	—

Instrument	1980	1981	1982	1983	1984	1985	1986	1987	1988	1989
L-5C	★	★	★	★	★	1	—	1	2	—
L-5CN	★	★	★	★	★	—	—	—	3	—
L-5CES	★	★	★	★	★	2	11	2	20	148
L-5CESN	★	★	★	★	★	2	1	6	4	52

★★L-5CT: George Gobel Model
†L-5 with Super 400 Neck
★Note: No data available from 1980–1984.

TABLE B-15
Prewar Acoustic L-5 Production

Model	Instrument	Years of Shipment						
		1935	1936	1937	1938	1939	1940	1941
First	L-5	70	6	23	—	—	—	—
Second	L-5	30	19	251	197	152	52	51
Second	L-5N	—	—	—	—	—	—	36
Third	L-5P	—	—	—	—	40	11	14
Third	L-5PN	—	—	—	—	—	40	13
Totals by Year		100	25	274	197	192	103	134

TABLE B-16
Prewar Acoustic L-5 Production Summary

Model	Instrument	Variation	Number Shipped
First	L-5	Noncutaway body, sunburst finish, 16-inch lower bout (1935–1937)	99
Second	L-5	Noncutaway body, sunburst finish, 17-inch lower bout (1935–1941)	752
Second	L-5N	Noncutaway body, natural finish, 17-inch lower bout (1939–1941)	36
Third	L-5P	Cutaway body, sunburst finish, 17-inch lower bout (1939–1941)	65
Third	L-5PN	Cutaway body, natural finish, 17-inch lower bout (1939–1941)	53
		Total, all models, 1935–1941	1,005

TABLE B-17
Postwar Acoustic L-5 Production

Model	Instrument	Years of Shipment									
										1948	**1949**
Fourth	L-5									49	29
Fourth	L-5N									38	17
Fifth	L-5C									23	23
Fifth	L-5CN									21	22
Seventh	L-5CT									—	—
	Totals by Year									131	91
		1950	**1951**	**1952**	**1953**	**1954**	**1955**	**1956**	**1957**	**1958**	**1959**
Fourth	L-5	17	29	20	15	12	5	7	7	3	—
Fourth	L-5N	4	11	7	1	3	8	—	4	2	—
Fifth	L-5C	18	17	17	19	26	11	9	16	15	33
Fifth	L-5CN	23	9	15	4	13	25	11	16	3	22
Seventh	L-5CT	—	—	—	—	—	—	—	—	—	23
	Totals by Year	62	66	59	39	54	49	27	43	23	78
		1960	**1961**	**1962**	**1963**	**1964**	**1965**	**1966**	**1967**	**1968**	**1969**
Fifth	L-5C	26	19	21	41	23	15	25	10	36	70
Fifth	L-5CN	13	5	12	4	9	1	9	—	3	19
Seventh	L-5CT	9	11	—	—	—	—	—	—	—	—
	Totals by Year	48	35	33	45	32	16	34	10	39	89
		1970	**1971**	**1972**	**1973**	**1974**	**1975**	**1976**	**1977**	**1978**	**1979**
Fifth	L-5C	8	10	6	2	—	40	34	39	13	12
Fifth	L-5CN	2	2	6	1	1	4	29	23	19	3
	Totals by Year	10	12	12	3	1	44	63	62	32	15
		1980	**1981**	**1982**	**1983**	**1984**	**1985**	**1986**	**1987**	**1988**	**1989**
Fifth	L-5C	★	★	★	★	★	1	—	1	2	—
Fifth	L-5CN	★	★	★	★	★	—	—	—	3	—
	Totals by Year						1	0	1	5	0

★No data from 1980–1984

TABLE B-18
Postwar Acoustic L-5 Production Summary

Model	Instrument	Variation	Number Shipped 1948–1979	1985–1989
Fourth	L-5	Noncutaway body, sunburst finish	193	—
Fourth	L-5N	Noncutaway body, natural finish	95	—
Fifth	L-5C	Cutaway body, sunburst finish	677	4
Fifth	L-5CN	Cutaway body, natural finish	349	3
Sixth	L-5CT	Cutaway body, 2⅛-inch depth, cherry finish	43	—
		Total, all models	1,357	7

TABLE B-19
Total Acoustic L-5 Production, Selected Summary Data

Model	Instrument	Variations	Number Shipped Prewar	Postwar	Total
First	L-5	Noncutaway body, sunburst finish, 16-inch lower bout	99★	—	99
Second, Fourth	L-5	Noncutaway body, sunburst finish	752	193	945
Second, Fourth	L-5N	Noncutaway body, natural finish	36	95	831
Third, Fifth	L-5P/C	Cutaway body, sunburst finish	65	681†	746
Third, Fifth	L-5PN/CN	Cutaway body, natural finish	53	352†	405
Sixth	L-5CT	Cutaway body (2⅛-inch depth), cherry finish	—	43	43
		Total, all models	1,005	1,364	2,369

★This does not include any 16-inch L-5s shipped prior to 1935; no production data are available for 1924–1934 L-5s.
†1980–1984 totals incomplete, not listed

TABLE B-20
Postwar Electric L-5 Production

Model	Instrument	1950	1951	1952	1953	1954	1955	1956	1957	1958	1959
Sixth	L-5CES	—	31	29	25	30	19	23	22	21	26
Sixth	L-5CESN	—	8	17	18	20	31	32	15	27	12
	Totals by Year	—	39	46	43	50	50	55	37	48	38

Model	Instrument	1960	1961	1962	1963	1964	1965	1966	1967	1968	1969
Sixth	L-5CES	45	22	30	51	42	34	23	102	189	170
Sixth	L-5CESN	17	13	11	21	10	10	1	5	11	55
	Totals by Year	62	35	41	72	52	44	24	107	200	225

Model	Instrument	1970	1971	1972	1973	1974	1975	1976	1977	1978	1979
Sixth	L-5CES	71	101	128	138	208	137	139	147	117	45
Sixth	L-5CESN	24	26	65	18	17	36	103	100	38	15
Eighth	L-5CES "Spl." (L-5 body with Super 400 Neck)	—	—	—	6	6	2	3	—	—	—
	Totals by Year	95	127	193	162	231	175	245	247	155	60

Model	Instrument	1980	1981	1982	1983	1984	1985	1986	1987	1988	1989
Sixth	L-5CES	★	★	★	★	★	2	11	2	20	148
Sixth	L-5CESN	★	★	★	★	★	2	1	6	4	52
	Totals by Year						4	12	8	24	200

★No data available from 1980–1984.

TABLE B-21
Postwar Electric L-5 Production, Summary

Model	Instrument	Variation	Period of Shipment			
			1951–First Half of 1960	Second Half of 1960–First Half of 1969	Second Half of 1969–1979	1985–1989
Seventh	L-5CES	Venetian cutaway, sunburst	248	—	—	—
Seventh	L-5CESN	Venetian cutaway, natural	188	—	—	—
Eighth	L-5CES	Florentine cutaway, sunburst	—	601	—	—
Eighth	L-5CESN	Florentine cutaway, natural	—	118	—	—
Ninth	L-5CES	Venetian cutaway, sunburst	—	—	1,316	183
Ninth	L-5CESN	Venetian cutaway, natural	—	—	470	65
Tenth	L-5CES	Venetian cutaway, sunburst, Super 400 neck	—	—	17	—
		Totals, all models	436	719	1,803	248

Grand Total: 3,206 (plus 1980–1984 missing data)

TABLE B-22
Postwar Electric L-5 Production, Early Pickup Variations

Instrument	Variation	Pickup Configuration Subtotal		
		P90 (1951–1953)	Alnico (1951–First Half 1958)	PAF (Second Half of 1958–First Half of 1960)
L-5CES	Venetian cutaway, sunburst finish	85	104	59
L-5CES	Venetian cutaway, natural finish	43	111	34
	Totals	128	215	93

Note: The above subtotals are approximations, based on observation and Gibson archival and anecdotal information.

TABLE B-23
Table of Relative Rarity of the L-5

Rank	Model	Instrument	Variation	Years Shipped	Number Shipped	Percent of Total
1	Tenth	L-5CES	L-5 body/Super 400 neck, sunburst	1973–1976	17	.3%
2	Seventh	L-5CESN	PAF pickups, natural	Second half of 1958–first half of 1960	34	.6%
3	Second	L-5N	Noncutaway, natural	1941	36	.6%
4	Sixth	L-5CT	Thinbody, cherry	1959–1961	43	.8%
5	Third	L-5PN	Cutaway, natural	1939–1941	53	1%
6	Seventh	L-5CES	PAF pickups, sunburst	Second half of 1958–first half of 1960	59	1.1%
7	Third	L-5P	Cutaway, sunburst	1939–1941	65	1.2%
8	Fourth	L-5N	Noncutaway, natural	1948–1958	95	1.7%
9	First	L-5	16-inch body, sunburst	1935–1937★	99	1.8%
10	Eighth	L-5CESN	Florentine cutaway, natural	Second half of 1960–first half of 1969	118	2.1%
11	Seventh	L-5CESN	P90/Alnico pickups, natural	1951–first half of 1958	154	2.8%
12	Seventh	L-5CES	P90/Alnico pickups, sunburst	1951–first half of 1958	189	3.4%
13	Fourth	L-5	Noncutaway, sunburst	1948–1958	193	3.5%
14	Fifth	L-5CN	Cutaway, natural	1948–1979, 1985–1989	352†	6.3%
15	Ninth	L-5CESN	Venetian cutaway, natural	Second half of 1969–1979, 1985–1989	535†	9.5%
16	Eighth	L-5CES	Florentine cutaway, sunburst	Second half of 1960–first half of 1969	600	10.8%
17	Fifth	L-5C	Cutaway, sunburst	1948–1979, 1985–1989	681†	12.2%
18	Second	L-5	Noncutaway, sunburst	1935–1941	752	13.5%
19	Ninth	L-5CES	Venetian cutaway, sunburst	Second half of 1969–1979, 1985–1989	1,499†	26.8%
			Totals		5,574†	100%

★Does not include 16-inch L-5s prior to 1935
†1980–1984 totals incomplete, not included

ADDENDUM
Super 400 and L-5 Production, 1990–1993

Super 400	Finish	1990	1991	1992	1993	Total, 1990–1993
Super 400CES	vintage sunburst	1	5	32	36	74
	natural	1	1	14	17	33
	wine red	0	0	9	10	19
	ebony	0	0	8	8	16
Super 400C	vintage sunburst	0	0	0	0	0
	natural	0	1	0	0	1
Super 400 1939 reissue						
	antique sunburst				17	17
	natural				4	4
Super 400P 1939 reissue						
	antique sunburst				6	6
	natural				5	5
Super 400 oval sound hole, antique white					1	1
Super 400 Western Sky (oval sound hole)						
	honeyburst				6	6
	polaris white				1	1
Totals by Year, Super 400		2	7	63	111	180

L-5	Finish	1990	1991	1992	1993	Total, 1990–1993
L-5CES	vintage sunburst	86	29	24	42	181
	natural	67	14	3	5	89
	wine red	0	1	9	10	20
	ebony	1	0	7	7	15
L-5C	vintage sunburst	0	0	0	0	0
	natural	0	0	0	0	0
L-5 non-cutaway 1934 reissue, sunburst					16	16
L-5CES Wes Montgomery						
	vintage sunburst				65	65
	ebony				2	2
	wine red				18	18
Totals by Year, L-5		154	44	43	165	406

Photography
Acknowledgments

Bill Crump: All color photography except 13 photographs noted below; all black and white closeup and catalog photography except Chapter 4.

Scott Grey: Color photographs on Plate 13 (last three) and Plate 15 (last four).

Charmaine Lanham: Color photograph on Plate 15 (upper left); all black and white photography in Chapter 4.

Malcolm Paisley: Color photograph on Plate 1 (bottom).

James D'Aquisto: Color photographs on Plate 24 (first three).

Robert Benedetto: Color photograph on Plate 23 (bottom right).

Instrument
Acknowledgments

Color Plate	Instrument	Owner
1	1938 Super 400 and case	Guitar Gallery, London
6	1967 Super 400C	Peter Wagener
6	1969 Super 400C	Daniel Weber
8	1978 Super 400	Freddy Pigg
8	1978 Super 400N	Freddy Pigg
17	1934 L-5	Joel Sanders
17	1940 L-5P	Willie Baker
17	1948 L-5P	Hap Kufner
18	1947 L-5	Larry Wexer
18	1948 L-5N	Guitar Gallery, London
19	1969 L-5CT	J.P. Ohnishi, Japan
20	1970 L-5CES	Leon Chester
20	1989 L-5CES	Gary Brunner
21	1984 L-5CESN "50th Anniversary"	Guitar Gallery, London
21	1960 D'Angelico Excel	Joel Sanders
22	1953 Epiphone Emperor Zephyr Regent	Craig Swancy
23	1989 Heritage Super Eagle	Dr. Ken Ciuffreda
23	1990 Benedetto Cremona	Bob Benedetto
24	1990 D'Aquisto New Yorker	James D'Aquisto
24	1990 D'Aquisto Classic	James D'Aquisto
24	1990 D'Aquisto Avant-Garde	James D'Aquisto

All other instruments photographed are from the author's collection.

Bibliography

Bellson, Julius. *The Gibson Story.* Kalamazoo, Michigan: Gibson, 1973.

Bellson, Julius. Personal interview, May 1984.

Blackburn, Bill. "The Strange Case of Dr. Vintage." *Guitar World,* July 1987, pp. 62–64, 72.

Calder, James. "Texas Round-up: The Dallas Guitar Shows." *Guitarist,* August 1989, pp. 67–71.

Casabona, Helen. "Opening Moves—How Collectors Get Their Start." *Frets,* February 1985, pp. 20–21.

Del Rey, Teisco. "Greater Southwest Guitar Show." *Guitar Player,* June 1986, pp. 129–132, 178.

Del Rey, Teisco. "10th Annual Greater Southwest Guitar Show." *Guitar Player,* June 1987, pp. 50–56.

Del Rey, Teisco. "Guitars Held Hostage." *Guitar Player,* June 1988, pp. 118–119.

Donnell, Ken. "Below the Bottom Line: It's Only Worth What Someone Will Pay." *Frets,* February 1985, pp. 22–23, 54.

Duchossoir, A. R. *Gibson Electrics, Volume I.* Paris: Mediapresse, 1981.

Duchossoir, A. R. *Guitar Identification.* Milwaukee: Hal Leonard Publishing Corporation, 1983.

Duchossoir, A. R. Personal communication, 1990.

Forte, Dan. "The Bull Market." *Guitar Buyer's Guide,* 1989–1990, pp. 137–141.

Gartner, Rick. "Good as Gold. . .?" *Frets,* February 1985, p. 17.

Gruhn, George. "Sunburst Gallery: Gibson's Classic Les Paul." *Guitar Player,* March 1985, pp. 16–23.

Gruhn, George. "The Vintage Market Today." *Guitar Player,* July 1986, pp. 102, 130.

Gruhn, George. "Vintage Market Feeding Frenzy." *Frets,* May 1988, pp. 9, 55–56.

Gruhn, George. "Prices Then and Now." *Frets,* November 1988, pp. 57, 70.

Gruhn, George. "Guitar Trading: Texas Style." *Frets,* February 1989, pp. 41, 59.

Gruhn, George. "The Last Word." *Frets,* February 1989, p. 11.

Gruhn, George. "The Vintage Instrument Market, I." *Guitar Player,* June 1989, pp. 22, 161.

Gruhn, George. "The Vintage Instrument Market, II." *Guitar Player,* July 1989, pp. 8, 177.

Gruhn, George, and Walter Carter. "The Texas Guitar Show from the Inside." *Guitar Player,* February 1989, p. 14.

Gruhn, George, and Walter Carter. "A Pair of Dallas Guitar Shows." *Guitar Player,* June 1989, pp. 15–16.

Gruhn, George, and Walter Carter. "Vintage Instrument Showdown in Dallas." *Frets,* July 1989, pp. 41, 52.

Hawkins, John. Personal interview, 1990.

Hood, Phil. "Buy, Sell, Trade: Inside Today's Vintage Market." *Frets,* February 1985, pp. 15–16.

Hood, Phil. "Fine-Tuning the Crystal Ball." *Frets,* February 1985, p. 18.

Humphrey, Mark. "Fake! Vintage Frauds and Forgeries." *Frets,* February 1985, pp. 32–40, 60.

Humphrey, Mark. "Are You Covered? The Question of Insurance." *Frets,* February 1985, pp. 45–46, 54.

Hutto, Jim. "Music Dealers and Vintage Instruments." *Frets,* February 1985, p. 25.

Hutto, Jim. "The Auctioneers—Sealed Bids and Six-Figure Strads." *Frets,* February 1985, pp. 28–30, 60.

Lanham, Marty. Personal interview, Nashville, 1988.

McCarty, Theodore. Personal interview, Kalamazoo, 1984.

Miller, Wade, and George Gruhn. "Musical Instruments: Old versus New." *Frets,* December 1988, pp. 12, 17, 32.

Obrecht, Jas. "Straight Talk from Fatdog." *Guitar Player,* March 1989, pp. 18–19.

Sandmel, Ben. "Sound Investment." *Spirit,* May 1990, pp. 42–56.

Scott, Jay. "Vintage Buyers Go Berserk in Texas." *Guitar World,* July 1987, pp. 12–14.

Schilling, Ed. "Appraised Value: How Pros Price an Instrument." *Frets,* February 1985, pp. 24–26.

Schmidt, Paul. "Acquired of the Angels: The Lives and Works of Master Guitar Makers John D'Angelico and James D'Aquisto." New Jersey: Scarecrow Press, 1991.

Smith, Richard. "An Early Fender in Dallas." *Guitar Player,* June 1989, pp. 136–137.

Smith, Richard. "Early Birds: The Sprung Collection." *Guitar Player,* July 1989, pp. 26–29.

Stromberg advertising brochure, late 1930s–early 1940s.

Tsumura, Akira. *Guitars: The Tsumura Collection.* New York: Kodansha, Limited, Harper & Row, 1987.

Turner, Dean. Personal interview, 1989.

Turner, Rick. "Sound Investments: The Silber Collection." *Frets,* June 1987, pp. 34–37.

Van Hoose, Thomas. "The Gibson Super 400 Acoustic Models." *Guitar Trader's Vintage Guitar Bulletin,* November 1983, pp. 2–3.

Van Hoose, Thomas. "The Gibson Super 400 Electric Models." *Guitar Trader's Vintage Guitar Bulletin,* December 1983, p. 2.

Van Hoose, Thomas. "The Gibson L-5 Guitar." *Guitar Trader's Vintage Guitar Bulletin,* August 1983, pp. 2–4.

Van Hoose, Thomas. "The Gibson L-5 Electric Models." *Guitar Trader's Vintage Guitar Bulletin,* September 1983, pp. 2–4.

Van Hoose, Thomas. "The Last of Kalamazoo's Finest: The 50th Anniversary Super 400CES and L-5CES Guitars." *20th Century Guitar,* July/August 1990, pp. 8–9.

Van Hoose, Thomas. "Greater Southwest Guitar Show—13 Years in Dallas and Still Going Strong." *Vintage Guitar,* June 1990, pp. 1, 9, 12.

Wheeler, Tom. *American Guitars.* New York: Harper & Row, 1982.

Wheeler, Tom. "Lone Star Bazaar: Big Guitars, Big Bucks." *Guitar Player,* January 1990, pp. 15–16.

Willcut, J. Robert, and Kenneth Ball. *The Musical Instrument Collector.* New York: The Bold Strummer Ltd., 1978.

Yasuda, Mac. *The Vintage Guitar, Vol. 2.* Tokyo: Shinko Music Publishing, 1988.

INDEX

Thomas A. Van Hoose, Ph.D., is a clinical psychologist whose avocation is guitar playing and collecting. Widely recognized as a leading authority on the Gibson Super 400, Van Hoose has assembled one of the finest and most extensive collections of these guitars in the world.